Marketisation and Forensic Science Provision in England and Wales

Marketisation and Forensic Science Provision in England and Wales

BY

KAREN MCGREGOR RICHMOND
University of Copenhagen, Denmark

emerald PUBLISHING

United Kingdom – North America – Japan – India – Malaysia – China

Emerald Publishing Limited
Howard House, Wagon Lane, Bingley BD16 1WA, UK

First edition 2023

British Library Cataloguing in Publication Data
A catalogue record for this book is available from the British Library

ISBN: 978-1-83909-124-7 (Print)
ISBN: 978-1-83909-123-0 (Online)
ISBN: 978-1-83909-125-4 (Epub)

Printed and bound by CPI Group (UK) Ltd, Croydon, CR0 4YY

This work is dedicated to my father, Gordon Black Richmond.

Contents

List of Abbreviations

CAI	Case Assessment and Interpretation
CJINI	Criminal Justice Inspectorate Northern Ireland
CJS	Criminal Justice System
DNA	Deoxyribonucleic Acid
EGPS	Early Guilty Plea Scheme
ERU	Evidence Recovery Unit
FSNI	Forensic Science Northern Ireland
FSP	Forensic Science Provider
FSR	Forensic Science Regulator
FSS	Forensic Science Service
LCN-DNA	Low Copy Number DNA
NDNAD	National DNA Database
NIDNAD	Northern Ireland DNA Database
PSNI	Police Service of Northern Ireland
RMP	Random Match Probability
SFR	Streamlined Forensic Reporting

Preface and Acknowledgements

The boundaries between this book and my ongoing research are not so rigidly demarcated that I can easily list those to whom I owe thanks. It would not have been possible without the engagement of staff at Edinburgh, Strathclyde, and Dundee, universities in Scotland, and research projects within the Leverhulme Research Centre for Forensic Sciences, Technical University Graz, and my current institution, iCourts (the Danish National Research Foundation's Centre of Excellence in International Courts, University of Copenhagen). I am grateful for their encouragement.

Special thanks, however, are due to Dame Professor Sue Black, Vice Chancellor at Lancaster University and Senior Member of the Royal Society of Edinburgh, for setting me on the right track; to Professor Nicolette Priaulx of Cardiff University for her continued inspiration; and to Professor Mikkel Jarle Christensen of University of Copenhagen, for opening new doors.

For their enduring interest, and enthusiastic participation in my research, I am grateful to: the Royal Society, the Royal Society of Edinburgh, Her Majesty's Inspectorate of Constabulary, the United Kingdom Accreditation Service, the Crown Prosecution Service, the Metropolitan Police, and the Office for the Forensic Regulator. Thanks also to the Scottish Police Authority, Scottish Institute for Policing Research, and the Faculty of Advocates. Greatest thanks are due to the staff of the forensic science providers in all four corners of the UK for sharing so freely of their time and expert knowledge.

I am likewise grateful to fellow doctoral students, researchers, and academics for the encouragement and engagement they offered, having enlisted their help in reading – and commenting on – early drafts and research papers. Thanks also to the Institute for Advanced Legal Studies, the Law and Society Association, the Socio-Legal Studies Association, the Chartered Society of Forensic Sciences, and the Society of Legal Scholars, for helping me to disseminate my research. And I owe a special debt to all those who took an interest in this project and who attended workshops and conferences to hear me speak about the results of my research.

The greatest thanks must go to my father, Gordon Black Richmond, who passed away before this book could be published, but who never doubted my potential, and whose hard work, resilience, and faith continue to inspire me. This work is dedicated to him.

Chapter 1

The Forensic Market

Introduction

Contrary to the portrayals of the forensic sciences beyond the scientific and legal domains, evidence does not speak for itself. Expert scientific evidence is generated from the convergence of investigatory, analytical, and interpretative processes, involving a diverse array of agencies. Thus, the ongoing stability, durability, and quality of the relationships between these institutional agents are of central importance to ensuring the accurate, efficient, and consistent production of expert scientific reports. It is therefore unusual to encounter a jurisdiction in which forensic science – generally perceived as a matter for public sector provision – is reconfigured around a fully marketised system of delivery[1]: England and Wales are unique in this respect.[2] Given that the scientist's ability to harness those objective scientific precepts on which the forensic sciences found, are prone to influence from interposing political, economic, and organisational factors,[3] the policy-driven transition from public to private forensic provision raises significant concerns regarding the potential for commercial markets not only to reliably support the criminal justice system (CJS),[4] but also to influence – and even distort – the very processes

[1]Partial marketisation has been introduced in the Netherlands, where, in 2017, the Dutch Ministry of Justice and Security awarded a contract for DNA testing to the Maastricht Forensic Institute and Eurofins. Retrieved from www.eurofins.nl/nl/contact-details/the-maastricht-forensic-institute-tmfi/. Accessed on May 7, 2022.

[2]For a US perspective, *see* McAndrew, W. P. (2012a). Are forensic science services club goods? An analysis of the optimal forensic science service delivery model. *Forensic Science Policy & Management: An International Journal, 3*(4), 151–158; McAndrew, W. P. (2012b). Is privatization inevitable for forensic science laboratories? *Forensic Science Policy & Management: An International Journal, 3*(1), 42–52.

[3]*See* Bijker, W. E., Bal, R., & Hendriks, R. (2009). *The paradox of scientific authority: The role of scientific advice in democracies*. Cambridge, MA: MIT Press.

[4]Hamilton, F. (2018, January 31). Police foot the bill after collapse of forensics firm. *The Times*. Retrieved from www.thetimes.co.uk/article/police-foot-the-bill-after-collapse-of-forensics-firm-key-forensic-services-limited-bg5nbxkxt; Devlin, H. (2018, December 6). Convictions for drug-driving quashed in forensics lab inquiry.

Marketisation and Forensic Science Provision in England and Wales, 1–16

Published under exclusive licence by Emerald Publishing Limited
doi:10.1108/978-1-83909-123-020221001

of forensic analysis and interpretation that characterise this public good.[5] Employing a critical realist, comparative case study approach, and utilising a palette of qualitative methods, the instant study – adapted from a doctoral research project – seeks to limn the contours of this unexplored domain of marketised scientific practice, rendering visible the links between novel governance structures and the performative practices of forensic expertise. The study also considers the impact of overarching regulatory incursions, analysing the ways in which forensic regulation seeks to manage risk through quality assurance. The results offer a unique insight into the ways in which institutional agents have adapted to changing relations, shifting priorities, and the imposition of market logics, within a sector historically unaccustomed to the obtrusions of market-based efficiency and external regulation. The data discussed in this monograph thus demonstrate not only how criminal justice agencies failed to respond collaboratively to the nascent introduction of commoditisation and competitive tendering but also illuminates the ways in which the market that developed in their wake began to influence and reconfigure the central processes of forensic strategy-setting and analysis. These market-driven distortions served to generate further challenges and phenomena – triaging, de-skilling, the introduction of inexpert streamlined reports, and research stasis – which together describe a decade-long trajectory from objective scientific analysis to productised 'regulatory objectivity'.[6] The study thereby demonstrates the ways in which the forensic sector, by reconfiguring itself around these indices of competition and efficiency, rendered itself unable to meet the challenges of a dynamic and evolving field. In such circumstances, the turn away from research-driven biomedicine to data-driven digital evidence – the subject of the final chapter – is no longer viewed as merely opportune but as a pragmatic turn necessary for the survival of the sector at large.[7]

The Guardian. Retrieved from www.theguardian.com/uk-news/2018/dec/06/forty-convictions-quashed-after-investigation-at-uk-forensics-lab

[5]*See* House of Lords Science and Technology Committee. (2019, May 1). *Forensic science and the criminal justice system: A blueprint for change*. 3rd report of session 2017–19 (HL Paper 333). Retrieved from https://publications.parliament.uk/pa/ld201719/ldselect/ldsctech/333/33302.htm. Accessed on July 23, 2021. At page 3:

> The delivery of justice depends on the integrity and accuracy of that evidence, and the trust that society has in it. The quality and delivery of forensic science in England and Wales is inadequate.

See also Forensic Science Regulator. (2019, March 15). *Annual report November 2017–November 2018*. Retrieved from www.gov.uk/government/publications/forensic-science-regulator-annual-report-2018. At page 3: '… profound changes to funding and governance are required to ensure that forensic science survives and begins to flourish rather than lurching from crisis to crisis'.

[6]*See* Cambrosio, A., Keating, P., Schlich, T., & Weisz, G. (2006). Regulatory objectivity and the generation and management of evidence in medicine. *Social Science and Medicine, 63*, 189–199.

[7]Morgan, R. M., & Levin, E. A. (2019). A crisis for the future of forensic science: Lessons from the UK of the importance of epistemology for funding research and

Forensic Science Provision in England and Wales

The governance of the provision of forensic science services, alongside the organisation, structuring, and management of individual forensic science laboratories, varies widely across regions and between individual countries and jurisdictions. Nonetheless, across this heterogeneous forensic landscape, forensic providers face shared scientific challenges and similar budgetary constraints.[8] Commercial imperatives have intermitted, to a greater or lesser extent, into a field of relative scientific autonomy, with many public forensic providers now recognising the need to demonstrate a willingness to embrace new management techniques, to internalise – and comply with – regulatory objectives,[9] and to enter into rudimentary forms of competition.[10] Nonetheless, despite the increasing recognition of commercial imperatives, the overwhelming majority of developed countries still choose to deliver vital forensic services through a system of public provision. The current system of forensic science provision operating in England and Wales is thereby exceptional, insofar as provision is achieved through a fully privatised model of delivery, instituted through the winding down and complete closure of the Forensic Science Service (Ltd.; FSS) in early 2012. However, in political and managerial terms, it may be posited that the journey towards privatisation commenced in the early 1980s, at which point the ethos of 'customer relations' – central to commercial organisation – gathered discursive power and began to influence the practices of an increasing number of government agencies.[11] This introduction of processes of economic rationalisation to the criminal justice sector and the 'ascendancy of market imaginaries'[12] thus began to alter the field of forensic science provision, which gradually became reconfigured around new

---

development. *Forensic Science International: Synergy, 1,* 243–252; Horsman, G., & Sunde, N. (2022). Unboxing the digital forensic investigation process. *Science & Justice, 62*(2), 171–180.

[8]Not least the shared challenge of establishing the foundational validity of a wide variety of scientific techniques and practices and the regional harmonisation of forensic evaluation. See Committee on Identifying the Needs of the Forensic Sciences Community, National Research Council. (2009). *Strengthening forensic science in the United States: A path forward.* Washington, DC: National Academy of Sciences; President's Council of Advisors on Science & Technology. (2016). *Forensic science in criminal courts: Ensuring scientific validity of feature-comparison methods.* Washington, DC: Executive Office of the President.

[9]Most notably, the Forensic Science Regulator Act 2021, c. 14. Retrieved from www.legislation.gov.uk/ukpga/2021/14/contents/enacted

[10]*See, for example,* the 2019 collaboration involving Forensic Science Northern Ireland (FSNI) and private forensic providers, funded through the Northern Ireland Department for Economy (DfE) Small Business Research Initiative (SBRE). Retrieved from www.justice-ni.gov.uk/articles/tenders-0

[11]*See* Whitehead, P., & Crawshaw, P. (Eds.). (2012). *Organising neoliberalism: Markets, privatisation and justice.* London: Anthem Press.

[12]Albertson, K., Corcoran, M., & Phillips, J. (Eds). (2020). *Marketisation and privatisation in criminal justice* (p. 1). Bristol: Policy Press.

goals, interests, and incentives. Thereafter, as this study illustrates, the normative objects of England's key public sector forensic agency came to be subsumed by the quantitative indices of marketised service delivery, characterised by entrepreneurial innovation, value for money, choice, and communication between stakeholders. The instant study measured the effect of these policy innovations within the forensic science sector in England and Wales, exploring the ways in which these profound shifts in public policy and management brought about an emphatic reorganisation of the provision of forensic services and of core scientific processes and outputs. The following section describes the privatised English and Welsh model of forensic service provision in greater detail.

Marketisation and Privatisation in England and Wales

For the purposes of this study, both marketisation and privatisation are considered as interrelated phenomena. Specifically, marketisation is understood in terms of a paradigmatic shift away from the values of post-war welfarism and the procedural benefits of centralised provision,[13] an equality of arms, and the objective evaluation of material evidence, towards an ideology of managerialism, competition, and efficiency, advanced through discourses of perceived costliness and a lack of sustainability. As Albertson, Corcoran, and Phillips note,[14]

> A market economy logic is evident in a myriad of different case studies having initially been introduced in order to fix a perceived problem such as a perception that the service was too expensive or inefficient, ineffective or lacking in accountability. However, with that came unintended consequences impacting on the delivery of justice and the effectiveness of the system, as well as the legitimacy of the institutions concerned.[15]

Thus, marketisation describes a broader reorganisation process involving the commoditisation of public services and the conversion of scientific labour and forensic processes into saleable products. Privatisation occurs when public resources and employment (generally but not necessarily subject to prior market reorganisation at the macro, meso, and micro levels) are transferred to private

---

[13]Centralisation and public ownership are common features of forensic science provision throughout Europe and across common law, and civil law, jurisdictions: for example, *Statens Kriminaltekniska Laboratorium* (Swedish National Laboratory of Forensic Science, SKL); Forensic Science Ireland; Netherlands Forensic Science Institute.

[14]*See, for example,* Smith, T., & Johnston, E. (2020). Marketisation and competition in criminal legal aid: Implications for access to justice. In K. Albertson, M., Corcoran, & J. Phillips (Eds), *Marketisation and privatisation in criminal justice* (pp.133–150). Bristol: Policy Press.

[15]Albertson, K., Corcoran, M., & Phillips, J. (Eds). (2020). *Marketisation and privatisation in criminal justice* (p. 2). Bristol: Policy Press.

enterprise through sale, lease, or the disposal of public resources in favour of tendering through an open market system. Beginning in the 1980s, the UK witnessed a profound shift in public policy, from autonomous public provision to for-profit enterprise. In its earliest 'experimental' phase, privatisation remained subordinate to fiscal policy imperatives, such that the initial phase of structural and cultural transformation focussed on the privatisation of profitable entities in order to reduce public sector borrowing. In later, comparatively aggressive, phases, the reorganisation of public service delivery through market culture was extended to the CJS, where it impacted across a wide range of contexts, from prison and probation to policing, migrant detention, rehabilitation, and community programmes.[16] However, it should be noted that the specific sectoral characteristics of marketisation and privatisation are situational, advancing through diverse processes and structures according to jurisdiction, service, and objective. Nonetheless, it should be stressed that the material calculus of marketisation and privatisation is such that they may distort behaviours and processes in such a way as to 'undermine the very aims of the organisation or context which the market was intended to "fix"'.[17] That process is the subject of the instant study.

Forensic Science Marketisation and Privatisation

Following an in-depth inquiry in 2019, focussing on the privatisation of forensic science and its aftermath, the House of Lords Science and Technology Committee concluded the following:

> In December 2010 the Government announced the closure of the Forensic Science Service, citing losses averaging £2 million per month as the reason. Following the announcement, the House of Commons Science and Technology Committee conducted an inquiry into the closure. It concluded that the Government did not give 'enough consideration to the impact on forensic science research and development (R&D), the capacity of private providers to absorb the FSS's 60% market share and the wider implications for the criminal justice system' when making the decision and warned of the possibility of serious market instability. They were right.[18]

[16]Albertson, K., Corcoran, M., & Phillips, J. (Eds.). (2020). Marketisation and privatisation in criminal justice. Bristol: Policy Press.

[17]Albertson, K., Corcoran, M., & Phillips, J. (Eds.). (2020). *Marketisation and privatisation in criminal justice* (p. 2). Bristol: Policy Press; Sandel, M. J. (2012). *What money can't buy: The moral limits of markets*. New York, NY: Farrar, Straus and Giroux.

[18]House of Commons Science and Technology Committee. *The forensic science service* (seventh report, session 2010–12, HC 855), at p. 3; House of Lords Science and Technology Committee. (2019, May 1). *Forensic science and the criminal justice system: A blueprint for change*. 3rd report of session 2017–19 (HL Paper 333), para. 42, p. 17.

The creation of the forensic market (from a system of public provision under the FSS, through an interim phase of quasi-private provision, culminating in the liquidation of the central government-operated forensic science agencies) was emblematic of exposure to new public management techniques and processes of economic rationalisation. The construction of consent to such processes of commercialisation can be traced back to the early 1980s, at which point the Home Office was opened up to discourses of 'modernisation' and 'economic rationality', and its character transformed by managerialist techniques, which valorised the concepts of 'economy, efficiency and effectiveness'.[19]

By the end of that decade, the ethos of 'customer relations' – central to commercial organisation – had begun to influence the practices of all government agencies, and the turn towards economic rationalisation began to influence, and distort, the field of forensic science provision, which would soon be reconfigured around new goals, interests, and incentives. Thus, the qualitative goals of public sector agencies were gradually subsumed within the indices of marketised service delivery: specifically, entrepreneurial innovation, value for money, choice, and communication between stakeholders. These profound shifts in public policy and management brought about an emphatic reorganisation of the provision of forensic services, the developing discursive framework of 'added value' service delivery – as vigorously promoted by the government's Audit Office – carrying serious implications for the governance of the publicly funded FSS. In 1987, an accounting firm, Touche Ross, was commissioned to draft a report on police scientific support. Prior to the commissioning of the Touche Ross report, forensic biologists related that,

> [...] the FSS was funded centrally so the Police didn't have to pay directly for any of their requested work. This resulted in forces often submitting very large numbers of items from each case, often waiting months for results.[20]

However, following the recommendations of the Touche Ross report, the FSS introduced direct charging to police forces. The costs of forensic services thus became visible to operational forces (henceforth to be regarded as 'customers'), and the FSS aligned itself with a more 'business-oriented' approach to service delivery, with a sustained focus:

> [...] on 'forensic strategy' and with far more careful triaging of items and agreeing target dates for court. Through all of this time,

[19]Lawless, C. (2010). *A curious reconstruction? The shaping of 'marketized' forensic science*. CARR Discussion Paper 63.

[20]King, D., Stangoe, C., & Cooke, L. (2012). *Scrutinising forensic services*. CPD Presentation to 25 Bedford Row.

> it was the scientists who determined what forensic examinations and analyses to make, in collaboration with the Police.[21]

In addition to managing internal change, the FSS was faced with a further challenge, when its monopoly on forensic science delivery in England and Wales came to an end, with two private companies (LGC Ltd. and Scientifics Ltd.) beginning to compete for FSS business. These companies had originated from within the public sector and were joined by the first fully private company, Forensic Alliance, in 1996.[22] During this period, the FSS had undergone a degree of internal reorganisation in order to bring it into line with the emergent market realities. Indeed, the FSS made it clear that the commercial considerations of the new forensic market were paramount in reshaping the relationship between FSS forensic experts and the requirements of the CJS:

> It is the belief of the FSS that the perception of such value for money should be that of the customer. These initiatives have the aim of not only providing better value for money, but also of achieving improvement through a genuine partnership in which the customer has a greater participation than hitherto in decisions about what work is done in the laboratory.[23]

The degree to which these changes altered the nature of FSS service delivery can be demonstrated by comparing the FSS 'mission statement' from 2001 – in which the agency defined its role in terms of a commitment to crafting a 'safer and more just society' – with later versions, which referred to the need:

> […] to retain and reinforce our leading position as the principal provider of forensic science to the UK criminal justice system (UKCJS), and use this platform to become the leading provider worldwide, thereby enhancing long term shareholder value.[24]

The alterations to policy and management – stimulated by both marketisation and productisation – were accompanied by structural changes. The FSS had

---

[21]King, D., Stangoe, C., & Cooke, L. (2012). *Scrutinising forensic services*. CPD Presentation to 25 Bedford Row, at p. 5.

[22]Lawless, C. (2010). *A curious reconstruction? The shaping of 'marketized' forensic science*. CARR Discussion Paper 63, pp. 3–6; Lawless, C. J., & Williams, R. (2010). *Helping with inquiries or helping with profits? The trials and tribulations of a technology of forensic reasoning. Social Studies of Science, 40, 731–755,* at pp. 736–738.

[23]Cook, R., Evett, I. W., Jackson, G, Jones, P. J., & Lambert, J. A. (1998). A model for case assessment and interpretation. *Science & Justice*, *38*, 151–156, at p. 152.

[24]*See* Lawless, C. J., & Williams, R. Lawless, C. J., & Williams, R. (2010). Helping with inquiries or helping with profits? The trials and tribulations of a technology of forensic reasoning. *Social Studies of Science, 40,* 731–755.

been awarded Trading Fund status in 1999. Thus, the service was able to recoup funds and to declare a profit, in the short term. However, as new competitors emerged, each reducing the FSS' market share, profits declined. The McFarland Review in 2003 found that the FSS was too heavily burdened by overhead costs and was thus unable to meet clients' needs. The Review recommended a further change in governance, to GovCo status, as a preliminary stage prior to restructuring as a public–private partnership. The McKinsey Review of 2008 further examined the sustainability of the forensic science market, concluding that the market was underperforming and was in need of urgent reform. It also noted that the costs of restructuring the FSS would be significant. As a result, the government announced its plans to wind down the FSS, following the advice of the House of Commons Science and Technology Committee. The service was eventually closed in 2011. With the closure of the FSS, forensic science provision in England and Wales became fully privatised, with work (including the 65% market share of the defunct FSS) now shared between 15 private companies. The consequences and effects of that decision are the subject of this comparative case study. Thus, in order to introduce a suitable comparator, discussion now turns to the public sector approach to forensic provision maintained in Northern Ireland.

Forensic Science Provision in Northern Ireland

In contrast with the privatised system of forensic science delivery currently operating in England and Wales, the provision of forensic science services in Northern Ireland has remained within the public sector. A forensic laboratory was first opened in the Province in 1956: this Department of Industrial and Forensic Science, situated in Belfast, was originally operated under the control of the Ministry of Commerce.[25] It was later renamed 'The Northern Ireland Forensic Science Laboratory'. On 1 September 1995, under the UK Government's Next Steps Initiative, the Forensic Science Laboratory became an Executive Agency within the Northern Ireland Office and was renamed 'The Forensic Science Agency of Northern Ireland'. A further alteration to nomenclature took place in April 2002 when the agency became 'Forensic Science Northern Ireland' (FSNI). Agency status was reconfirmed following a quinquennial review, stage one of which was completed in January 2002, and on 12 April 2010, as a direct consequence of the devolution of policing and justice responsibilities to the Northern Ireland Executive, FSNI became an agency within the newly formed Department of Justice.

These changes reflect the shifting sociopolitical landscape in the province, with its changing operational pressures, shifting priorities, and advancing social conditions. If the foregoing brief account suggest a lack of stasis that is not reflective of forensic-scientific instability. When compared with other parts of the UK, the provision of forensic science services in Northern Ireland has never been subject

[25] Lawless, C. (2016). *Forensic science: A sociological introduction* (p. 45). London: Routledge.

to radical market-driven interventions. Nonetheless, it should be noted that from its inception – and throughout its 50 years of service – the agency has demonstrated a strong commercial orientation, beginning with its industrial-scientific roots in Belfast, and continuing through to its recent incorporation of waste-reduction methodologies.[26]

The agency has – on a number of occasions – faced the added pressure of managing public perceptions consequent to the use of forensic techniques in high-profile criminal cases and was subject to intense media scrutiny focussing on the validity of new forensic techniques, in the context of the 'Omagh bomb' case.[27] The agency has demonstrated an ability to respond reflexively to public scrutiny and criticism and – since the devolution of Criminal Justice in Northern Ireland – has placed an imperative on transparency and demonstrable scientific objectivity. Any study of criminal justice procedures in Northern Ireland must take into account the diminishing terrorism, and security, situation that has affected the province over past decades. While 'the troubles' have had a profound effect on the security of the agency, and its staff, the latter highlight the positive effect that such demands have had on the quality of forensic outputs. Board members highlighted the fact that, throughout this period, FSNI were forced to take a more holistic approach to evidence collection, analysis, and evaluation. Thus, the agency was able to develop enhanced capabilities based on an appreciation of the need for joint recovery of evidence and the spatial correlation of heterogeneous evidence types. As a result, the agency has become less reliant on DNA profiling as an isolated forensic solution.[28]

The agency defines its purpose in terms of the provision of 'professional, independent and objective scientific expertise in support of Justice',[29] a role which it interprets widely, and holistically, given that it retains the ability to deal with the full range of forensic services 'under one roof'. FSNI has acknowledged the complexity of its role and an awareness that the agency is situated within a complex matrix of public – and private – actors, whose interactions, expectations, and engagements shape the forensic science field. In operational terms, the agency recognises two equally onerous areas of responsibility. The first of these is its duty to 'key paying customers': the Police Service of Northern Ireland (PSNI), Police

---

[26]*See, for example,* Northern Ireland Department of Justice. (2015, October 21). Justice Minister congratulates FSNI on winning quality award. Retrieved from www.justice-ni.gov.uk/news/justice-minister-congratulates-fsni-winning-quality-award

[27]*See, R.* v. *Sean Hoey* [2007] NICC 49, in which the trial judge raised concerns regarding the scientific validation of methods used to evaluate mixed samples of LCN-DNA (Low Copy Number DNA): an innovation which had, in that instance, been utilised by the Forensic Science Service in England.

[28]These forensic developments were elicited in response to the actions of criminals involved in domestic terrorism, whose growing familiarity with forensic capabilities led to comprehensive attempts to evade detection. Source: Chief Executive, FSNI (September 2015).

[29]*FSNI fourteenth annual report & accounts 1st April 2008–31st March 2009* (p. 7). (2009, July 15). London: The Stationary Office.

Ombudsman for Northern Ireland (PONI), and the State Pathologist's Department (SPD). The second is to a network of stakeholders, including the Public Prosecution Service (PPS), defence solicitors, the Northern Ireland Courts and Tribunal Service (NICTS), the judiciary, and the rest of the CJS. The agency also recognises its responsibility towards a broader field of actors, including prosecutors, defence representatives, victims and their families, defendants, suspects, society at large (and its political representatives).[30]

The agency's role, as a provider of forensic science services, is neither demarcated by its geographical position nor delineated by its administrative alignment. However, these factors significantly influence the nature of FSNI's customer base, with 94% of annual income being derived from PSNI.[31] Nonetheless, FSNI continues to articulate its strong commitment to commercial values, routinely employing the rhetoric of business efficiency: efficiencies, through which 'paying customers'[32] achieve 'demonstrable value for money'[33] as a result of 'business-like' procedures, guided by a reflexive management system capable of 'redefining ... performance measures and targets, using the [Strategy Map and] Balanced Scorecard tool'.[34] Nonetheless, as a public sector agency, FSNI is subject to routine inspection (every four to five years) by the Criminal Justice Inspectorate of Northern Ireland (CJINI). Following the 2009 CJINI report, the agency embarked on a Transformation Programme, designed to 'build capacity, improve speed, create efficiency and develop a culture of innovation and continuous improvement ...'.[35] This Transformation Programme took place as part of the Northern Ireland Administration's drive for 'Fairer, Faster Justice'. As a critical part of the Transformation Programme, FSNI participated in a detailed process review called the Service Improvement Platform. This review entailed a detailed examination of all business, and scientific, processes, and the identification of more efficient working patterns and potentially innovative areas, using a management methodology known as the 'Lean Six Sigma' process. The agency thereby sought to streamline and re-engineer processes in conformation with the administration's overarching programme of economic rationalisation.

A major capital investment, the Perseus system, was allocated under the Transformation Programme, with the aim of developing an integrated case management system. The Perseus system (costing over £3 million) has a target date for implementation of 2016 and aims to improve functionality with regard to

[30]*FSNI fourteenth annual report & accounts 1st April 2008–31st March 2009* (p. 1). (2009, July 15). London: The Stationary Office.
[31]*Source*: Internal 'FSNI Operational Background' document: 2014.
[32]Internal 'FSNI Operational Background' document: 2014, at p. 17.
[33]See *FSNI annual reports & accounts 1st April 2008–31st March 2015* (p. 7). London: The Stationary Office.
[34]*FSNI Annual Reports & Accounts 1st April 2008–31st March 2015* (p. 7). London: The Stationary Office.
[35]*Source*: Internal 'FSNI Operational Background' document: 2014.

> Laboratory Information Management (LIMS) and Quality Electronic Document and Records Management (EDRMS), in addition to developing an Activity Based Costing and Workflow Management System and implementing a system of Management Information Reporting.[36]

The agency states that,

> Locard, Perseus and SIP are together designed to improve the responsiveness, capacity, capability and efficiency of the Agency, which will be essential if [FSNI] are to meet the service requirements of the Criminal Justice System in this time of pressurised public expenditure.[37]

The transformation programme extended beyond the administration of forensic science provision, to include substantive improvements in forensic technological capability. Thus, FSNI began to utilise the potential of DNA-17 technology in December 2013, six months ahead of similar laboratories in England and Wales.[38] Under the Transformation Programme, the agency also allocated a second major capital investment of £13.9 million for the construction of a new 'high care laboratory'. This facility (known as the Locard Building, in reference to the 'founding father of forensic science, Edmond Locard)'[39] was opened in March 2016.

---

[36]FSNI response to *Criminal Justice Inspectorate of Northern Ireland FSNI Inspection Report*. Laid before the Northern Ireland Assembly: February 2014.

[37]*FSNI annual report and accounts for the year ended 31 March 2015* (p. 7). (2015, July 3). London: The Stationary Office.

[38]The science of DNA profiling is based around the targeted 'amplification' of a number of areas within an individual's DNA. Each region is known as a *locus* (plural *loci*). A number of separate loci can be analysed simultaneously, using what is referred to as a 'multiplex' chemical test. By increasing the number of loci that are targeted for multiplication, the discriminatory power (i.e. the ability to differentiate one individual from another) of the multiplex is proportionally increased. It is this ability to identify individuals that is fundamental to the use of multiplex DNA tests within forensic sciences. The DNA profile produced from these tests is stored as a set of numbers.

The first such test deployed in the early 1990s, using four loci, was known as the 'Quad'. This was superseded in 1994 by a seven-loci test, known as the Second Generation Multiplex, or SGM. A further development in 2001, adding four additional loci to the seven-loci system, was the SGM Plus. This system (with a discriminating power of over one in one billion) is still in use today. In December 2013, DNA 17 was deployed which includes a further six tests looking at 17 loci in total. DNA 17 technology consists of 16 STR loci samples and one gender identifier. It is more sensitive than its predecessor (SGM Plus) and routinely picks up 'touch DNA'. This leads to more numerous reports of 'mixed' DNA samples.

[39]Dr Edmond Locard (13 December 1877–4 May 1966) was a French criminologist, credited as the progenitor of modern forensic-scientific practices.

The new laboratory is designed to facilitate the efficient recovery (and subsequent analysis) of trace evidence – including DNA samples – under strictly controlled environmental conditions.[40]

Police Force Forensic Science Provision in the UK

An account of the effect of marketisation on the forensic science sector in England and Wales would be incomplete without a consideration of the contribution made by in-house police laboratories. As Lawless notes, the maintenance of in-house police laboratories across each of the 43 force areas of England and Wales – and in neighbouring Scotland with its centralised police authority – is reflective of the priorities of police budget holders, faced with market instability.[41] The variegated nature of forensic delivery across the 43 forces, the unique character of individual forces, and their divergent priorities are such that it is not feasible to find a paradigm example for analysis. Nor was a consideration of in-house police provision central to the instant study, not least due to notable gaps in provision relating to DNA analysis and a lack of accreditation and regulatory oversight. However, for the purposes of completing an account of provision across the UK, and as an example of centralised in-house provision, discussion focusses on provision of forensic services within Scotland.

Although the delivery of forensic science services in Scotland has remained within the public sector, Scotland has no independent forensic science service. While the employees of FSNI are civil servants owing a duty to the courts and to the administration of justice, able to carry out work for defence practitioners, the members of SPA Forensics operate as part of the police authority. Just as the majority of police forces in England and Wales have developed their own in-house laboratories – whose regulation has been a long-standing cause of concern – so the unitary Police Scotland operates a centralised forensic support service, based primarily at the Scottish Crime Campus in Gartcosh.[42] The statutory provision of forensic-scientific services in Scotland is governed by Section 31 of the Police and Fire Reform (Scotland) Act 2012, which requires that 'The [Scottish Police] Authority must provide forensic services to the Police Service, the Police Investigations and Review Commissioner and the Lord Advocate and procurators fiscal'. As such, the Scottish forensic provider – SPA Forensic Services – does not come under the direct control of the Chief Constable. This, alongside the

[40]The focus on demonstrable anti-contamination measures may be seen as a response to the trial verdict in *The Queen* v. *Colin Francis Duffy and Brian Patrick Shivers* [2012] NICC 1. This complex trial raised questions regarding the provenance of 'touch' DNA, deposited on a latex glove in the course of a terrorist murder. The accused, Colin Duffy, claimed that DNA was planted on the glove and was exonerated. However, it may be posited that an issue relating to the 'transfer and persistence' of the defendant's DNA may have been misconstrued by the court as one of contamination.

[41]Lawless, C. (2016). *Forensic science: A sociological introduction* (p. 70). London: Routledge.

[42]Satellite laboratories are located in the cities of Aberdeen, Dundee, and Edinburgh.

introduction of 'a "sterile corridor" ... in place between Forensic Services SPA and Police Scotland', the provider claims, 'ensures a suitable degree of independence and impartiality'.[43] However, the Scottish Police Authority is legislatively responsible for maintaining policing in Scotland and for promoting the principles of policing. Further, it has been stated that the day-to-day operations of SPA Forensics are directed, to a not insignificant degree, by the Crown Office (e.g. the imposition of limits on evaluative DNA reporting), to whom tits employees owe a duty.[44] Given the importance of absolute independence, and impartiality, in the provision of expert forensic-scientific services – and the public's perception of the same – the provider's claim that its governance structure ensures 'suitable independence and impartiality' requires further evaluation and may be viewed in light of a comparison with the degree of administrative separation – and expert autonomy – subsisting in Northern Ireland.[45]

The Police Scotland forensic support service is centrally funded and governed by a Scottish Police Authority board. The SPA Board operates four laboratories,[46] which provide all of the forensic science services required by the Crown Office Procurator Fiscal Services. Geographical specialisation is evident, with the majority of the 'volume' work being performed at the Scottish Crime Campus in Gartcosh. Defence work in Scotland is sent to providers in other jurisdictions. In addition to mainstream work done at the SPA Forensic laboratories, there are also specialist groups, which are located in universities or research institutes, to whom the police and defence will go directly. SPA Forensic Services are not governed by the Forensic Science Regulator but do support that office and have claimed an adherence to the guidelines, although there are no requirements to do so. The authority maintains partial accreditation under the United Kingdom Accreditation Service.[47]

Thus, Forensic Science Provision in Scotland can be said to proceed according to a 'technical support', or 'structural' mode,[48] under which the provision of forensic services are framed in adjunctive terms *qua* policing. Although such provision remains largely within the public sector, this does not entail that the sector is free of those same emerging imperatives of economic rationality, that have led to the creation of a forensic science market in England and Wales. In Scotland, the nature and contours of economic rationalisation may not be so starkly delineated, but there is ample evidence of a reshaping of forensic labour

---

[43]Scottish Police Authority. Retrieved from www.spa.police.uk/forensic-services/

[44]Source: Director, SPA Forensic Services (2015).

[45]The Director of Forensic Services concedes that the impartiality, and independence, of the Scottish service is a cause for concern and could be improved through instituting strict administrative separation from the police service.

[46]These are located in Gartcosh Scottish Crime Campus, Aberdeen, Edinburgh, and Dundee. The Scottish DNA Database (SDNAD) is also located at the Dundee Harbour facility.

[47]Scottish Police Authority. Retrieved from www.spa.police.uk/forensic-services/quality/

[48]Lawless, C. (2016). *Forensic science: A sociological introduction* (pp. 61, 75). London: Routledge.

processes in line with rationalising ideologies, not least the commoditisation of forensic products for sale to Police Scotland, the institution whom the Scottish Police Authority is also required to govern and support.

When comparing different models of forensic science provision within the UK, it is important to avoid the application of a reductive politico-economic binary, categorising according to purely private, or public, provision. More important is the need to resist applying normative judgements to such categorisations. Indeed, some commentators highlight a perception that has been allowed to develop, which tends to view the 'Scottish model' of public sector provision as being qualitatively different, if not better, than that which subsists in the rest of the UK.[49] Lee and Woodward argue that such differences in approach may be directly attributable to the process of constitutional devolution.

> The politics of depoliticisation … which has confined devolution in England to more prescriptive administrative delegation, is in contrast to the re-politicisation of the implementation process, and the greater political autonomy over both the design of policy and the allocation of resources, which has resulted from devolution to Scotland, Wales and Northern Ireland.[50]

However, Poole and Mooney are more cautious in their treatment of the subject, noting that,

> […] whilst devolution has undoubtedly increased the *potential* for a distinctively Scottish social policy agenda to emerge, in practice [distinctive] social policy development north of the border has been constrained by a number of factors …[51]

They trace changes to public sector provision in Scotland in the 1990s to a broader agenda, as introduced by the Labour Government of the late 1990s, whose policy initiatives made frequent recourse to market-based solutions. This agenda was notable for its ideological commitment to the opening up of public services throughout the UK to market forces. Despite public opposition in Scotland, the 'modernisation' agenda received widespread support at a local governmental level and was enthusiastically pursued by the Scottish Executive.

---

[49]Christie, C. (2011). *Commission on the future delivery of public services*. Edinburgh: Scottish Government. Retrieved from http://www.scotland.gov.uk/Resource/Doc/352649/0118638.pdf

[50]Lee, S., & Woodward, R. (2002). Delivering public services – Mechanisms and consequences: Implementing the third way: The delivery of public services under the Blair Government. *Public Money & Management, 22*(4), 49–56.

[51]Poole, L., & Mooney, G. (2006). Privatizing education in Scotland? New labour, modernization and 'public' services. *Critical Social Policy, 26*(3), 562–586.

Thus, Poole and Mooney question 'the often taken for granted view that Scottish social policy-making is necessarily informed by a more "public service" and collectivist ethos'.[52]

The significant changes made to public sector provision in Scotland – in line with those inculcated elsewhere in the UK – are closely associated with New Labour's 'third way' approach to public sector service delivery, which served to blur the distinction between the state and the market. The 'third way' approach incorporated the concepts of 'best value' – an exhortation to achieve economically rational goals through improvements in efficiency – alongside a belief that 'what matters is what works', a pragmatic, though equally ideological, focus on achieving the delivery of effective, high-quality public services. The seeming pragmatism of third way thinking required that the public sector be restructured and reorganised by way of a blurring of the boundaries between public and private provision. This was to be achieved through the forging of partnerships between responsibilised stakeholders. Governmental reform, and modernisation of the public sector in Scotland, was achieved through the reform and modernisation of public sector workers, and the risks associated with the placing of private interests at the heart of public service delivery were offset through managerialisation and increased regulation.

It might be argued that public sector working practices in Scotland, including those of forensic science provision and continuing under the devolved Scottish National Party (SNP)-led Scottish government, display a significant degree of penetration by commercialised management techniques, objectives, and incentives.[53] Indeed, the public sector is a crucial arena, if not *the* crucial arena, within which to gauge the influence and impact of measures of economic rationality, both at theoretical and procedural levels.[54] However, it is also a site of resistance and contestation. Thus, it is not uncommon to discover that discourses regarding the provision of forensic services expose a tension between traditional views of the role of public services and the countervailing imperatives of economisation:

> It is clear that financial matters must be considered. We must achieve best value – but the need to protect our communities by ensuring that we prosecute the people who perpetrate crime is at

---

[52]Poole, L., & Mooney, G. (2006). Privatizing education in Scotland? New labour, modernization and 'public' services. *Critical Social Policy, 26*(3), 562–586.

[53]The SPA speak of the benefits of adopting an integrated approach 'from crime scene to courtroom'. Retrieved from www.bbc.co.uk/programmes/profiles/4SNV7PJDHsH874vGFd69BNb/tom-nelson-director-of-spa-forensic-services

[54]McCafferty, P., & Mooney, G. (2010). Resisting the neoliberal 'modernisation' of public services in contemporary Scotland: The case of public sector workers. In N. Davidson, P. McCafferty, & D. Miller. *Neo-liberal Scotland: Class and society in a stateless nation*. Newcastle: Cambridge Scholars Publishing.

> the root of the current process … The Scottish Police Services Authority is currently engaging with its customers and stakeholders on the future delivery of police forensic services.[55]

The above is illustrative of the view that the provision of forensic support services in Scotland's police laboratory – despite remaining within the public sector – reflects the influence of the same commercial discourses which drove thoroughgoing privatisation of provision in England and Wales, albeit that in-house provision remains the norm in Scotland. Having outlined the variegated nature of forensic science provision across the UK – focussing on the governance models, societal roles, and particular features relating to provision in each of its constituent jurisdictions – discussion now turns to the exercise of forensic-scientific expertise.

[55]MacAskill, K. Scottish Justice Minister. (2010, January 28). Extract from minutes of the Scottish Parliament.

Chapter 2

Forensic-Scientific Processes

DNA and Epistemological Privilege

The centralised laboratories considered in the course of this study aim to satisfy the requirement for a range of services encompassing biology, DNA analysis, toxicology, chemistry, firearms, fingerprints, toolmarks and sundry lesser crafts and techniques. However, it should be stressed that during the past two decades, deoxyribonucleic acid (DNA)-profiling techniques have achieved an unparalleled epistemological status to the detriment of a number of less efficient but nonetheless complimentary techniques. Indeed, it may be posited that knowledge claims derived from a number of cognate forensic techniques enjoy a comparatively low status as compared with DNA, since many are derived from practices which fail to meet the criteria applicable to progressive forms of research science. As will be shown in relation to the problem of DNA mixtures, alongside DNA 'transfer and persistence', criticisms that focus on the relative status of forensic, and 'normal', science cannot fully account for the problematic and heterogeneous nature of the forensic field. Indeed, while standard accounts claim that the diminished status routinely applied to forensic craft practices does not apply to those DNA-profiling techniques borrowed from the biosciences, this fails to account for more complex iterations. Nonetheless, such techniques are widely regarded as conforming to the positivist ideals of research science and may even be viewed as the means through which the larger body of forensic science practices have been rehabilitated (at least within the public sphere).

It is clear that, in the eyes of the law alongside those of the general public, DNA-profiling techniques and Bayesian analytical methods together constitute 'an exceptionally scientific form of evidence',[1] which may be easily contrasted with a body of 'subjective and pre-scientific' forensic craft practices. As such, the introduction of DNA/Bayes may be construed as heralding a 'paradigm shift'[2]

[1]Lynch, M. (2013). Science, truth, and forensic cultures: The exceptional legal status of DNA evidence. *Studies in History and Philosophy of Biological and Biomedical Sciences, 44*, 8.

[2]Saks, M. J., & Koehler, J. J. (2005). The coming paradigm shift in forensic identification science. *Science, 309*, 892–895, at p. 893.

Marketisation and Forensic Science Provision in England and Wales, 17–31

Published under exclusive licence by Emerald Publishing Limited
doi:10.1108/978-1-83909-123-020221002

in forensic science. However, commentators have recommended caution in this regard. Saks and Koehler[3] argue that – by Kuhnian criteria – DNA profiling has not inculcated a paradigm shift within the forensic science field, insofar as DNA-profiling techniques do not overthrow an existing conceptual framework, thereby generating a new stream of 'normal' science. However, accepting Saks and Koehler's position, it is still possible to claim that there has been a non-Kuhnian 'revolution' in forensic science, insofar as an array of expert forensic-scientific practices has managed to achieve, if not surpass, scientific status.[4]

Nonetheless, the emergent 'scientific' status of the DNA/Bayes network may serve to make forensic knowledge claims more resistant to the interposition of contextual factors and thereby help to shape the forensic-scientific profession. That DNA profiling has achieved scientific status may be inferred from the achievements of those analysts and researchers associated with the process. Focussing on the academic, and career, trajectories of those involved in 'normal' scientific culture, as against those of forensic science practitioners, Saks and Koehler noted that routine forensic practices – though 'graced with an aura of science' – are held to be of significantly lower status than those conducted within the field of 'real' science (in accordance with Merton's normative approach). DNA profiling is, therefore, both significant and unusual, insofar as it has risen to the status of normal science. This achievement may be attributed to its transparency with regard to its hypotheses, its application of knowledge 'derived from core scientific disciplines' – including chemistry, biology and mathematics – and its harnessing of 'data-based, probabilistic assessments'[5] in order to structure evaluation.

What is not clear from the literature is whether, or to what extent, forensic practices in general have begun to be regarded as nominally scientific 'on the coat-tails' of DNA profiling and its 'elite' status. A consideration of the epistemological basis for such claims – resting on increasingly indefensible concepts, such as 'uniqueness' and 'individualisation' – would suggest that, for this to be the case, forensic identification practices would have to overcome significant hurdles.[6] This will be the subject of further discussion in Chapter 3.[7]

[3]Saks, M. J., & Koehler, J. J. (2005). The coming paradigm shift in forensic identification science. *Science, 309*, 892–895, at p. 893.

[4]Saks, M. J., & Koehler, J. J. (2005). The coming paradigm shift in forensic identification science. *Science, 309*, 892–895, at p. 893; see also Cole, S. A. (2013). Forensic culture as epistemic culture: The sociology of forensic science. *Studies in History and Philosophy of Biological and Biomedical Sciences, 44*, 36–46.

[5]*Ibid*, at p. 893; see also Lynch, M. (2013). Science, truth, and forensic cultures: The exceptional legal status of DNA evidence. *Studies in History and Philosophy of Biological and Biomedical Sciences, 44*, 60–70.

[6]Cole, S. (2009). Forensics without uniqueness, conclusions without individualization: The new epistemology of forensic identification. *Law, Probability and Risk, 8*, 233–255.

[7]For a full discussion of contemporary media representations of forensic practices, see Lawless, C. (2016). *Forensic science: A sociological introduction* (p. 20). New York, NY: Routledge.

Returning to the DNA/Bayes, it is clear from the literature that, beyond the core set of forensic-scientific practitioners (and associated institutional actors), DNA-profiling techniques have been accorded an exceptional – if not unassailable – epistemological status. Evidence derived from DNA profiling has been described, variously, as 'infallible', furnishing 'irrefutable proof' and as a 'truth machine' or 'revelation machine'.[8] Characteristically hyperbolic statements, commending the hitherto-unparalleled discriminatory potential of forensic bio-identification techniques, reach a zenith with the claim – from the president of the *Deutschen Gesellschaft für Rechtsmedizin* (German Society for Forensic Medicine) – that 'a DNA match identifies a perpetrator with 100% certainty'.[9] Such statements are not uncommon among the literature, more frequently the secondary sources, devoted to forensic DNA profiling. However, the epistemological privileging of knowledge claims derived from such techniques is by no means limited to the claims of institutional actors.[10]

Insofar as forensic-scientific knowledge claims, based upon DNA/Bayes[11] techniques, have been held to possess the epistemological status of objective 'natural' facts, the development of this branch of forensic inquiry follows the trajectory of prior forensic identification techniques, particularly that of latent fingerprint analysis. In a seminal example of social-constructivist Science and Technology Studies scholarship – one whose historical, and disputational, focus exhibits features common to both the Edinburgh and Bath schools – Cole has chronicled the contentious history and development of friction ridge examination (fingerprinting).[12] His account begins in the early twentieth century, when

---

[8]See Lynch, M., Cole, S. A., McNally, R., & Jordan, K. (2008). *Truth machine: The contentious history of DNA fingerprinting*. Chicago, IL: University of Chicago Press.

[9]Lindsey, S., Hertwig, R., & Gigerenzer, G. (2003). Communicating statistical DNA evidence. *Jurimetrics, 43*, 147–163, at p. 150.

[10]'DNA – deoxyribonucleic acid – is God's signature. God's signature is never a forgery'. Prison inmate Loyd, E.-J., quoted in Wilgorin, J. (2002). Confession had his signature; DNA did not. *The New York Times*, August 26.

[11]The use of 'DNA/Bayes' terminology prefigures discussion of the probabilistic interpretation of biological identification techniques as constituting an actor–network (see Chapter 3).

[12]Cole, S. A. (2001). *Suspect identities: A history of fingerprinting and criminal identification*. Cambridge, MA: Harvard University Press; see also Cole, S. A. (1998). Witnessing identification: Latent fingerprint evidence and expert knowledge. *Social Studies of Science, 28*(5/6), 687–712; Cole, S. A. (2000). The myth of fingerprints: A forensic science stands trial. *Lingua Franca,* November, pp. 54–62; Cole, S. A. (2003). Fingerprinting: The first junk science? *Oklahoma City University Law Review, 28*(1), 73–92; Cole, S. A. (2004). Grandfathering evidence: Fingerprint admissibility ruling from Jennings to Llera Plaza and back again. *American Criminal Law Review, 41*(3); Cole, S. A. (2007). Twins, Twain, Galton & Gilman: Fingerprinting, individualization, brotherhood and race in Pudd'nhead Wilson. *Configurations, 15,* 227–265; Cole, S. (2009). Forensics without uniqueness, conclusions without individualization: The new epistemology of forensic identification. *Law, Probability and Risk, 8*, 233–255.

'fingerprinting' was regarded as both a reliable, and reputedly infallible, source of expert evidence in criminal trials. Courts demonstrated a willingness to accept the testimony of fingerprint examiners, with little – or no – inquiry into the scientific and epistemological basis of their judgements, insofar as the latter claimed to be able to make correct source attributions. All elements of the criminal justice system accepted the proposition (flowing from the philosophical concept of 'uniqueness'), that no two individuals exhibit the same friction ridge patterns. Further (in an example of institutional actors articulating the second limb of the 'forensic imaginary', discussed *infra*), it was accepted that trained examiners could detect 'matches' without error.[13] The courts therefore allowed examiners to express 'unqualified certainty' when making testimonial claims and did not require them to supply error rates or other probabilistic estimates normally associated with scientific procedure.[14]

However, the first challenge to friction ridge examination arose from the application of new admissibility tests laid out in *Daubert* v. *Merrel Dow Pharmaceuticals* and *Kumho Tires* v. *Carmichael*,[15] which required expert testimony to exhibit, and meet, verifiable scientific standards (see below). The second challenge arose from the introduction of DNA 'fingerprinting' techniques and the application of a new 'gold standard' in forensic science. Mnookin et al.[16] point out distinct similarities between the ways in which the courts treated friction ridge analysis and later treatment of DNA 'fingerprinting'. Both of these bio-identification techniques relied on an analyst's ability to make strong discriminatory assertions in respect of suspect populations and to link these to an ineradicable bodily substrate. Thus, both fingerprints, and DNA evidence, were widely regarded as being derived directly from nature, with human mediation a mere triviality. Mnookin's research (which draws on Cole's historical study of fingerprint analysis[17]) throws light on the problems that were faced by forensic identification experts and which would later be faced by those advancing DNA-based knowledge claims. Both faced initial challenges with regard to the precision of their claims. Indeed, DNA analysts – whose methods for calculating random match probabilities were based

[13]Uncritical acceptance of dogmatic concepts, e.g. uniqueness and the 'science of individualisation', is attributed to a long-standing failure to articulate a defensible epistemological foundation for the testimonial claims of forensic bio-identification experts. See Cole, S. (2009). Forensics without uniqueness, conclusions without individualization: The new epistemology of forensic identification. *Law, Probability and Risk, 8*, 233–255.

[14]Lynch, M., & Cole, S. A. (2005). Science and technology studies on trial: Dilemmas of expertise. *Social Studies of Science, 35*(2), 269–311, at p. 270.

[15]See below.

[16]Mnookin, J., Cole, S., Fisher, B. A. J., Dror, I. E., Houck, M., Inman, K., … Siegel, J. (2010). The need for a research culture in the forensic sciences. *UCLA Law Review, 58*, 725.

[17]Cole, S. A. (2001). *Suspect identities: A history of fingerprinting and criminal identification*. Cambridge, MA: Harvard University Press.

upon dubious statistical assumptions – weathered robust criticism in both scientific journals and legal hearings.[18]

However, Cole highlights the way in which the same forms of techno-legal controversy, which had been deemed problematic for fingerprinting, came to be regarded as strengths when applied to DNA profiling. The controversies and contretemps of the 'DNA wars' led, not to debunking, but to peer-reviewed publication, scientific status and closure.[19]

Critics of standard identification techniques, such as latent print analysis, might assert that the diminishing status of these techniques in the face of DNA evidence was both deserved and overdue. Indeed, Cole contends that the nature and magnitude of the claims made by latent fingerprint analysts could only be achieved through a 'leap of faith'[20] through which the analyst becomes 'subjectively certain that the patterns could not possibly be duplicated by chance'.[21] He contends that such 'leaps of faith' render individualisation unscientific, irrational and unnecessary. In counterpoint, DNA profiling – presented in probabilistic terms – 'has shown that non-individualising evidence can have it both ways: convey a significant probative value *and* transparently convey information … to fact-finders'.[22]

Nonetheless, these studies left much to be done. While they addressed a series of structural problems which had hampered the forensic-scientific production of knowledge claims – primarily from a scientific-realist perspective – they did not fully account for the efficient and routinised iterations of DNA-profiling techniques which have subsequently been developed.

Probability and Statistical Evidence in Criminal Proceedings

The evaluation of DNA-profiling evidence is constructed around a form of inferential reasoning derived from Bayes' theorem. It must be stressed that 'the

[18]Lynch, M. (2013). Science, truth, and forensic cultures: The exceptional legal status of DNA evidence. *Studies in History and Philosophy of Biological and Biomedical Sciences, 44*, 60–70.

[19]Of particular interest in this regard is an article in the science journal *Nature* by Lander and Budowle, which has been viewed as an attempt to create the illusion of scientific consensus, with the specific intention of facilitating the use of DNA-based evidence in the landmark *Simpson* trial. See Lander, E. S., & Budowle, B. (1994, October 27). DNA fingerprinting dispute laid to rest. *Nature, 371*, 735–738.

[20]Cole, S. (2009). Forensics without uniqueness, conclusions without individualization: The new epistemology of forensic identification. *Law, Probability and Risk, 8*, 233–255, at p. 247.

[21]Stoney, D. A. (1991). What made us ever think we could individualize using statistics *Journal of the Forensic Science Society, 31*, 197–199.

[22]Cole, S. (2009). Forensics without uniqueness, conclusions without individualization: The new epistemology of forensic identification. *Law, Probability and Risk, 8*, 233–255, at p. 247.

Bayesian approach' is not a direct application of Bayes' theorem. Indeed, it may be argued that many iterations of Bayesian philosophy are better considered as sophisticated forms of hypothetico-deductivism developed from causal Markov chains.[23] Indeed, Bayesian probabilistic methods should be seen as a form of inferential reasoning rather than a strict calculus. The method is based on the proposition that while it is impossible to state with absolute certainty that a trace comes from a particular source, it is possible to draw inferences from the analytical results. Since there can only be two possibilities (match and non-match), the task for the forensic scientist is to evaluate the likelihood that each of these two mutually exclusive possibilities is correct. This is achieved by comparing pairs of propositions, in order to arrive at a likelihood ratio.

The likelihood ratio balances the likelihood of obtaining the particular analytical result (e.g. a DNA match) given that one proposition is true (e.g. the DNA from the blood found on the suspect's clothes comes from the victim), against the likelihood of obtaining the same result (a DNA match) given that the alternative proposition is true (the DNA from the blood found on the suspect's clothes does not come from the victim). Thus, the likelihood ratio expresses the weight of the evidence, rather than its accuracy.

The above example deals with a relatively common and straightforward pair of propositions. In such an example the pair of propositions typically translates to the respective prosecution, and defence, versions of events. However, more than one set of propositions can be constructed depending on the complexity of the case and the availability of information. Further, the Bayesian approach allows for the incorporation of contextual information, which may lead to the modification of propositions, and the creation of successive hypotheses, which serve to nullify prior hypotheses. As such, the Bayesian 'inference engine' exhibits Popperian falsification (discussed below). The unique features of this calculus of causal reasoning are explored in the following section.

Standardisation through Probabilistic Evidence Techniques

Epistemological theories of causality find their most concise expression in Hume, who notes that,

> after a repetition of similar instances, the mind is carried by habit, upon the appearance of one event, to expect its usual attendant, and to believe that it will exist. This connexion, therefore, which we feel in the mind, this customary transition of the imagination from one object to its usual attendant, is the sentiment or impression from which we form the idea of power or necessary connexion.

The mapping of the connections between causal beliefs and commonly perceived effects allows for the modelling of predictions, diagnoses and accurate decisions, which allows agents to reason in the face of uncertainty. Within the

[23]Discussed in the following chapters.

forensic-scientific domain, such reasoning is expressed through the use of probabilistic tools. Statistical translations thereby comprise the strategic means by which the particular epistemic cultures stabilises and standardises the practice of forensic-scientific expertise.[24]

The literature relating to the use of probability models in forensic science – and the presentation of statistical evidence in court – is extensive and predates the use of DNA 'fingerprinting' as a forensic tool. It is clear that the appearance of DNA on the forensic-legal field served merely to crystallise pre-existing debates relating to the accurate interpretation and exposition of probabilistic evidence and to throw ongoing concerns into sharp relief. The body of literature devoted to the forensic use of statistics and probabilistic reasoning thus represents an ongoing attempt, by both academics and practitioners, to develop a coherent approach to the presentation of evidence derived from forensic techniques. In recent years, this project has been most closely associated with a method of statistical reasoning based on the use of Bayes' theorem.[25]

As stated above, Bayes' theorem offers forensic scientists the means to reason in the face of uncertainty. While probabilistic reasoning always starts with a hypothesis and follows a series of well-defined arguments to reach a conclusion that is guaranteed to be true, statistical reasoning starts with some observations and tries to use them to infer something about the wider world. This inference is not guaranteed to be true and so we say that it has a probability of being true. Note that the use of probability is not the same as probabilistic.

Inductive inference means that we take some available evidence and extend it to form a conclusion. Because this is inductive inference, we cannot be 100% certain that the conclusion made is a result of well-defined logical steps from a hypothesis. Therefore, we attach a likelihood or a probability of our conclusion being true. Therefore, inductive inference falls under the umbrella of statistical reasoning. This kind of inference involves reasoning in the face of uncertainty and hence a probability that the result will be true.

Bayes' theorem is a mechanism which allows us to infer something about A (which we cannot observe) from B (something we can observe). Since we are making an inference about A using the available evidence given by B, we have some uncertainty that A is really true. Bayes' theorem calculates the probability of A being true given that we know B is true. There is no guarantee that B being true will imply that A is also true, and as a result, this method must belong to inductive inference.

Redmayne describes the widespread use of such methods as 'the Bayesian Turn in forensic science'.[26] He traces the 'Bayesian turn' to a paper presented

---

[24]Haack, S. (2009). *Irreconcilable differences? The troubled marriage of science and law.* 72 Law and Contemporary Problems 1.

[25]Bayes' theorem is a mathematical formula that can be applied to update probabilities of particular issues in the light of new evidence. Bayesian methods are further explained at Section 1.4.4.

[26]Redmayne, M. (2001). *Expert evidence and criminal justice*. Oxford: Oxford University Press.

to the Royal Statistical Society in 1977, in which Lindley[27] – using the example of the interpretation of glass evidence – championed the use of Bayesian, as opposed to classical, statistics. In this paper, Lindley laid out the problems associated with the use of classical statistics. The main problem can be put in statistical terms, as follows: when attempting to place a value within a normal distribution curve around the benchmark value, the standard deviation limits (i.e. the limits of error) around the mean are treated – in classical statistics – as absolute limits. What this means is that the scientist can only declare two possibilities: a match and a non-match. If a source sample and a reference sample are compared and the data fall within a certain range, they will be treated as matching perfectly and vice versa. Conversely, a value falling just beyond these limits is completely discounted. This 'fall-of-the-cliff' effect appears to be predicated on an arbitrary criterion: the standard deviation limit set by the examiner. Lindley's approach was to employ Bayesian statistics in order to prevent evidence from falling of the probabilistic cliff.

The Bayesian approach is markedly different. As stated above, it incorporates similarities and differences between two samples, in addition to other factors, expressing these differences in terms of a likelihood ratio, which measures the probative force of a particular piece of evidence relative to two hypotheses. Without going into the technicalities of Bayesian analysis (of which there are many), it will serve present purposes to state that Bayes' theorem adds precision but is still dependent on contextual background information and invites the scientist to ask different questions regarding the object of analysis. It also requires that the investigator solicits different sorts of information with regard to the crime. However, the use of Bayesian statistical methods does not dispense with the need to make assumptions, and the results will be affected by those assumptions.

The persistence of subjectivity in arriving at assumptions against a background of incomplete and imperfect knowledge has been the subject of concern among academics. Evett,[28] Redmayne[29] and Taroni and Aitken[30] addressed this issue, while Hacking[31] and Cohen[32] attempted to add philosophical context, raising awareness that there exists a long-running philosophical dispute with regard to the qualitative nature of probability.

---

[27]Lindley, D. V. (1977). Probability and the law. *The Statistician, 26*, 203, at p. 211.

[28]Evett, I. W. (1996). Expert evidence and forensic misconceptions of the nature of exact science. *Science and Justice, 36*, 118.

[29]Redmayne, M. (2001). *Expert evidence and criminal justice*. Oxford: Oxford University Press.

[30]Taroni, F., & Aitken, C. G. G. (1997). Forensic science at trial. *Jurimetrics, 37*, 327–337; Taroni, F., & Aitken, C. (1998). Probabilistic reasoning in the law. Part 1: Assessment of probabilities and explanation of the value of DNA evidence. *Science & Justice, 38*(3), 165–177.

[31]Hacking, I. (1999). *The social construction of what?* Cambridge, MA: Harvard University Press.

[32]Cohen, J. L. (1981). *Can human irrationality be experimentally demonstrated? Behavioural and Brain Sciences, 317*, 329–330.

The problem crystallises around the use of Bayesian statistics to arrive at a 'likelihood ratio' based on the prior and posterior odds relating to a particular proposition. In order to determine the likelihood ratio, it will be necessary to determine the size of the 'suspect population' from which the crime sample is believed to originate. 'Suspect population' is a problematic term insofar as it suggests that all people within a defined group are equally likely (before any other evidence is obtained) to have committed the crime, and that those outside the group could not have committed the crime. However, common sense would suggest that a suspect living within 5 miles of the locus might be more likely to have committed the libelled crime than a suspect 500 miles distant.[33] It is clear that the use of Bayes' theorem in the criminal justice system is subject to evidential premises that carry broad implications. As Tillers states, 'it is in fact the case that the most complex argument about inferences from evidence rests on almost innumerable personal and subjective judgements'.[34]

These implications were recognised before the advent of DNA profiling. As early as 1970, Finkelstein and Fairley proposed the use of Bayes' theorem in criminal cases.[35] Their suggestion prompted a 'rhetorically powerful and multi-pronged attack' from Professor Laurence Tribe of Harvard Law School on what he called 'trial by mathematics'.[36] Tribe's criticisms of the use of probability theory to model factual inferences were as follows:

1. Bayes' theorem makes precise what is inherently imprecise.
2. Bayes' theorem makes objective what is subjective.
3. Trial by mathematics and statistics is morally and socially offensive.
4. Lay triers-of-fact cannot understand Bayes' theorem.
5. Numbers tend to dwarf soft variables.
6. Bayesian analysis ignores the possibility of source uncertainty.

Tribe's arguments are interesting insofar as they go beyond mere technicalities, drawing on moral, social and philosophical grounds relating to the nature of subjective human reasoning and its place in the criminal trial. They were also largely successful, at least in the short term. Despite a flurry of rejoinders from Finkelstein and Fairley, it seemed to most legal scholars that Tribe had succeeded in putting the lid back on Pandora's box.

---

[33]Donnelly, P., & Friedman, R. D. (1998–1999). DNA database searches and the legal consumption of scientific evidence. *Michigan Law Review, 97*, 931.

[34]Tillers, P. (2011). Trial by mathematics – Reconsidered. *Law, Probability & Risk, 10*, 167–173.

[35]Finkelstein, M. O., & Fairley, W. (1970). A Bayesian approach to identification evidence. *Harvard Law Review, 83*, 489.

[36]Tribe, L. (1971). Trial by mathematics: Precision and ritual in the legal process. *Harvard Law Review, 84*, 1329.

As Twining notes,[37] since 1977, the debate has centred around a more fundamental issue. Cohen[38] has suggested that there is more than one form of probabilistic reasoning. He posits the existence of a non-mathematical mode which he terms Baconian probability, in addition to the standard mathematical mode which he terms Pascalian probability. Further, he asserts that Baconian probability is commonly used by lawyers when reasoning about facts under conditions of uncertainty, in forensic contexts. Cohen's arguments have drawn criticism from both Eggleston[39] and Glanville-Williams,[40] who retort that there can be no more than one mode of probabilistic reasoning and that Cohen's conclusions are unsupported by his reasoning. Further, that the Baconian mode may be accounted for within the Pascalian mode.[41]

The appearance of DNA-profiling evidence on the forensic field has altered the nature of the debate considerably, and those moral, social and philosophical arguments – which had previously characterised the debate – have tended to wilt in the face of new developments. From the advent of DNA profiling, academic debate has become grounded in more pragmatic concerns, particularly around the 'correct' presentation of DNA-profiling evidence. Academics have attempted to posit a variety of guidelines for the exposition of statistical evidence, as have the courts. The literature on the presentation of evidence – and the ability of the trier-of-fact to understand such evidence – is quite considerable, the debate centring around the communication of statistical information, which can be constructed in a variety of ways. It may be communicated as a match probability or a likelihood ratio, though a brief survey of cases has thrown up a whole variety of terms (statistical probability, statistical likelihood, likelihood ratio, frequency ratio, frequency, random occurrence ratio), and the latter term has now gained widespread acceptance.

However, the purpose of this study was not to consider the relative utility of alternative forms of inferential reasoning and their translation and expression (though this forms an integral part of the discussion and analysis). Rather, it aligns with Lawless indication of

> the potential for qualitative ethnographic studies to uncover finer practices which underpin performative aspects of consciously 'Bayesian' reasoning, but which evade the gaze of philosophical accounts and models presented in technical journal articles.[42]

---

[37]Twining, W. (2006). *Rethinking evidence* (p. 127). Cambridge: Cambridge University Press.

[38]Cohen, L. J. (1977). *The probable and the provable*. Oxford: Oxford University Press.

[39]Eggleston, R. (1978). *Evidence, proof and probability*. London: Weidenfeld & Nicolson.

[40]Glanville-Williams. (1979). *The mathematics of proof I. Criminal Law Review, 297.*

[41]See Twining, W. (1980). Debating probabilities. *The Liverpool Law Review*, *2*(1), 51–64.

[42]Lawless, C. (2016). *Forensic science: A sociological introduction* (p. 97). London: Routledge.

With this in mind, the discussion turns to the harnessing of Bayesian methods within the Case Assessment and Interpretation (CAI) process.

The CAI Method

A central feature of the Bayesian approach is its flexibility and its capacity to assimilate new facts under fresh hypotheses. Rather than simply applying a formula, the forensic scientist – taking into account the surrounding facts of the case – may construct various sets of alternative propositions. Therefore, the construction of propositions under the Bayesian approach is highly dependent on context. Although this approach is designed to promote a balanced view of the evidence, and achieves a degree of transparency in respect of its underlying assumptions, the framing of alternative propositions remains a difficult process. As Cook (1998) states,

> In practice, the propositions that are addressed will depend on the circumstances of the case, the observations that have been made, background data that is available and the domain of expertise of the scientist.[43]

These propositions fall into three major categories, which together form a 'hierarchy of propositions': Source (Level I), Activity (Level II) and Offence (Level III). Examples of propositions from these generic classes are given below:

III	Offence	Miss X assaulted Mr Y
II	Activity	Miss X is the person who stabbed Mr Y
I	Source	The blood on Miss X's clothing came from Mr Y

Level I propositions are made from observations, measurements and analyses. The prosecution proposition will be determined from a comparison between two samples, and the defence proposition will be determined by considering one of these samples in reference to an external population (such as the National DNA Database, NDNAD).

Level II propositions relate to activities. They too are based on observations, measurements and analyses. However, in order to construct an activity proposition, the scientist must take account of the circumstantial framework. The scientist will need to exercise judgement in relation to the construction of Level II propositions and will require as much information as possible regarding the circumstances of the case. This will entail some degree of interaction between the forensic scientist and the investigator or prosecutor.

Another notable feature of Level II propositions is that they may be constructed in respect of a complete absence of source material. They might also take into account the possibility of contamination or the manufacture of evidence.

[43]Cook, Evett, Jackson, Jones (1998), at p. 151.

Level III propositions relate to the commission of offences. The forensic scientist, in his capacity, as expert witness, is forbidden from expressing an opinion on the ultimate issue. However, the three generic grades are not rigidly demarcated, and it may be possible to construct propositions which approach the ultimate issue without encroaching on the responsibilities of the trier-of-fact.

The CAI model may appear relatively unproblematic when presented in its basic form. However, its history and practical application reveal some areas of concern. CAI was developed by a management and advisory working group within the Forensic Science Service. The objective of the model was,

> To enable decisions to be made which will deliver a value for money service meeting the needs of our direct customers and the Criminal Justice System.[44]

CAI proceeds through three interlinked phases – customer requirement, case pre-assessment and service delivery – all of which are inscribed with those discourses of economic rationality discussed in the opening section: During the first phase (customer requirement), the customer's needs are determined in relation to economic imperatives. This requires that the scientist open up a dialogue with the customer in order to form an appraisal of the circumstances of the case, the kinds of examinations which can be conducted and what might be expected from them. The scientist also solicits information with regard to the suspect in order to maintain a balanced view, though this is mediated through the investigative authorities.

An analysis based on Level II (activity) propositions will be of greater use to the customer than a Level I analysis that is confined to source material and may also offer greater value for money. Forensic scientists are therefore encouraged to address their analyses to the highest propositional level possible, stopping short of an opinion on the ultimate *probandum*:

> [...] in some cases the scientist might be able to address propositions which are quite close to the deliberations of the court such as 'this is the person who murdered the victim'; in other cases it might be necessary to settle for propositions further removed from the ultimate issue such as 'these fibres came from that garment'.[45]

As the forensic scientist ascends the scale of propositions, she must solicit a greater amount of contextual information from the customer. However, the shift in focus from Level I (source) to Level II (activity) propositions may also be

---

[44]Cook, R., Evett, I. W., Jackson, G, Jones, P. J., & Lambert, J. A. (1998). A model for case assessment and interpretation. *Science & Justice, 38*, 151–156, at p. 153.

[45]Cook, R., Evett, I. W., Jackson, G, Jones, P. J., & Lambert, J. A. (1998). A model for case assessment and interpretation. *Science & Justice, 38*, 151–156, at p. 153.

viewed as an attempt by forensic experts to claim ownership of the actual process of contextualisation, in preference to lawyers or triers-of-fact.

> The probative value of scientific findings depends on the propositions that they are taken to be addressing. If scientists were always to restrict their interpretations to *source* level issues and propositions they would effectively be trusting other criminal justice professionals, or fact-finders themselves, to contextualise the scientific findings and interpret them correctly. But … the probative value of scientific findings addressed to source level propositions may *appear* considerably weaker … than if the same findings are presented in terms of activity level propositions. It must at least be seriously open to question whether lawyers and courts are currently sufficiently well-informed about the relational nature of scientific evidence or calculations of likelihood ratios to perceive these evidential subtleties, and fully to appreciate their forensic significance, without expert assistance.[46]

Thus, a shift in the balance of power between lawyer and scientist takes place as the latter ascends the propositional ladder, and scientists demarcate an indispensable role within the criminal justice system.

The next phase, case assessment, is seen as a natural extension of the determination of customer requirements. At this point, the scientist is required to tighten up the formulation of pairs of propositions in light of the information solicited from the customer and the latter's requirements. At this stage, the scientist is encouraged to document his expectations, these notes forming an integral part of the final written report.

The final phase, service delivery, accounts for the forensic scientist's main examination. Products are commissioned in light of prior assessments and following a consultation with the customer. Source material is analysed, results are interpreted and a report is drafted. The fact that the expectations were noted before the examination is carried out is a measure designed to counter any accusations of post hoc rationalisation. However, this safeguard is compromised by the recursive, as opposed to linear, nature of the CAI process.

The CAI model, being designed to meet customer requirements, has a strong iterative element. The propositions and expectations laid down in the second phase are subject to review, reframing and modification in light of the results of the material analysis and the availability of new information. The FSS stated that,

> There are many reasons why both propositions and expectations might change as a result of unexpected developments during the

[46]Para 2.40 of Jackson, G., Aitken, C., & Roberts, P. (2015). *Practitioner guide 4 – Case assessment and interpretation of expert evidence*. Royal Statistical Society's Working Group on Statistics and the Law.

> examination. There should be a continuous process of review and, where necessary, further consultation with the customer.[47]

Evett et al.[48] provide a series of case studies, which illustrate the ways in which mutually exclusive pairs of propositions may be revised and refined in order to take account of new information. The following example is adapted from one such study.

An armed robbery was carried out on a post office by masked men, who left the incident in a stolen vehicle. Eyewitnesses saw clothing being discarded from the car as it drove off. One of the items of clothing was a balaclava. The following day, a suspect was interviewed. He denied any involvement in the robbery. He said that the balaclava was not his and that he had never worn such an item. A DNA swab was taken from the suspect and submitted for examination against traces found on the balaclava.

The circumstantial framework in this case concerns material that may have been transferred from the suspect to an object associated with the locus, and time is relevant to the interpretation of the evidence. The scientist is tasked with framing a pair of propositions, and the framework of circumstances suggests that she is justified in addressing Level II propositions, which might take the form:

> The suspect was wearing the balaclava on the day of the robbery.
>
> The suspect has never worn the balaclava.

These two propositions represent the prosecution and defence accounts of the incident. In this case, the likelihood ratio will be determined by considerations based on the presence of DNA on fibres.

The above example shows how the propositions are determined to a significant degree by anything the suspect might say. If, under further questioning, the suspect changes his story, then the propositions must change to account for the change. If the suspect revises his story, claiming that he does own the balaclava but that he was not wearing it on the day of the robbery – and had not worn it for some weeks – then the propositions must now be expressed as follows:

> The suspect was wearing the balaclava on the day of the robbery.
>
> The suspect was wearing the balaclava a few weeks before the robbery.

---

[47]Cook, R., Evett, I. W., Jackson, G, Jones, P. J., & Lambert, J. A. (1998). A model for case assessment and interpretation. *Science & Justice, 38*, 151–156, at p. 153.

[48]Evett, I. W., Jackson, G., & Lambert, J. A. (2000). More on the hierarchy of propositions: Exploring the distinction between explanations and propositions. *Science & Justice, 40*(1), 3–10.

In this revised analysis, the likelihood ratio will be determined by considerations based on the *persistence* (rather than the *presence*) of DNA on fibres.

The above example demonstrates the significance of ongoing communication and collaboration between the investigating authorities and the forensic scientist, allowing the latter to construct case propositions that accurately reflect the existing case theory and which can be adapted to take account of, and incorporate, new contextual information. Evett et al. prescribe an ideal mode of forensic investigation and evaluation. As demonstrated above, collaboration and feedback are also regarded as necessary for the efficient and timely management of the casework process. The customer 'has a greater participation than hitherto in decisions about what work is done in the laboratory'[49] and dictates the direction of the evaluative process by ordering a particular forensic test or 'product'. Before ordering a test (or series of tests) to be carried out, the forensic scientist will provide some indication as to the sorts of inferences that can be made from the possible results and their potential probative value. This allows the customer to make an informed decision as to the desirability of conducting particular tests and to allocate resources accordingly.

The 'customer-directed' nature of the casework process thereby introduces economic and commercial factors into the process of forensic analysis which may impinge on the evaluative process: since the creation of propositional pairs is highly dependent on the availability of contextual information, and the collection of samples and background information is determined by economic factors (and a perceived scarcity of resources), then it may be argued that the evaluative process itself might be directly affected by operational determinations.[50]

Analytical problems associated with the allocation of limited resources may be aggravated by technological and physical factors, both of which can increase the cost, complexity and probative value of a forensic analysis. The dramatic increase in the sensitivity of DNA-profiling systems has enabled them to construct DNA profiles from very small quantities of 'touch' or low template DNA. However, when dealing with minute traces of DNA evidence, it can become difficult to differentiate 'signal' from 'noise'. This can place demands on the CAI process which are exacerbated when DNA-profiling evidence is transferred to the courtroom.

Having introduced the central governance and procedural features of marketised forensic science provision in the UK, the next chapter turns to a discussion of the unique challenges encountered when attempting to conduct interdisciplinary empirical research within this forensic field.

---

[49]Cook, R., Evett, I. W., Jackson, G, Jones, P. J., & Lambert, J. A. (1998). A model for case assessment and interpretation. *Science & Justice, 38*, 151–156, at p. 152.

[50]Lawless, C. J., & Williams, R. (2010). Helping with inquiries or helping with profits? The trials and tribulations of a technology of forensic reasoning. *Social Studies of Science, 40*, 731–755; Lawless, C. (2010). *A curious reconstruction? The shaping of 'marketized' forensic science*. CARR Discussion Paper 63; Lawless, C. (2011). Policing markets; the contested shaping of neo-liberal forensic science. *British Journal of Criminology, 51*, 671–689.

Chapter 3

Exploring the Forensic Field

This monograph is founded upon doctoral research which sought to illuminate the landscape of forensic science provision in England and Wales since the announced closure of the Forensic Science Service (FSS) in December 2010, with a sustained focus on the introduction of complete privatisation, as the central feature of the process of marketisation. In so doing, the study demonstrates the ways in which forensic scientists working within the marketised forensic have had to respond to the influence of marketisation. These informants provide evidence of the problematic influence of marketisation on the introduction of standardised practices and commodification of forensic products and services; of the restructuring of forensic expertise and labour conditions; of the streamlining of forensic analyses, most notably deoxyribonucleic acid (DNA) profiling, and the introduction of non-expert reporting; and of the regulation of these processes in an attempt to ensure quality and reliability across a febrile market. These findings are given fresh impetus by recent tumultuous events within the forensic market, most notably the collapse of one of the main forensic providers, and its subsequent resuscitation by the Metropolitan police, followed closely by the discovery of criminal practices among forensic analysts leading to the collapse of a number of trials. These data, discussed in the substantive sections of this study, amply demonstrate the structural problems which afflict the market and the inability of the regulator to effectively assure the quality of marketised forensic analysis. A sophisticated understanding of the effects of marketisation on the evidential trajectory is therefore timely and an essential contribution to understandings of the privatised forensic sector. The informants' testimony further suggests that marketised forensic science has followed a circular trajectory from scientific objectivity to regulatory objectivity, from epistemological validity to instrumental efficiency, and in reconfiguring itself around the indices of competition and efficiency has rendered itself less able to meet the challenges of a dynamic and evolving biomedical field. However, the forensic market – based upon triaging and low-skill repetitive analyses – may be configured to ably exploit the potentials of digital forensic evidence. Further research will therefore be necessary to inform debates around the future of marketised forensic science, as it begins to grapple with new methods and fresh challenges. However, before embarking on a focussed analysis and discussion of the empirical evidence, it is first necessary to discuss

Marketisation and Forensic Science Provision in England and Wales, 33–52

Published under exclusive licence by Emerald Publishing Limited
doi:10.1108/978-1-83909-123-020221003

the research process and the unique challenges encountered when interrogating expert scientific processes, which transect disciplinary boundaries.

Methods

The instant study proceeded from an objectivist ontological commitment and a critical realist epistemological perspective, utilising a comparative case study design with multiple embedded units. The nature of the phenomenon, the contextual conditions, and the research question – which sought to explore the influence of marketisation on the forensic science sector – was determinative in adopting the case study paradigm and met the criteria enumerated by leading proponents of case study methods.1 The case studies selected from within the forensic science sector in England and Wales represented the two dominant categories of private forensic organisation: private companies acting as large-scale government forensic science providers (FSPs) (Tier 1 FSPs) and small- to medium-sized private FSPs primarily serving legal defence requirements (Tier 2 FSPs). Participants were selected according to limiting criteria, and one public sector FSP was included to act as a control. This approach aligned with the 'most similar' case study method, which typically focusses on two or more cases. In its paradigmatic form, a pair of cases are chosen, both of which are similar on all measured variables, with the exception of the independent variable of interest. Table 3.1 outlines the typical approach.

In this model, both cases display similarity across all background conditions (relevant to the outcome of interest). This is signified by X_2, the vector of control variables. However, the cases differ on one main dimension (X_1) and on the outcome (Y). A logical inference, drawn from this pattern of co-variation, is that the presence, or absence, of X_1 is the cause of variation acting on Y. In the instant case, two cases (fully marketised, and publicly funded, forensic providers) were chosen due to the fact that these cases displayed variance across the variable of interest (degree of marketisation). The background variables (provision of forensic analysis and evaluation services to the criminal justice system) were similar. Thus, the predicted outcome would be divergent, indicating that the public sector/marketised variable would be responsible for the differences in outcome with regard to the divergent processes of forensic analysis and evaluation. Such a strategy answers the research objectives as directly and efficiently as is possible when using qualitative case study methods focussed on small-*n* paradigm case samples.

The study utilised a palette of qualitative methods, specifically documentary analysis and semi-structured fieldwork interviews, the latter conducted with experienced forensic professionals within the administrative facilities of the selected FSPs. Focus groups and strategic conversations were also held at a number of locations including The Home Office, Scottish Crime Campus, and New Scotland

[1] Yin, R. K. (2003). *Applications of case study research* (2nd ed.). Thousand Oaks, CA: Sage; Flyvberg, B. (2006). Five misunderstandings about case study research. *Qualitative Enquiry, 12*(2), 219–245, at p. 222.

Table 3.1. Most Similar Case Study Analysis with Two Cases.[2]

	Variable		
Case	X_1	X_2	Y
1	+	+	+
2	–	+	–

Yard. In addition to forensic scientists, interviews were conducted with allied institutional agents including senior professional members of the Judiciary of England and Wales, Her Majesty's Inspectorate of Constabulary, the Office of the Forensic Science Regulator, the Crown Prosecution Service, the Royal Society, The Royal Society of Edinburgh, Her Majesty's Inspectorate of Constabulary, the United Kingdom Accreditation Service, the Crown Prosecution Service, the Metropolitan Police, and the Chartered Society of Forensic Sciences. The period of data collection lasted from 2015 to 2021. Data collected from the study were subject to analysis and triangulation, prior to writing up and dissemination. Having specified the methodology, the following sections now proceed to detail the findings from the qualitative study, beginning with an account of pre-marketisation forensic analyses within the public sector FSS.

Interdisciplinary research, and the collaborative co-production of knowledge claims across disciplinary boundaries, has engendered a large, and diverse, body of scholarship: it is clear that interdisciplinary practices are enacted across a disciplinary landscape marked by diversity and variegation; that the practices, of which interdisciplinary study is comprised, are diverse; and that those practices are enacted within a multitude of institutional contexts. Research into interdisciplinary practices, while enjoying an unparalleled degree of popularity, has also tended to cluster around a set of underlying assumptions. Frickel, Albert, and Prainsack's analysis[3] of interdisciplinary collaboration in the social sciences identifies three of the most common underlying misconceptions:

1. Interdisciplinary knowledge is better than disciplinary knowledge.
2. Disciplines are silos that constrain the free development of disciplinary knowledge.
3. Interdisciplinary interactions are unconstrained by the status hierarchies, and power asymmetries, which operate within disciplines.

[2]Note that plusses and minuses represent the score demonstrated by a case on a particular dimension (variable). These are coded dichotomously. X_1 = the variable of theoretical interest (public sector organisation); X_2 = the background/control variable, or vector (forensic analysis); Y = the hypothetical outcome.

[3]Frickel, S., Albert, M., & Prainsack, B. (2016). *Investigating interdisciplinary collaboration: Theory and practice across disciplines* (p. 7). New Brunswick: Rutgers.

The authors do not seek to challenge these implicit assumptions so much as highlight the degree to which social science research has taken them for granted. They go on to present a general critique of these implicit assumptions, which they claim may threaten the 'academic and scientific institutions that [interdisciplinarity] claims it can strengthen'.[4] The critique is necessary, but may itself be misconceived, and based on flawed assumptions. For example, the authors challenge the degree to which disciplinary boundaries remain impermeable 'to outside ideas or social accountability'. The degree of permeability of institutional silos is of central importance to the current study – therefore, the researcher shares the authors' concern that this claim may be too often based on anecdotal evidence lacking strong empirical support. The authors highlight,

> recent bibliometric analyses conducted by Jerry Jacobs (2013: Jacobs and Frickel; 2009), which suggests that, at the very least, the assumption of disciplinary boundaries is potentially flawed: ideas, concepts, theories, and methodological tools seem to travel quite fluidly, even between far-flung disciplines.[5]

In counterpoint, it may be argued that the above statement does little to challenge the assertion of cross-disciplinary impermeability. The current study demonstrates that concepts and ideas may flow across disciplinary boundaries. However, the task of empirical research is to examine the ways in which these shifting concepts and ideas are used, within an interdisciplinary environment marked by normative and epistemological fluidity. That task lies beyond the capabilities of bibliometric analysis.

The above example is cited solely to demonstrate the complexities of interdisciplinary research. Nonetheless, interdisciplinary research is as rewarding as it is challenging, offers significant advantages and benefits, and is the sole means to respond to the research needs of collaborating legal, and scientific, institutions.

The instant study focusses on what might be regarded as a paradigmatic example of interdisciplinary collaboration: the co-production of forensic-scientific knowledge claims, derived from DNA-profiling techniques, for consumption by the criminal justice system. It is posited that the results drawn from this analysis of law's relationship with science can provide valuable insights regarding the opportunities, and pitfalls, encountered during interdisciplinary studies of the interactions between competing disciplines. Thus, it is hoped that the instant study may offer some useful perspectives, which may be relevant not only to those responsible for charting the future direction of legal research but also those responsible for shaping the future direction of legal education.

---

[4]Frickel, S., Albert, M., & Prainsack, B. (2016). *Investigating interdisciplinary collaboration: Theory and practice across disciplines* (p. 7). New Brunswick: Rutgers, at p. 10.
[5]Frickel, S., Albert, M., & Prainsack, B. (2016). *Investigating interdisciplinary collaboration: Theory and practice across disciplines* (p. 7). New Brunswick: Rutgers, at p. 14.

To return to the research topic, the purpose of the current study is to explore the shaping of DNA profiling within a criminal justice system *vis* marketisation. Clearly, the scientific processes which underpin this body of forensic techniques plays an increasingly central role in criminal investigations, and subsequent proceedings, and their deployment now requires the mobilisation of expert knowledge drawn from disparate fields: law, forensic science, and research science. Specialists in forensic disciplines must combine with associated institutional actors within the criminal justice system, and each phase of the evidential trajectory (from the collection and stabilisation of trace samples to their conversion into graphical representations and statistical probabilities) revolves around material objects and graphical representations, all of which are contingent, constructed, and shaped by contextual factors. The current study is concerned with exploring, and revealing, the particular series of laboratory translations, which convert raw material samples into a probabilistic inscriptions.

The ultimate purpose of the forensic-scientific output – the expert evidence – is to guide and assist the court and to aid the trier-of-fact in their deliberations. Thus, the law clearly regards knowledge derived from interdisciplinary collaboration as being of a higher quality than that which could be derived from intra-disciplinary analysis. That belief is consistent with a general assertion of quality (some may say assumption) which is frequently made with regard to interdisciplinary knowledge claims. It is often claimed that interdisciplinarity leads to better quality outputs and greater impact. This claim is only partially true. If it is done correctly, it can lead to significant gains. If it is done badly, it can lead to the 'enslavement of one domain of knowledge production to another', and the instrumental use of scientific knowledge claims, devoid of context.[6] What this study aims to reveal is a body of data which may allow researchers and practitioners to more readily differentiate between productive practices and unproductive, instrumental ones, thereby producing higher quality outputs, with more consistency, while avoiding the associated pitfalls.

Achieving these aims entails a degree of correspondence between the academic research context, the work environment, and the research field. Not merely correspondence but prolonged immersion in each field. As Frickel et al. state,

> [...] many [interdisciplinary researchers] have appointments in, or affiliations with, more than one discipline. The nature of such jobs requires that we maintain dual positions in the academic field, with one foot planted in the bedrock of traditional disciplinary departments and the other foot treading across less stable interdisciplinary terrain. Thus we come to our investigations of interdisciplinary research as practitioners of the same.[7]

---

[6]Tata, c

[7]Frickel, S., Albert, M., & Prainsack, B. (2016). *Investigating interdisciplinary collaboration: Theory and practice across disciplines* (p. 7). New Brunswick: Rutgers.

This research project is born from a similarly prolonged, and ongoing, 'lived experience of developing interdisciplinary knowledge, practices, and sensibilities'. This lived experience has enabled the researcher to enter into meaningful discourses with forensic biologists, statisticians, managerial staff, and associated institutional actors within the criminal justice system. However, it should be highlighted that while this body of institutional actors may be diverse, they are united by their expertise. Therefore, in order to derive meaningful data from these agents, it was first necessary not merely to build knowledge of the forensic-scientific domain but to acquire a degree of necessary expertise in forensic science. In this regard, the novice researcher's experiences followed those described by Collins and Evans, in their sociological studies of gravitational wave physicists.

> Typically, sociologists who want to study areas of scientific knowledge that are new to them have to try to grasp something of the science itself. The sociologist begins with no specialist expertise – which is a level insufficient to do sociological analysis of scientific knowledge. The sociologist is likely to move rapidly through public understanding and primary source knowledge, which are also inadequate to allow for competent social analysis of scientific knowledge. With luck, however, interactional expertise, which does allow for social analysis of scientific knowledge, will eventually be attained.[8]

However, the researcher was aware of the necessity of attaining a deeper level of interactional expertise than that envisaged by Collins and Evans. The latter study was restricted to one field of scientific research, whereas the instant study was highly interdisciplinary, requiring an ability to conduct a reflexive analysis of the heterogeneous epistemic cultures which contribute to the production of forensic-scientific knowledge and their embedding in particular institutional contexts. The problem was theoretical, as well as methodological, since these competing domains apply divergent sets of norms. This poses a particular challenge for the interdisciplinary researcher: how is it possible to achieve interdisciplinary understanding and expertise in an alternate discipline, which is underpinned by a different normative framework? There is only one possible answer: ontological, cognitive, and epistemological understanding (within the context of interdisciplinary research) is only possible through long-term immersion in two, or more, disciplines.[9] This requirement is also consistent with a relational approach to expertise posited above.

---

[8]See Collins, H., & Evans, R. (2007). *Rethinking expertise* (p. 32). Chicago: University of Chicago Press.

[9]An appreciation of the need for immersion in both disciplines, illuminated by the research data, led to the development of a relational theory of interdisciplinary expertise (*supra*).

Therefore, the necessary preparation for empirical interdisciplinary research began some years prior to the commencement of the instant project, with the completion of a Diploma in Forensic Medical Science. Later, the fieldwork stage was prefaced with a number of conversations with forensic scientists, lawyers, academics, and members of the judiciary. As a direct result, the researcher was invited – by the directors of the Leverhulme Research Centre for Forensic Science – to attend their Scientific Discussion meeting at the Royal Society in London. The event brought together forensic scientists and legal practitioners from around the world, in order to discuss *The Paradigm Shift for UK Forensic Science*. Drawing upon the experience of the judiciary, expertise in change management, and the knowledge of world-renowned forensic science researchers, the participants at this two-day meeting sought to develop a robust, efficient, and effective forensic capability that could serve the interests of justice within a changing landscape. A variety of perspectives were aired – on subjects as diverse as analytical forensic chemistry, cognitive neuroscience, biometrics, and the logical foundations of scientific enquiry, and following the discussion meeting in London, I was invited to join a closed meeting at The Royal Society's Chicheley Hall, home of the Kavli Royal Society Centre. Over the next two days, five groups of practitioners from the worlds of law and science sought to map out the emerging forensic landscape, understand each other's perspectives, identify areas requiring further research, and gain a clearer understanding of the capabilities and limitations of their respective fields. Members of the bar and the bench (including the then Lord Advocate, Lord Mulholland, Lord Carloway, Lord Eassie, Lord Kitchin, Lord Hughes, Judge Wall, and Justice Binnie) brought their legal expertise to bear alongside research scientists from a variety of geographic and disciplinary backgrounds.

These types of interactions proved invaluable in achieving a deep familiarity with the conceptual framework, and epistemological outlook, of forensic-scientific practice. Nonetheless, this was a slow and steady process of reflexive assimilation rather than a rapid, interactional apotheosis. As Collins states,

> The transition to interactional expertise is accomplished, crucially, by engaging in conversation with the experts. Interactional expertise is slowly gained with more and more discussion of the science … Where interactional expertise is being acquired, there will be a progression from 'interview' to 'discussion' to 'conversation' as more and more of the science is understood … Its steady acquisition can … be recognized.[10]

This experience informed the decision to opt to utilise semi-structured qualitative interviews. Nonetheless, early conversations, and pilot interviews, had tended to be formulaic, and lacked conversational flow, only later becoming far more

[10]See Collins, H., & Evans, R. (2007). *Rethinking expertise* (p. 33). Chicago: University of Chicago Press.

discursive and interactional. Finally, in conformity with Collins' experiences, a stage was reached when respondents '[gave] studied consideration to critical comments'. In this later phase, respondents would ask the researcher's own opinion on a particular matter or enquire as to the standard practice of attitudes prevalent in other jurisdictions. This echoes Collins experiences:

> the sociologist who has just come from visiting scientist X may be able to tell scientist Y something of *the science* that X is doing or the kind of thinking that X is engaged in respect of some common problem.[11]
>
> By this stage, what were once 'interviews' have become 'conversations', not markedly dissimilar to the conversations the analyst will have with social scientist colleagues and, presumably, not that different to the conversations that one scientist will have with another.[12]

Notably, research in this area also necessitated the assimilation of knowledge and expertise from associated areas. The researcher was required to develop a high degree of statistical literacy, knowledge of quantitative methods, and an ability to discuss the intricacies of Bayesian reasoning, and random match probabilities, as well as their practical applications in the courtroom. Having outlined the novel requirements of interdisciplinary research, the discussion focusses on situating the research project within a broader strategy.

Science and Technology Studies (STS) and Forensic-Scientific Knowledge

Returning to the general history, and development, of STS scholarship (see Chapter 1), it is evident that – despite a small number of notable exceptions[13] – early STS scholarship almost completely overlooked the forensic field. The task of filling the research gap fell to socio-legal scholars, who embarked on broad, but piecemeal, critiques of the forensic field. A notable example is Redmayne,[14] who, in his treatment of expert evidence, makes a significant contribution. However, in an early paper calling for sociological work in the field of DNA profiling,

---

[11]See Collins, H., & Evans, R. (2007). *Rethinking expertise* (p. 33). Chicago: University of Chicago Press. Whilst maintaining informants confidentiality.

[12]See Collins, H., & Evans, R. (2007). *Rethinking expertise* (p. 34). Chicago: University of Chicago Press.

[13]Wynne, B. (1989). Forensic pathology, scientific expertise, and the criminal law. In R. Smith & B. Wynne (Eds) *Expert evidence: Interpreting science in the law* (pp. 56–92). London: Routledge.

[14]Redmayne, M. (1997). Expert evidence and scientific disagreement. *UC Davis Law Review, 30*, 1027–1080.

Thompson[15] criticises him for not taking the sociological perspective far enough. Jasanoff[16] reiterates Thompson's argument, stating that 'our understanding of the nature of DNA evidence cannot be considered complete until we have gained a fuller understanding of the sociology of forensic technique'. This assertion echoes Redmayne's statement that

> there might be areas of DNA science [beyond the technology itself] where talk of construction would lead to the sort of profitable debunking of assumptions that it does in other areas.

These early engagements hinted at the need to develop in-depth social-constructivist accounts of the co-production of forensic-scientific knowledge claims, Therefore, in the early 1990s, STS scholars increasingly began to turn their attention towards the subject. The 'forensic turn' paved the way for a significant line of research, which can be categorised under the following headings[17]:

- The incorporation of economic imperatives into forensic analyses.[18]
- The writing of attributes such as race into forensic traces.[19]
- The contestability of all forensic knowledge claims.[20]

---

[15]Thompson, W. C. (1997). A sociological perspective on the science of forensic DNA testing. *UC Davis Law Review, 30*, 1113–1136.

[16]Jasanoff, S. (1995). *Science at the bar: Law, science & technology in America*. Cambridge, MA: Harvard University Press.

[17]Mnookin, J., Cole, S., Fisher, B. A. J., Dror, I. E., Houck, M., Inman, K., ... Siegel, J. (2010). The need for a research culture in the forensic sciences. *UCLA Law Review, 58*, 725.

[18]Daemmrich, A. (1998). The evidence does not speak for itself: Expert witnesses and the organization of DNA-typing companies. *Social Studies of Science, 28*, 741–772; Lawless, C. J., & Williams, R. (2010). Helping with inquiries or helping with profits? The trials and tribulations of a technology of forensic reasoning. *Social Studies of Science, 40*, 731–755.

[19]Cole, S. A. (2007). Twins, Twain, Galton & Gilman: Fingerprinting, individualization, brotherhood and race in Pudd'nhead Wilson. *Configurations, 15*, 227–265; Kahn, J. (2008). Race, genes and justice: A call to reform the presentation of forensic DNA evidence in criminal trials. *Brooklyn Law Review, 74*, 325–375; M'Charek, A. (2006). Technologies of population: Forensic DNA testing practices and the making of differences and similarities. *Configurations, 8*, 121–158; M'Charek, A. (2008). Silent witness, articulate collective: DNA evidence and the inference of visible traits. *Bioethics, 22*, 519–528.

[20]Jasanoff, S. (1995). *Science at the bar: Law, science & technology in America*. Cambridge, MA: Harvard University Press; Lynch, M. (1998). The discursive production of uncertainty: The OJ Simpson 'dream team' and the sociology of knowledge machine. *Social Studies of Science, 28*, 829–868; Lynch, M., Cole, S. A., McNally, R., & Jordan, K. (2008). *Truth machine: The contentious history of DNA fingerprinting*. Chicago, IL: University of Chicago Press; Mnookin, J. L. (2001). Fingerprint evidence in an age of DNA profiling. *Brooklyn Law Review, 67*, 13–70.

- The ethnographic (or historical) tracing of forensic practitioners on the journey from laboratory to courtroom.[21]
- The effort to discipline forensic practitioners and objects through quality assurance mechanisms.[22]

Further studies began to explore the emergent realities of productisation and marketisation, within the UK forensic science sector. An example is Daemmrich,[23] who embarked on a detailed study of the construction of forensic-scientific knowledge claims, prior to the introduction of the 'casework' model of forensic interpretation. His research offered insights into the ways in which companies were able to control the production of forensic knowledge through investment in research and new technologies, and the subsequent widespread standardisation of practices in conformation with those technologies: phenomena which he termed 'upstream', and 'downstream', integration.

While Daemmrich's study opened the door to further research, it must now be placed in historical context. The 'casework model'[24] – as adopted by most commercial companies and public sector laboratories – has altered the degree to which the forensic scientist can exert control over the production of forensic knowledge within the laboratory. Thus, the features which Daemmrich unearthed may be seen to be confined to an emergent phase of DNA profiling. Nonetheless, subsequent developments were anticipated in his observation, that:

> there no longer is an 'inside' and an 'outside' to the testing laboratory: instead, company practices shape the structure of the legal and social environments as much as the former are shaped by the latter.[25]

The theme of emergent marketisation was developed by Lawless and Williams, whose ethnographic study of the Case Assessment and Interpretation (CAI) process considered the ways in which commercial imperatives may 'condition the use of forensic science in support of criminal justice'.[26] It should be noted that in the

---

[21]Jordan, K., & Lynch, M. (1998). The dissemination, standardisation and routinisation of a molecular biological technique. *Social Studies of Science, 28,* 773; Timmermans, S. (2006). *Postmortem: How medical examiners explain suspicious deaths.* Chicago, IL: University of Chicago Press.

[22]Leslie, M. (2010). Quality assured science: Managerialism in forensic biology. *Science Technology Human Values, 35*, 283.

[23]Daemmrich, A. (1998). The evidence does not speak for itself: Expert witnesses and the organization of DNA-typing companies. *Social Studies of Science, 28*, 741–772.

[24]Cook, R., Evett, I. W., Jackson, G, Jones, P. J., & Lambert, J. A. (1998). A model for case assessment and interpretation. *Science & Justice, 38*, 151–156, at p. 152.

[25]Cook, R., Evett, I. W., Jackson, G, Jones, P. J., & Lambert, J. A. (1998). A model for case assessment and interpretation. *Science & Justice, 38*, 151–156 at p. 759.

[26]Lawless, C. J., & Williams, R. (2010). Helping with inquiries or helping with profits? The trials and tribulations of a technology of forensic reasoning. *Social Studies of Science, 40*, 731–755.

intervening years between Daemmrich's study and their own, CAI had become firmly embedded in the architecture of forensic service provision. Their empirical study – limited to the private sector and conducted solely through interviews with forensic scientists – sought to explore the relationship between commerce and science, focussing on forensic practitioner's attempts to negotiate the CAI process. Their research establishes an explicit connection between CAI and emergent forms of economic rationalisation. However, it must be reiterated that CAI was intended, from the outset, to bring economic imperatives to bear on knowledge production, and the intention to integrate commercial imperatives into the investigative process was made publicly and explicitly.

Lawless and Williams' study provides a comprehensive account overview of the introduction, and early development, of the CAI process (prior to the low template (LT) DNA controversy).[27] At that time, they viewed CAI as a 'boundary object': one which provided a standardised form of communication between 'the different epistemic worlds of science and policing'.[28] However, it is doubtful to what extent such insights remain relevant in the wake of the subsequent introduction of efficient forms of forensic reporting (discussed below).

Lawless returns to the subject in later papers,[29] exploring the ways in which commercialised forensic science provision is shaped around constructions of 'providers' and 'customers'. These later studies reiterate the link between measures of economic rationalisation and the production of forensic knowledge. However, some of the most promising aspects of these studies remain unexplored. Lawless work is largely descriptive and does not attempt to place the contextual shaping of forensic knowledge claims in theoretical perspective. Nor does his work explore the nature of forensic-scientific expertise in any detail.

Indeed, the majority of accounts of the production of forensic-scientific knowledge claims rest on a narrative, which highlights the lack of meaningful communication between forensic scientists and legal professionals. The corollary of this 'contest and communication' narrative is that many of the difficulties encountered by these two discrete fields may be overcome through improved communication and a mutual appreciation of both context and milieu. Solutions have therefore tended to be practical and pragmatic, rather than theoretical and epistemological.

The 'contest and communication' narrative is generally associated with the view that the forensic, and legal, fields operate from within discrete 'silos', and that the degree to which professionals become 'silo-ed' is exacerbated in an adversarial

---

[27]Discussed, *infra*.

[28]Lawless, C. J., & Williams, R. (2010). Helping with inquiries or helping with profits? The trials and tribulations of a technology of forensic reasoning. *Social Studies of Science, 40*, 731–755, at p. 745.

[29]Lawless, C. (2010). *A curious reconstruction? The shaping of 'marketized' forensic science*. CARR Discussion Paper 63; Lawless, C. (2011). Policing markets; the contested shaping of neo-liberal forensic science. *British Journal of Criminology, 51*, 671–689.

context.[30] Such views, routinely expressed in the forensic-scientific field, are echoed by members of the judiciary and the legal profession. Lord Thomas, the Lord Chief Justice of England and Wales, perceives a similar communication problem, and likens it to the challenge facing comparative lawyers, whom he commends for their success in unearthing common legal concepts.

> It is now accepted that the work of comparative lawyers, whose discipline was based on finding differences, and the globalization of many legal concepts, particularly the rule of law as applicable to all governmental action and the right to a fair and open trial, have brought about a considerable narrowing of the differences.[31]

It may be argued that the desire to share common concepts is based on an idealised conception of underlying similarity between two heterogeneous disciplines whose normative basis is completely divergent. This will be the subject of further discussion below.

A further contribution to the sociology of forensic science has been made by Kruse, whose extended empirical studies attempt to recreate the 'biography' of forensic evidence by following its trajectory from crime scene to courtroom. Her ethnographic analysis of 'the social life of forensic evidence' leans heavily on the social-constructivist scholarship of 'Wave Two' STS and borrows from Latour's theories of material agency. However, Kruse methodological approach owes more to Arjun Appadurai's homologous concept of 'the social life of things',[32] which 'allows for the combining of a theoretical focus on human actors … with a methodological focus on objects … travelling through [the criminal justice system]'.

Undoubtedly, a culturally focussed analysis of the social life of forensic evidence may be greatly facilitated by 'recognising the material agency'[33] of forensic evidence. However, it may be argued that this is a partial, and limited, approach, and that an obverse approach may prove more fruitful, insofar as it would allow for a focus on those interposing contextual factors which condition the practice of relational forms of forensic-scientific expertise. Such an approach – utilising theoretical perspectives from Latour, rather than Appadurai – would require that we ascribe material agency, not to the evidence, but rather to the DNA/Bayes casework process itself. Such an approach will be outlined in the following chapter.

Kruse further admits that her work is culturally circumscribed, in terms of both its subjects and its perspective. Rather than following the traditional focus

---

[30]See Kelty, S. F., Julian, R., & Ross, A. (2013). Dismantling the justice silos: Avoiding the pitfalls and reaping the benefits of information-sharing between forensic science, medicine and law. *Forensic Science International, 230*(1–3), 8–15.

[31]Thomas, L. C. J. (2015). *The legal framework for more robust forensic science evidence*. Philosophical Transactions of the Royal Society, *B 370*, 20140258, p. 1.

[32] Appadurai, A. (Ed.) (1986) The Social Life of Things, (Cambridge University Press: Cambridge).

[33]See Kelty, S. F., Julian, R., & Ross, A. (2013). Dismantling the Justice Silos: Avoiding the pitfalls and reaping the benefits of information-sharing between forensic science, medicine and law. *Forensic Science International, 230*(1–3), 8–15.

on the resolution of scientific controversy, she adopts a constructive outlook, which – she concedes – is culturally inflected. Both she and her interlocutors 'share a language and live under the same public administration'.[34] Thus, their shared perspectives are conditioned by the Nordic social-democratic model of governance, which places a great emphasis on the openness and transparency of governmental institutions and activities. However, Kruse foregoes the opportunity to make explicit connections between the overarching mode of governance and the production of forensic-scientific knowledge claims.

This omission has ramifications on the procedural level. Kruse ethnographic studies were conducted solely within the Swedish state forensic laboratory: an institution, which shapes forensic-scientific knowledge claims in preparation for their entry onto a non-adversarial legal field. This inquisitorial system practices complete freedom of evidence and requires that the prosecutor present both inculpatory and exculpatory evidence, in relation to the accused. Further, the requirements of formal adjudication procedures within the Swedish jurisdiction are such that they do not entail extensive use of expert witnesses (though the courts may make occasional recourse to skilled consultants). Nor are scientists routinely required to produce witness statements.

These local procedural elements shape an epistemic culture, in which forensic knowledge claims from statens kriminaltekniska laboratorium (SKL) (the state laboratory) are greeted with almost unquestioning acceptance. Kruse quotes a member of the Swedish judiciary as saying:

> you don't question DNA profiling, whether the SKL did it right, you don't question that. It leads too far to … go in [to the laboratory] and look at their work …

Given the above, it is questionable to what extent Kruse' empirical work – which remains highly descriptive of local practices – may translate to an adversarial context. Further, Kruse does not engage with regulatory factors, quality assurance regimes, and audit protocols, which are a regular feature of forensic-scientific practice in the UK, except to say that – outwith the casework process – 'SKL works correctly and impartially'.[35] Thus, a major contextual factor is absent from her analysis. Finally, while her empirical studies capture the conceptual fluidity, and diverse terminology, deployed by institutional actors, these factors are not placed in a theoretical context.[36]

Nonetheless, Kruse does offer some valuable insights into narrative theories of evidence production. These flow from her understanding of the centrality of the concept of the 'chain of evidence' and of the need for socio-legal studies to

[34]Kruse, C. (2016) *The Social Life of Forensic Evidence* (University of California Press: Oakland, California), at p. 13.
[35]Kruse, C. (2016) *The Social Life of Forensic Evidence* (University of California Press: Oakland, California), at p. 28.
[36]*See* Chapter 1, *supra*.

account for the co-production of evidence prior to its arrival at the administrative border of the courtroom. In the first of a series of studies,[37] she uses the theory of 'legal story-telling' to explain the work of the forensic scientist, as (s)he attempts to reason in the face of uncertainty.[38] Kruse notes that, whatever the source, science does not enter the court as bare facts, or as claimed truths, but as evidence (within a Swedish jurisdictional context). For evidence to be considered relevant, it must deliver answers that are germane to the legal case. Therefore, facts must be placed in context in order to gain meaning and significance: the disjointed facts must be transformed into propositions, and representations, which bind together to form a credible narrative. These familiar stories may be drawn from a catalogue of stock scripts and may be peopled with archetypal characters. Such an approach – she suggests – may be useful to the court, insofar as the forensic-legal narrative helps to associate people, and actions, with legal categories, in an attempt to account for all of the available evidence.

Shifting her focus to the production of forensic knowledge, Kruse observes that legal storytelling does not only happen in the courtroom. It is a central part of the investigative process: beginning at the crime scene and continuing within the forensic laboratory. She posits that 'story-telling' is now so central to criminal investigation that forensic scientists have developed a particular form, which they call 'casework'. Casework, she observes, accounts for that activity which we most closely associate with forensic inquiry – the analysis of source material. More importantly, it provides a narrative framework in order that the scientist may order those material analyses in ways that makes sense.

In a later paper, Kruse[39] returns to the topic of legal 'story-telling' through casework, adding further theoretical detail. Kruse acknowledges the uncertainty inherent in the 'story-telling' process and asserts that casework functions as a means of distributing responsibility for these uncertainties between the scientific and legal fields.[40] In contrast to many commentators, she speaks of the shared understanding that exists between scientists and lawyers and the unity of purpose which allows for a substantial degree of transparency to exist: a transparency which allows those practices and activities, which normally take place within the

---

[37]Kruse, C. (2012). Legal storytelling in pre-trial investigations: Arguing for a wider perspective on forensic evidence. *New Genetics and Society, 31*(3), 299–309.

[38]Bennet, W. L., & Feldman, M. S. (1981). *Reconstructing reality in the courtroom*. New Brunswick: Rutgers University Press; Jackson, B. S. (1988). *Law, fact and narrative coherence*. Liverpool: Deborah Charles Publications; Wagenaar, W. A., Van Koppen, P. J., & Crombag, H. F.M. (1993). *Anchored narratives: The psychology of criminal evidence*. London: St. Martin's Press; White, J. B. (1973). *The legal imagination*. Chicago, IL: Chicago University Press.

[39]Kruse, C. (2013). The Bayesian approach to forensic evidence: Evaluating, communicating and distributing responsibility. *Social Studies of Science, 43*, 887.

[40]This section of Kruse' analysis – though unacknowledged – owes much to Moreira, T., May, C., & Bond, J. (2009). Regulatory objectivity in action: Mild cognitive impairment and the collective production of uncertainty. *Social Studies of Science, 35*(9), 665–690, at p. 678.

'black box' of DNA profiling, to become visible to the courts. Nonetheless, Kruse acknowledges that the maintenance of a state of increased (if not complete) transparency is a difficult task.

It is clear that Kruse takes a more optimistic approach to the subject of interdisciplinary knowledge creation than do other STS scholars. Kruse finds co-operation where others unearth contestation, and – in conversation – Kruse admits that this constructive outlook may flow from the overarching Nordic, social-democratic model of governance, which places great emphasis on the openness and transparency of governmental institutions and activities. However, it remains highly questionable to what extent Kruse account of the casework process accords with its original aims, as conceived within the UK FSS. Further, Kruse account of the co-operative enterprises, and shared understandings, of scientists and lawyers – though feasible within the Swedish criminal justice system – runs counter the 'contest and communication' narrative advanced by authors within adversarial jurisdictions and is of limited application in the UK.

STS and Studies of Expertise and Experience (SEE)

In order to pursue socio-legal enquiries related to the development of forensic identification techniques – and their operation within the criminal justice system – it is first necessary to outline a subsisting body of literature, broadly classified as STS. STS is an umbrella term used to describe a corpus of anthropological, sociological, and historical, studies of science: one which also contains developed subcategories associated with Studies of Scientific Knowledge (SSK) and SEE. The majority of works within this diverse group of studies share a social-constructivist perspective and proceed on the understanding that scientific truth claims, and technological artefacts, are co-produced through a variety of natural, cultural, and social practices. The STS corpus thus tends to demonstrate – through empirical methods – the extent to which contingent historical factors, social values, and group interests are embedded in the production of scientific practices, artefacts, and truth claims.

Attempts to categorise the field of STS tend to revolve around certain common themes, which may be categorised chronologically, doctrinally, or thematically. Part 1 of the thematic review – which blends all three approaches – will describe, and analyse, the development of a category of STS scholarship devoted to the development of theories of scientific expertise. Beginning with Merton's scientific norms, it charts the rise of social constructivism in the wake of Kuhn's theory of scientific revolutions. It follows the programmatic shift of sociologies of science from the Weak, to the Strong, and explores the doctrinal distinctions between the Edinburgh, and the Bath, schools. It critically analyses the Third Wave of STS scholarship – devoted to SEE – and demonstrates the deficiencies of the current theory, before concluding by suggesting ways in which these deficiencies may be overcome, through the application of relational theories drawn from historical epistemology and the philosophy of knowledge acquisition. The following chapter will focus on the literature relating to the application of STS, and related theories, within the forensic-scientific field.

The Common Origins of Law and Science

Lynch contends that law and science are separated by a common language. Their shared vocabularies feature similar terms, including 'investigation', 'proof', 'law', 'test', 'inquiry', 'fact', and 'evidence'.[41] These terms may carry distinct meanings, particular to their respective fields. However, Lynch argues that the use of parallel terms, in both the legal and scientific fields, indicates a common origin. A number of scholars have attempted to trace this common origin. Their conclusions achieve little by way of consensus, excepting the fact that such studies may point to the dominant historiographical preoccupations of the time. For example, at the dawn of the Scientific Revolution, in the late seventeenth century, religion was widely held to have provided the formative basis of both law and science.[42] This view persisted through the Enlightenment, into the twentieth century,[43] when it was complemented by a similarly determinative theory based around the significance of economic forces.[44] In the modern era, scholars have embarked on more radical departures from classical social theory, developing arguments, which highlight the significance of disciplinary power and the evolution of governmentality.[45] These 'genealogies of fact' have unearthed more complex – though no less compelling – narratives.

Shapiro, for example, has traced the *fons et origo* of scientific inquiry back to legal procedures and shared institutional structures. She posits that the commensurate nature of these corresponding institutional arrangements allowed for the easy transmission of common values between discrete fields, both of which were based around a particular mode of objectivity. According to her thesis, it was neither God nor Mammon – but legal bureaucracy – which provided the model for scientific method. Shapin[46] and Schaffer[47] adopt a similar post-structuralist perspective, citing the congruence between the courtroom and the scientific experiment, both of which serve as discrete sites of knowledge-making, in which d

---

41Lynch, M. (2013). Science, truth, and forensic cultures: The exceptional legal status of DNA evidence. *Studies in History and Philosophy of Biological and Biomedical Sciences, 44*, 60–70.

42Faigman, D. (1999). *Legal alchemy: The use and misuse of science in the law*. New York, NY: W.H. Freeman.

43Thomas Merton's 1936 doctoral dissertation – 'The Merton Thesis' – outlines the links between a particular mode of religious pietism and early experimental science. The thesis continues to form the subject of academic debate. See Shapin, S. (1988). Understanding the Merton thesis. *Isis, 79*(4), 594–605.

44See, for example, Freudenthal, G., & McLaughlin, P. (Eds). (2009). *The social and economic roots of the scientific revolution: Texts by Boris Hessen and Henryk Grossmann*. New York, NY: Springer.

45See Foucault, M. (1997). *Society must be defended: Lectures at the Collège de France, 1975–1976* (pp. 243–244). New York, NY: St. Martin's Press.

46Shapin, S. (1994). *The social history of truth*. Chicago, IL: Chicago University Press.

47Shapin, S., & Schaffer, S. (1985). *Leviathan and the air pump*. Princeton, NJ: Princeton University Press.

participants apply impersonal rules, within the context of a body transparent and 'rational' procedures, all of which are designed to produce 'morally certain' resolutions on 'matters of fact'.[48]

Thus, in 1659, when Robert Boyle completed the construction of his *machina Boyleana*,[49] and embarked on a programme of experimentation in order to 'solicit and interrogate the testimony of nature',[50] his determinations were – at that time – deemed to lack the epistemological authority of those derived as a result of inferential legal reasoning. However, Shapiro[51] has noted that – by the mid-eighteenth century – a distinct split had developed between the moral certitude of the courtroom (expressed as 'a satisfied conscience' or proof 'beyond reasonable doubt'), and the 'mathematical certainty' to which science aspired.[52]

This distinction became more pronounced throughout the course of the twentieth century, as science began, increasingly, to become characterised by a particular set of norms. The 'norms of science', as described by Merton,[53] may be listed as follows: communalism, universalism, disinterestedness, and organised scepticism. Paradoxically, it should be noted that Merton's normative categorisation – which sees science as striving towards an ideal of impartiality and rationality – was heavily influenced by Boyle, whom – as we have shown above – had been heavily influenced by the 'rational bureaucracy' of the courtroom. Thus, it is posited that the normative roots of science may be traced to the fountainhead of legal inference.

As with legal positivism, the scientific method – as Merton describes it – is composed of an accrescence of normative outputs, which – in the social context – combine to produce a privileged scientific *leitkultur*. The scientist thus speaks as an authoritative representative of a body of privileged truth claims, which are both esoteric and positivistically inflected. Collins, describing the widely held, Mertonian view of scientific method, goes as far as to assert that (until the 1960s) 'it was inconceivable that decision-making in matters that involved science and

---

[48]Shapin, S., & Schaffer, S. (1985). *Leviathan and the air pump*. Princeton, NJ: Princeton University Press.

[49]A pneumatic engine designed to facilitate experimentation.

[50]Shapiro, B. J. (1991). *"Beyond reasonable doubt" and "probable cause": Historical perspectives on the Anglo-American law of evidence*. Berkeley, CA: University of California Press.

[51]Shapiro, B. J. (1991). *"Beyond reasonable doubt" and "probable cause": Historical perspectives on the Anglo-American law of evidence*. Berkeley, CA: University of California Press.

[52]Shapiro, B. J. (1986) To a moral certainty: Theories of knowledge and Anglo-American juries 1600–1850. *Hastings Law Journal, 38*, 153–193; Shapiro, B. J. (1991). *"Beyond reasonable doubt" and "probable cause": Historical perspectives on the Anglo-American law of evidence*. Berkeley, CA: University of California Press.

[53]Merton, R. K. (1973) [1942]. The normative structure of science. In R. K. Merton (Ed.), *The sociology of science: Theoretical and empirical investigations*. Chicago, IL: University of Chicago Press.

technology could travel in any other direction than from the top down'.[54] Further, that the role of social science was to reinforce the nostrums of positivist science, rather than to question their basis.

Merton thus provided the means by which to recognise legitimated scientific expertise. However, studies of normative science also needed to account for the changing – and often contradictory – nature of scientific truth claims. This development is attributed to Thomas Kuhn, whose work provided the first comprehensive account of the nature of scientific revolutions.[55] Kuhn argued that paradigm shifts in the natural sciences are best viewed as tectonic conceptual changes, which are – at first – resisted, later achieving the momentum necessary to overthrow the prevailing dogma and gaining widespread acceptance. The classic example is provided by the Scientific Revolution, which swept away the earth-centred Aristotelian universe and replaced it with a Heliocentric model, thus inculcating a mode of inquiry through which all natural phenomena could be tested by way of scepticism, empiricism, and mathematisation. In addition to generating epistemological changes, Kuhn demonstrated that scientific paradigm shifts may inculcate profound, frequently anomic, social changes.[56] Kuhn attributed such anomic effects to the incommensurability of competing paradigms. The 'old' and 'new' paradigms would stand in opposition, and – following a brief struggle – one view would prevail, to the exclusion of the other. The dominant view, once embedded, would then generate its own body of 'normal science'.

Ironically, Collins claims that Kuhn's work was itself responsible for a paradigm shift in STS, breaking the wave of 'positivism' and ushering in the era of 'unbridled social constructivism'.[57] However, Collins' 'First Wave of Social Studies of Science' must be approached with caution. It is a neat categorisation: one, which Collins concedes, may do violence to the subject through the compression of the 'work of many authors and thinkers into a few simple formulae'.[58] Nonetheless, Collins and Evans were not dissuaded, for such broad categorisation was deemed necessary in order to initiate their own – programmatic – paradigm shift in STS. Collins and Evans' 'Third Wave' theory will form the subject of comprehensive discussion below. However, for present purposes, it is sufficient to note that any attempt to periodise this diverse body of studies – particularly a chronological

[54]Collins, H. M., & Evans, R. (2002). The third wave of science studies: Studies of expertise and experience. *Social Studies of Science, 32*(2), 235–296, at p. 239.
[55]Kuhn, T. (1962). *The structure of scientific revolutions*. Chicago, IL: University of Chicago Press.
[56]The poet John Donne wrote of the anomie of the Copernican Revolution. See also John Keats' *Lamia* (1884), in which the poet laments the fact that Sir Isaac Newton had 'unweaved the rainbow' by using a prism to split light into its constituent parts.
[57]Jasanoff, S. (2003). Breaking the waves in science studies: Comment on H. M. Collins and Robert Evans, 'The Third Wave of Science'. *Social Studies of Science, 33*(3), 389–400, at p. 390.
[58]Collins, H. M., & Evans, R. (2002). The third wave of science studies: Studies of expertise and experience. *Social Studies of Science, 32*(2), 235–296, at p. 237.

attempt to portray the development of 'the problem of scientific legitimacy' in Hegelian terms (thesis, antithesis, and synthesis) – may be misleading.[59]

Auopoiesis and the Systems Theory of Interdisciplinary Knowledge

Any account of interdisciplinary expertise and knowledge transfer would be incomplete without taking account of legal autopoiesis (a sub-branch of systems theory). It may be posited that the emergent field of forensic science has achieved a level of codification, complexity, and functional differentiation, such that it may now be described as a unified system, distinct from both research, and applied science, as commonly defined. While commentators have focussed on the creation of 'hybrid sets' of actors, none has thus far utilised systems theory to discern the existence of a uniquely interrelated network of actors, and agencies – extending beyond the hierarchy of formal criminal justice institutions which forms the system's core – encompassing a heterogeneous matrix of laboratories, private enterprises, courts, (non) governmental regulatory agencies, populated by scientific, juridical, criminological, and allied institutional agents. These nodes structure the space, and shape the dynamics, of the forensic subsystem, and the adjacent justice system. The dominant stream of socio-legal research in the forensic field has hitherto focussed upon the challenge of making the social structure of the forensic field analytically intelligible through both structural and agent-centred approaches, or through comparatively complex neo-Weberian methods, which bridge the lacuna between the two. It is proposed that these social scientific approaches may be further enhanced, through the implementation of theories of legal autopoiesis, whose focus upon functional differentiation and organisation may better reveal the dynamic relations of the forensic science subsystem, albeit at a high level of abstraction.

The objective is therefore to assess, using empirical social scientific methods, whether the forensic field can be said to constitute a fully autopoietic social subsystem. The analysis of the field founds upon a conception of society as a complex system of meaning and communication, comprising a set of functionally differentiated subsystems. Teubner posits that these 'social subsystems acquire increasing autonomy if their components (element, structures, process, identity, boundary, environment, performance, function) are self-referentially defined via reflexive communication'.[60] The central question is thus whether – like law, politics, or science more broadly defined – the forensic field exhibits the features and dynamics essential for such autopoiesis. Thus, the subsequent discussion attempts to discern the 'cyclical combination of cyclical self-description of self-reference' which signals the presence of a legal hypercycle, hence complete functional differentiation. In practice, this requires the researcher to determine the existence

[59] *Infra.*

[60] Teubner, G. (1989). *Recht als autopoietisches System.* Frankfurt/Main: Suhrkamp (English translation: *Law as an autopoietic system.* Oxford: Blackwell Publishers.

of, *inter alia,* specific elements (parts), structures (networks), processes (production), the system boundary and environment (space), and a self-conception of the system as a whole (unity), through the coding and analysis of representative samples of documentary evidence (relating to the various elements of the forensic system, its doctrines, actions, procedures, and norms).

In addition to discerning the existence – or otherwise – of a functionally differentiated forensic subsystem, the project will illuminate the process through which the posited autopoietic subsystem selects messages from a competitive field of nodal points, apprehending those environmental interactions which create 'perturbations', and selecting those whose subsequent resonations are reproduced in accordance with the system rationality and encoding of the forensic subsystem. Further, how structural coupling between the forensic and the legal, political and economic, subsystems allows the forensic subsystem to more efficiently maintain its autopoiesis. Lastly, it is argued that the project may lead to clearer understandings of the interactions between the emergent forensic subsystem, and domestic legal systems – against a backdrop of normative expectations – and will reveal the strategies employed in order to maintain autopoiesis, and promote system efficiency, necessitating an increased the flow of cognitive information, drawn from the environment, and reproduced within the subsystem.

Having laid out the necessary groundwork of discussing underlying theoretical perspectives and showing the unique challenges of conducting empirical socio-legal research in this area, the following chapter – the first of the substantive core of this monograph – turns to the commoditisation of forensic products and the ways in which the creation of the forensic product allowed for an externally imposed standardisation of the field and facilitated the introduction of 'triaging'.

Chapter 4

The Commodification of Forensic Science

Chapter Summary

Forensic science provision in the UK has undergone comprehensive, though uneven, restructuring over the past two decades. Most notably, in England and Wales, where forensic-scientific support is now delivered through a commercial market. As a result of this innovation, police forces (and other forensic 'customers') have become increasingly concerned with sourcing efficient, standardised products, and services. Meanwhile, forensic science providers (FSPs) have been tasked with maintaining a high-quality service that conforms to the overarching regulations.

Interviews with forensic biologists within the criminal justice system (CJS) reveal that a significant number of informants view standardisation as beneficial, in terms of quality assurance, predictability, and economic efficiency. However, they also reveal concerns regarding the creation of standardised forensic products; informants highlight the frequently problematic process of implementing standards which they deem as having been designed to conform to customer expectations. This chapter focusses on the ways in which organisational restructuring contributed to the creation of this 'menu' of standardised forensic products and explores the contingent historical factors, which shaped this new forensic standards environment. Crucially, it exposes the ways in which power differentials between stakeholders in the developing market may have contributed to incomplete standardisation. This chapter explores the extent to which the proposed arrangement may have been intended primarily to benefit 'customers' and exposes perceptions relating to the ways in which perceived gains have been subverted by partial standardisation, inadequate planning, and problems related to implementation.

This chapter thus aims to provide answers to the stated research questions, with a specific focus on the early market environment. It reveals and exposes, for the first time, the process of forensic standardisation and – in so doing – contributes to a small, but growing, number of sociologies of standardisation: studies whose empirical grounding and careful empirical analysis reveals rich descriptions of

Marketisation and Forensic Science Provision in England and Wales, 53–72

doi:10.1108/978-1-83909-123-020221004

the specific and unintended consequences of different forms of standards developed in the context of an emerging commercial market.

In broader terms, through its contribution to the nascent, but expanding, body of literature concerned with sociologies of standards, and standardisation, this chapter aims to answer Timmerman and Epstein's call 'for … analyses of the specific and unintended consequences of different sorts of standards operating in distinct social domains'.[1]

Introduction

As stated above, this data analysis chapter sets out to systematically, and critically, examine the forensic standard-making process, emphasising the complex negotiations required by both forensic scientists and allied professionals within the CJS. Further, it exposes the material, historical, and organisational contingencies, which led to the creation of standardised forensic products. It surveys their implementation and explores the reported benefits of standardisation, in addition to the ways in which these standards reportedly became subverted in site-specific contexts. The resulting analysis may be situated within a wider Science and Technology Studies, *corpus*. Additionally, it is hoped that the instant case – which focusses on forensic productisation and standardisation – may provide comprehensive answers to the research question(s), which may resonate with socio-legal scholars, providing the departure point for further research.

Specifically, this chapter focusses on the creation of standardised forensic 'products' within the marketised forensic science sector in England and Wales. This 'menu' of standardised forensic products emerged during a period of significant economic, and organisational, disruption, within the forensic science sector. If the perceptions of a significant proportion of forensic practitioners are accurate, then implementation of these codified products created further tensions; thus, this chapter may serve to demonstrate the (unintended) consequences, which may flow from incomplete application of standards, incomplete understanding of their effect, and the instrumental use of these same standards, not to achieve efficiencies or harmonisation, but to effect particular institutional goals, which are not shared across the wider community of practice. This section invites us to ask fundamental questions regarding the creation of informal standards within the marketplace; who should set such standards, and whom should they serve? Ultimately, it lays the groundwork for the following chapter, demonstrating the ways in which standardisation facilitates triaging and streamlining of forensic provision.

This chapter follows Timmerman's recommended approach, subdividing the informal standardisation process into phases of creation, implementation, and resistance, followed by a discussion of outcomes. This chapter utilises the case

[1]Timmermans, S., & Epstein, S. (2010). A world of standards but not a standard world: Toward a sociology of standards and standardization. *Annual Review of Sociology, 36*, 69–89.

study methodological perspective and draws upon results gleaned from documentary analysis, and from original empirical research, conducted throughout the forensic science sector in all four corners of the UK. While standardisation is regarded as practically beneficial, if the preponderance of informant perspectives are accurate, this chapter may serve to demonstrate the problems which can potentially arise when standards creation is dominated by one agency, when it does not emerge from consensus among stakeholders, when delivery is skewed towards the demand side, and when those who bear the cost of implementation have little input into the standards creation process.

Forensic Science Provision in England and Wales

The governance of the provision of forensic science services, and the organisational structure and management of individual forensic science laboratories, varies widely between different countries, regions, and jurisdictions. Nonetheless, across this varied forensic landscape, providers face similar economic challenges. Since the restructuring and closure of the Forensic Science Service (FSS), commercial imperatives have intruded, to a greater or lesser extent, on scientific autonomy, with most forensic providers now recognising the need to demonstrate a willingness to embrace new management techniques, to internalise regulatory objectives, and to enter into rudimentary forms of competition. However, despite the increasing pressure of commercial imperatives, the overwhelming majority of developed countries still choose to deliver vital forensic services through a system of public provision.[2] The current system of forensic science provision operating in England and Wales is therefore quite, exceptional, insofar as it is achieved through a system of marketised delivery.

The development of marketised forensic provision in England and Wales mirrors similar developments across the domestic sector, where the state is no longer viewed as the only agency suitable to be tasked with the provision of services to the CJS. Within the forensic science sector – as across many other domains – the limitations of the state's capacity to manage the organisational complexities of social life has been relentlessly highlighted, and long-standing institutional arrangements have been transformed through volatile patterns of policy development and innovation. Hence, what were once state-monopolised powers have increasingly been transferred to private, 'for-profit' contractors. These actors are allowed to pursue commercial interests provided that they remain within the constraints established by their contract with the government authorities (and with their private customers) and submit to various forms of monitoring and regulation.

[2]Centralisation and public ownership are common features of forensic science provision throughout Europe and across both common law and civilian jurisdictions: for example, *Statens Kriminaltekniska Laboratorium* (Swedish National Laboratory of Forensic Science, SKL), Forensic Science Ireland, Netherlands Forensic Science Institute, and the *Bundeskriminalamt* Forensic Science Institute.

Economic Rationalisation in the UK

The privatisation of forensic services correspond precisely to the fiscal and ideological principles of (putatively 'Thatcherite') economic rationalisation, which have affected other state institutions within the UK. The reformation of subsisting modes of production has been achieved through the creation of new ideological categories, cognate with a theory of political-economic practice which proposes that human well-being can best be advanced by liberating individual entrepreneurial freedoms and skills within an institutional framework that is characterised by strong private property rights, free markets, and free trade. The role of the state under this system is thus merely to create, and preserve, an institutional framework appropriate to such practices.

Although degrees of commercialised forensic science provision exist in the majority of developed countries, only in England and Wales have the government sought to reorganise the delivery of such services around an exclusively market-based model. However, it should be noted that the process of forensic market-creation (from public ownership, through a gradual blending of public and private provision, culminating in the removal of government-operated forensic science agencies) is typical of any sector which has been exposed to 'new public management' techniques and processes of economic rationalisation.

This is not a recent phenomenon. The construction of consent to these processes of commercialisation began in the early 1980s, the point at which the Home Office was opened up to discourses of 'modernisation' and 'economic rationality', and its character transformed by self-negating management techniques, which valorised the concepts of 'economy, efficiency and effectiveness'.[3] By the end of that decade, the ethos of 'customer relations' – central to commercial organisation – had began to influence the practices of all government agencies, and the turn towards processes of economic rationalisation began to influence, and alter, the field of forensic science provision, which slowly became reconfigured around new goals, interests, and incentives. Thus, the normative goals of a public sector agency – the FSS – were gradually subsumed by the quantitative indices of marketised service delivery, marked by entrepreneurial innovation, value for money, choice, and communication between stakeholders.

The FSS: Transition and Closure

In the decades preceding marketisation, forensic science provision in England and Wales had been achieved solely through the publicly funded FSS (and a small number of 'in-house' police laboratories). This organisation, acting under the aegis of the Home Office, operated several facilities throughout the country; work was distributed across seven main laboratories, distributed from London to the Midlands and the North of England. The FSS provided scene-of-crime and

---

[3]Lawless, C. (2010). *A curious reconstruction? The shaping of 'marketized' forensic science*. CARR Discussion Paper 63.

forensic investigation services to police forces in England and Wales, as well as to the Crown Prosecution Service, HM Revenue and Customs, HM Coroners' Service, Ministry of Defence Police, British Transport Police, and worldwide forensic services. It also maintained a research laboratory at Aldermaston (previously the Central Research and Support Establishment), where the FSS developed 'low copy number' (LCN) techniques, advanced deoxyribonucleic acid (DNA) profiling, and established the National DNA Database (NDNAD).

From its inception, the FSS operated as a publicly owned service. However, profound shifts in public policy and management were to bring about an emphatic reorganisation of the provision of forensic services. Further, the developing discursive framework of 'added value' service delivery – as vigorously promoted by the government's Audit Office – would carry serious implications for the governance of the publicly funded FSS. Prior to 1987,

> [...] the FSS was funded centrally so the Police didn't have to pay directly for any of their requested work. This resulted in forces often submitting very large numbers of items from each case, often waiting months for results.[4]

In 1987, an accounting firm, Touche Ross, was commissioned to draft a report on police scientific support, concluding that police management of scientific support services was 'generally poor'. However, the Touche Ross report also explored the scope for organisational changes, and new funding methods, within the FSS. Following the recommendations of the report, the FSS introduced direct charging to police forces.

Restructuring and DNA Analysis

With the advent of direct charging, the costs of forensic services became visible to operational forces (henceforth to be regarded as 'customers'). Further, the FSS aligned itself with a more 'business-oriented' approach to service delivery, with a particular focus on 'forensic strategy', advocating more careful triaging of submitted items and agreeing target dates for court reporting. This involved a more customer-facing approach. Nonetheless, during this period, 'it was still the scientists who determined what forensic examinations and analyses to make, in collaboration with the Police'.[5]

The majority of FSS employees interviewed were able to provide evidence to support the view that they regarded 'pre-codification' forensic analyses carried out by the FSS as being both comprehensive and contextual. A lead biologist described the process:

---

[4]King, D., Stangoe, C., & Cooke, L. (2012). *Scrutinising forensic services*. CPD presentation to 25 Bedford Row.

[5]King, D., Stangoe, C., & Cooke, L. (2012). *Scrutinising forensic services*. CPD presentation to 25 Bedford Row, at p. 5.

> [...] essentially what would happen is that you would have almost a service provision, so in the FSS we dealt with pretty much everything ... whenever there was a case that came in the door there would be a huge bag of exhibits and the police would essentially say 'can you forensic those please' and we would say '... this is the overarching strategy, we'll start with Test A, we'll do Test B, C and D' and then once we've done that, our work hasn't impacted on the work of someone else, so we then hand over the case to that individual, and they'll do their Tests 1, 2 & 3 and once they've finished that work we can then shave off part of it into toxicology, or some other department, and ... after a few months of ... very clever science, you write a very large report that says ... we've done this to death: these are the opportunities available, these are the findings that we've got, and if necessary, if all of this falls down, we've actually retained material in these departments so we could ... go down [an alternative] avenue if you wish. (Interview with Lead Scientist: Tier 2 FSP, 2015)

This typical response, illustrating a standard FSS workflow, highlights the exhaustive nature of forensic investigatory processes, as carried out within the FSS. A lack of supervening concerns regarding economic costs, or value, on the part of the investigatory authorities, reputedly allowed for the submission of a large amount of initial samples. Further, the investigation, evaluation, and reporting process are presented as comparatively exhaustive (to a degree which might later be conceived of as excessive and surplus to 'customer requirements'). Another notable feature of these claims was the holistic nature of the investigation and analysis, which was not – at that time – solely dependent on DNA-profiling techniques. DNA profiling is thus viewed as contributing to a palette of forensic practices, with no evidence of the privileging of one method over another. The informant also highlights the possibilities for recursion, and review, at a later stage, in order to take account of updated contextual information. In summary, the response suggests a significant degree of forward planning, a high granularity of inference, contextual awareness, and flexibility, allowing for the compilation of exhaustive reports, written by expert forensic scientists. Further, it should be noted that that the investigatory authorities did not direct the course of the FSS examination, at this time: nor did they participate directly in the formulation of a forensic investigatory strategy.

Notably absent from this expert's response were concerns regarding the overarching importance of turn-around-times (TRTs) or the imposition of economic efficiencies. Rather, the report of the investigation, and comparatively rigorous forensic evaluation, appears to conform to normative representations of scientific method. They are indicative of universalism, insofar as the truth claims are subjected solely to pre-established impersonal criteria. They are communalist insofar as the 'customer' does not dictate the course of the investigation. And they are disinterested insofar as they are free from institutional motivations.

Indeed, such responses were routinely encountered and may thus be regarded as typical of expert perspectives of non-marketised forensic-scientific analysis. Indeed, there were clear and notable similarities between the description of exhaustive forensic analysis offered above – by a former employee of the FSS – and the contemporary observations of forensic scientists working within the publicly funded forensic sector in Northern Ireland, as indicated below:

> Where I would see … the big change is in what's requested in the first place. And that's not altogether a bad thing because, back in days of yore, where the police weren't, in any sense, paying for it, a truck would hiss to a halt outside, the doors would open, a hundred items would come out, and the forensic strategy would be 'forensicate that!' 'Well, what is it you want?' 'Everything'. 'Well, that's alright for you to say but I've got another fifty cases …' And a consequence of that was that we were reporting cases months, and months, and sometimes years after they came in. And how much of that output remained valuable at that stage? Who knows! So [the introduction of pricing and an appreciation of evidential value] has focussed the police onto trying to get the best return, and, of course, DNA – bit of a buzzword – tends to be one of the things they reach for first, though actually, not always sensibly. But that's what people think ….' (Interview with Lead Scientist: Forensic Science Northern Ireland, 2015)

To return to the process of organisational reform within the FSS, in addition to managing internal change, the FSS was – in the mid-1990s – faced with further challenges. Its monopoly on forensic science delivery in England and Wales came to an abrupt end when two private forensic companies (LGC and Scientifics Ltd.) emerged and began to compete directly for FSS' business. These companies had originated in the public sector and were joined – in 1996 – by the first fully private company, Forensic Alliance.[6]

During this period, the FSS had undergone a degree of reformation in order to bring it into line with the emergent market realities. Indeed, the FSS made it clear that the commercial considerations of the new forensic market were paramount in reshaping the relationship between FSS forensic experts and the requirements of the CJS:

> It is the belief of the FSS that the perception of such value for money should be that of the customer. These initiatives have the aim of not only providing better value for money, but also of

[6]Lawless, C. (2010). *A curious reconstruction? The shaping of 'marketized' forensic science*. CARR Discussion Paper 63, pp. 3–6.; Lawless, C. J., & Williams, R. (2010). Helping with inquiries or helping with profits? The trials and tribulations of a technology of forensic reasoning. *Social Studies of Science, 40*, 731–755, at pp. 736–738.

> achieving improvement through a genuine partnership in which the customer has a greater participation than hitherto in decisions about what work is done in the laboratory.[7]

The degree to which these changes altered the reported nature of FSS service delivery, and ethos, may be gauged by comparing the FSS 'mission statement' from 2001, in which the agency defined its role in terms of a commitment to crafting a 'safer and more just society', with later versions, which referred to the need to:

> retain and reinforce our leading position as the principal provider of forensic science to the UK criminal justice system (UKCJS), and use this platform to become the leading provider worldwide, thereby enhancing long term shareholder value.[8]

The alterations to policy and management – characterised by marketisation and productisation – were accompanied by deeper structural changes. The FSS had been awarded Trading Fund status by the government, in 1999. Thus, the service was able to recoup funds, and to declare a profit, in the short term. However, as new competitors emerged, each contributed to a reduction in the FSS' market share and profits declined. The McFarland Review, in 2003, found that the FSS was too heavily burdened by overhead costs and was thus unable to meet clients' needs. The Review recommended a further change, to GovCo (Government Company) status, as a preliminary stage prior to restructuring as a public–private partnership.

The later McKinsey Review, of 2008, examined the sustainability of the forensic science market as a whole, concluding that the market was underperforming and was in need of urgent reform. It also noted that the costs of restructuring the FSS would be significant. As a result, the government announced its plans to wind down the FSS, following the advice of the House of Commons Science and Technology Committee in December 2010. The service was eventually closed in 2011. With the closure of the FSS, forensic science provision in England and Wales became fully marketised, with work (including the 65% market share of the defunct FSS) now to be shared between 15 private companies.

The Forensic Science Market

The dissolution of the FSS having been completed, the forensic science sector now comprised a rudimentary market, which had emerged during the latter stages

---

[7]Cook, R., Evett, I. W., Jackson, G., Jones, P. J., & Lambert, J. A. (1998). A model for case assessment and interpretation. *Science & Justice*, *38*, 151–156, at p. 152.

[8]See Lawless, C. J., & Williams, R. (2010). Helping with inquiries or helping with profits? The trials and tribulations of a technology of forensic reasoning. *Social Studies of Science*, *40*, 731–755, at p. 737.

of FSS rundown; a market comprising a diverse number of commercial FSPs of varying sizes, boasting varying specialisms, and displaying varying abilities. The sector was, from the outset, dominated by four large companies, who together accounted for the largest share of the market. These were Key Forensic Services,[9] Cellmark,[10] Environmental Scientifics Group,[11] and LGC Forensics.[12] These four companies also comprised the founding commercial members of the Association of Forensic Service Providers,[13] with the stated aim of furthering the interests of the forensic services industry. The four large providers offered a wide range of forensic services. The remainder of the market consisted of medium-sized, and niche, organisations, such as ROAR, Principal Forensic Services,[14] Manlove Forensics,[15] Randox, and Hayward Associates Forensic Science (which provides only DNA-profiling services and specialises in criminal defence work).[16] In addition, it should be noted that each of the 43 police forces in England and Wales operated their own private testing laboratories, a state of affairs which subsists to the current day.

Procurement and the National Forensic Framework Agreement (NFFA)

The creation of a rudimentary forensic science market, and the introduction, by the FSS, of direct charging to customers, heralded an emphatic turn towards commoditisation within the forensic science sector. Therefore, in response to the imperatives of progressive marketisation, the FSS began to restructure service delivery. From this point, forensic services began to be organised in terms of the provision of products, which began to be defined by category of expert activity, chargeable units of time, cost, standards, and expected outcome. The demand side experienced similar commercial restructuring, and in 2006, the government announced a pilot procurement exercise. The exercise was initially limited to three police forces. However, this pilot project quickly grew to involve 14 police forces in England and Wales, a group which came to be known as the 'West-Coast Consortium'. The resulting SWNWW Tender (encompassing South Wales, North Wales, and the West of England) established fixed prices for a range of standardised and codified forensic products, which were to be purchased from FSPs on a bulk basis. Meanwhile, on the customer side, purchasing

---

[9]http://www.keyforensic.co.uk (in insolvency as of 2018).
[10]http://www.cellmarkforensics.co.uk
[11]http://www.esg.co.uk/services/forensic-services-overview/
[12]http://www.lgcgroup.com/sectors/forensic science/ (rebranded EuroFins as of 2017)
[13]http://www.afsp.org.uk/node/33/The non-commercial members are Scottish Police Authority Forensic Services and Forensic Science Northern Ireland.
[14]http://www.principalforensicservices.com/This company is noteworthy as it employs the incoming UK Forensic Science Regulator, Dr Gill Tully.
[15]Now ArroGen Forensics, merging with Forensic Access in 2018.
[16]http://www.haywardforensics.co.uk/

of forensic services shifted, from police Scientific Support Managers (most of whom had been scene-of-crime officers with experience of quality assurance and financial management in relation to forensic science) to police procurement departments. As will be shown, informants report that the introduction of this codified system for the purchase of fixed-price forensic products carried serious implications for the provision of forensic science services. Prior to the West Coast Consortium Tender police forces had submitted items to their forensic provider,

> [...] in discussion with a scientist, and the scientist then decided, using their skills, independence and experience, on what items to examine, using what techniques and what analytical technique, if any.[17]

Following communication between the investigatory authorities, and the forensic science provider, a TRT would be agreed, based on practical considerations (e.g. case complexity, supporting evidence, offence type, and court date). The work would then be charged on an hourly basis, with a degree of fixed-price charging in respect of analytical tasks. However, the competitive tendering process introduced by the West Coast Consortium Tender was largely customer led. It required FSPs to quote substantial efficiencies in the TRTs for both analysis and the evaluation of forensic samples. In addition, the tendering process saw the introduction of a range of standardised, and codified, forensic products. Rather than develop the codes in tandem with scientific experts, it was the police forces themselves who drew up the codes, using ex-forensic submissions administrators. Thus, under Association of Chief Police Officers (ACPO) guidance, the police created a 'menu' of forensic products and provided forensic scientists with instructions on when and how they were to be applied.

An example is as follows:

> *01BF (Body Fluids) – DNA (Deoxyribonucleic Acid) Crime Scene Stains – Standard:* To process recovered biological samples/material using the most appropriate means to successfully obtain the optimum Short Tandem Repeat (STR) Second Generation Multiplex Plus (SGM+) profile for – Comparison against an individual's DNA profile and/or submission onto the United Kingdom DNA Database (NDNAD).

With the publication of the tender document, forensic providers were required to rapidly reorganise their service delivery models to fit with the new regime: a process which required a thorough examination of each of the listed products, and attendant protocols, in order to determine the necessary business, and

[17]King, D., Stangoe, C., & Cooke, L. (2012). *Scrutinising forensic services.* CPD presentation to 25 Bedford Row, at p. 12.

operational, restructuring in order to deliver the product in accordance with the accompanying protocol. Additionally, providers were required to ascertain an appropriately competitive price to submit for each code. The codification process thus imposed new challenges on providers, not least due to the fact that some of the products were not clearly defined, leading to diverse interpretations – and ongoing disagreements – between customers and providers. This will form the subject of further discussion, *supra*.

Returning to the initial tendering process, forensic experts began to express concerns regarding the way in which the pilot project was allowed to increase in size and complexity. Untrammelled growth presented the Consortium with significant challenges when attempting to evaluate, and compare, each of the tenders against the requirements of the 14 individual forces involved. This led to consequent delay, and the process – which had been estimated to last a few months – took 18 months to reach completion. During this time, providers were precluded from approaching police forces to solicit further work, and market development therefore came to a halt, leading to increased tension between customers and providers. As the market began to stagnate, and pressures grew, commercial managers within the provider companies began to involve themselves in service delivery, taking control away from forensic scientists. This is reported as having led to diminishing morale among forensic scientists, who also harboured concerns over the quality of service delivery.

Contracts under the SWNWW tender were finally awarded in January 2008, with FSP's awarded contracts under a series of lots, each corresponding to a particular forensic activity (e.g. Lot 209, Questioned Documents). Under the contract, single forensic service providers were tasked with providing services to various police forces. These contracts were generally arranged on a large-scale 'volume' basis – normally in terms of tens of thousands of units, each unit corresponding to a forensic product – with the open market structure allowing forces to change providers with relative ease. Conversely, police forces might typically have contracts with a variety of providers, in order that the latter provide a range of different services. One provider may provide DNA-profiling information, another may do work relating to the analysis of footwear impressions, and a third may provide computer, and telecommunications, services. Thus, different elements of a complex case would inevitably be sent to different providers. Further, it is alleged by a number of practitioners that since the market structure actively precluded communication between rival companies, the articulation of rich contextual detail that had been shown to be essential to providing accurate results was impacted. While the productised model of delivery was limited to so-called volume crime, it is nonetheless the case that routine work on high-volume crime may throw up the same complexities and difficulties as those relating to serious crime. However, the ability to fully investigate these complexities would henceforth be impacted to a significant degree by organisational capabilities and budgetary constraints.

Returning to the initial tender, this provided the stimulus for further restructuring of the FSS, the organisation having lost a significant amount of work to LGC Forensics and Cellmark Forensic Services. Meanwhile, Key Forensic

Services[18] were tasked with providing assistance with initial resource problems across the industry. However, the previous decision to allow the tender to grow in size, and complexity, was to lead to further problems. The tender had been intended to be a small pilot, the results of which were to be analysed carefully, before the next round of tendering was instituted. Thus, improvements and modifications had been planned to be taken into account in order that lessons learned from any problems encountered during the pilot tender could be absorbed. However, due to the long delay in the tender evaluation and award process, there was insufficient time to consider operational feedback from both the FSPs and the police forces before the next round of tenders were instituted.

The National Policing Improvement Agency (NPIA)/NFFA

As outlined above, problematic contingencies became structurally embedded in the standardised procurement procedures and were expressed in the subsequent tendering process. This latter process came under the control of the NPIA and became known as the NFFA. The NFFA represents a government attempt to implement standardisation measures in respect of the services offered to the police by the new body of FSPs. It was launched in August 2008. The agreement sought to bring much-needed organisation to the system of police procurement of forensic services while ensuring compliance with overarching European Union requirements regarding transparency. A dozen FSPs including the FSS, participated in the original agreement. The structure and content of the NFFA was broadly similar to that of the West Coast Tender. Under this agreement, in August 2008, 12 FSPs – including the FSS – were to take part in the initial NFFA tender. The introduction of the NPIA/NFFA also allowed small private forensic science suppliers to bid for particular lots (such as DNA crime scene stains or sexual offence casework). This enabled niche providers to bid for contracts in areas, which had previously been dominated by full-service providers, while providing customers with a greater degree of choice and flexibility.[19] While the government were able to introduce a level of standardised practice across the market, implementation difficulties are reported as contributing to a further set of problems.

Forensic Productisation – Implementation and Resistance

As Lawless has previously observed, the NFFA 'placed cognitive practices of evidence interpretation alongside mechanical and technical procedures', allegedly leading to opposition, and resistance, from forensic scientists. Further, scientists raised concerns regarding what they regarded as the partial, and incoherent, manner in which standardisation had been implemented.

---

[18]Cellmark, LGC, and Key Forensic Services comprise the top tier of marketised forensic science provision in the UK.

[19]Lawless, C. (2016). *Forensic science: A sociological introduction* (p. 71). New York, NY: Routledge.

During the data collection process, a significant number of respondents highlighted the difficulties faced by FSPs, when attempting to negotiate the standardised forensic product system. In particular, they noted that while there had been a degree of standardisation with regard to products, the process was incomplete and was characterised by deep meso-level diversification with regard to the application of those standards. Specifically, it was claimed that each of the 43 police force 'customers' wished to apply the codes in a bespoke manner which would maintain, and serve, the latter's unique force identity.

> [The codes] are broadly similar but … they're incompatible. The turn-around times, the delivery of the report, the way in which the report findings should be delivered, whether it's an SFR, an abbreviated statement, all of these change between force, even within the same consortium. So, you're effectively re-inventing the wheel for every customer. (Interview with Lead Scientist: Tier 2 FSP, 2015)

> [Police] procurement dictate the codes. So, for example, 'mixed sample' is A6. A6 is broken into different tiers but it's an over-simplification of the job and there are too many levels. Further, the police can manipulate the codes. So, an A6 for the Met and an A6 for Cambridge may mean different things, as they tender individually. There's no direct comparison. (Interview with Lead Biologist: Tier 1 FSP, 2015)

Standardisation under the NFFA, occurring at force level, thus led to a multitude of standards being enforced between different force areas, Forensic scientists associated such problems as being directly related to the non-unitary nature of policing in England and Wales:

> The only driving force behind police forces coming together to tender for work was cost, but what they didn't do was change their own internal procedures, or lose their own force identity, because they've all got their own management, their own Chief Constable, their own ACC, their own forensic… Avon and Somerset may want an SFR sent to a CJSM account sent to an individual by post. [Conversely] if you're working in Devon you [compile] an abbreviated statement, but only for footwear …. (Interview with Managing Director: Tier 2 FSP, 2015)

However, the problems also extended beyond England and Wales, to allied jurisdictions within the UK.

> Our product coding system is based on that original ACPO/NPIA coding system … The codes don't necessarily fit the request or the item. It doesn't easily fit the processes we do and [the product

> codes] have been adjusted over the years. So, each lab interprets them in a different fashion. Each lab adjusted [the codes] according to their own protocols and interpretation. (Interview with Lead Scientist: FSNI, 2015)

Further, scientists highlighted concerns relating to the ways in which productisation now afforded individual police forces with the means to direct forensic strategy within the context of a criminal investigation, often in the absence of supporting contextual information.

> You might have an item from a suspect's jumper. The jumper has three obvious dark brown stains on the sleeve that appear to be blood. So the police tell you to test those stains to tie them to the victim. But the stains could be from the suspect – he may have had a bleeding nose. And beside those large stains may be a small stain more consistent with low-velocity splatter. That may be the crucial item to test that ties the suspect to the victim. (Interview with Lead Scientist: Tier 2 FSP, 2015)

Biologists were especially concerned that laboratory testing processes had become visible to the police, through productisation, but that the latter lacked the necessary expertise to understand when and how to use forensic products. Conversely, scientists felt less able to approach investigations in a rigorous, scientific manner. In practical terms, this was often related to a lack of provision of necessary contextual information.

> In practice, the police have budgets and scientists have turnarounds. You need thinking time … or experience [to carry out a thorough analysis]. So, when time is short, the tendency is just to do what the police ask. You have targets to meet. You have to complete a number of allocations. (Interview with Lead Scientist: Tier 1 FSP, 2015)

Such problems were reputedly exacerbated by poor communication between FSPs, and the investigatory authorities, compounded by the supposed incommensurability of each agency's role.

> If you are needing further information you can only contact certain named people. Often they will be named on the contract. Ideally, you contact the budget holder, who has to sign off on the work. Otherwise you don't get paid. You have to provide an estimate. The estimate has to correspond to product codes. So the codes allow the police to control budgets and compare providers. (Interview with Managing Director: Tier 1 FSP, 2015)

> The problem is that police procurement are monitoring for performance, and scientists are carrying out the work governed by different criteria. The key is good communication between the different layers. (Interview with Lead Scientist: Tier 1 FSP, 2015)

Lastly, scientists reported encountering implementation problems within the police force, directly related to the 'triaging' of forensic investigations.

> The code system doesn't apply to serious crimes such as murder. They are charged under a bespoke system according to an hourly rate. You may have an item from a jumper that's been taken from a suspect in a homicide. The police may try to put that item through under a volume crime code. The police assume that it's the same test. So there has to be a triaging process of monitoring submissions from the police. (Interview with Lead Scientist: Tier 2 FSP, 2015)

This triaging process will form the subject of further discussion, *supra*.

Triaging of Forensic Investigations

Since the majority of products allotted during the tendering process were assigned a fixed price, forensic providers were forced to allocate work to their scientists as directed by the investigative authorities, categorising work according to particular product codes. Thus, the triaging of cases could be seen to be a direct response to (or was at least heavily influenced and facilitated by) the introduction of categories defined by non-expert 'customers' from outwith the forensic-scientific domain, who themselves were propelled by financial considerations. Further, the tight TRTs associated with each product process significantly reduced the time available for expert interpretation and evaluation, while putting pressure on scientists to deliver particular results.[20] If testimony is accurate, then it may be claimed that a reduction in 'thinking time' meant that scientists faced a significant loss in the primary resource necessary in order for them

> to use their skills and experience to look at a case and determine what techniques to use, and to carefully examine the results, interpret them and to write a clear and robust statement.[21]

[20]Arbitrary three- or four-day 'turn round times' are both common in, and unique to, the UK forensic market and do not reflect the time taken for a case to reach court. Equivalent analyses may take up to 90 days in the United States.

[21]King, D., Stangoe, C., & Cooke, L. (2012). *Scrutinising forensic services*. CPD presentation to 25 Bedford Row, at p. 16.

As demonstrated above, scientists discerned further problems related to the shift in administrative control, from the forensic-scientific expert, to the 'customer'; primarily, the fact that the 'customer' was now able to dictate which product was to be used. Although the scientist retained the ability to recommend the use of alternative – or additional – products, these requests were increasingly viewed as purely advisory and were often outweighed by cost concerns. Conversely, some scientists expressed a reluctance to suggest viable alternatives, as these might diminish the provider's contracted TRTs. Therefore, it may be concluded that the introduction of commoditisation led to perceptions of a significant loss of scientific autonomy in the setting of the forensic strategy necessary for case evaluation and investigation,[22] to that extent that larger providers increasingly began to follow customer recommendations, even where these were perceived to be mistaken or merely inefficient.

> It is dependent on the contract ... the wording of that contract, what falls under [the contract], or the scientist's interpretation of what that is ... some scientists previously have read a certain code to me in a source-level only interpretation ... and especially because of the perceived price difference between a lower code and a higher code, they don't get that added value ... I'm not going to give them that activity level interpretation because they're not paying for it, but really, my view is that [I should]. (Interview with DNA Reporting Scientist: Tier 1 FSP, 2015)

One interviewee (a lead biologist) discussed the ways in which commoditisation might create issues for expert forensic analysis,[23] providing the example of a common assault, following which the police submit one blood-stained item of clothing – taken from a suspect – to the forensic science provider. The investigating authorities request that product 01BF (a DNA test for body fluids) be used. The forensic scientist examines the item and submits one blood stain for DNA analysis. The DNA is found to 'match' that of the alleged victim.[24] A report is produced in those terms, stating that a DNA profile was obtained and found to 'match' that of the victim.

---

[22]Productisation might therefore be seen as having a negative impact on the scientist's ability to carry out casework interpretation and analysis, given that the Case Assessment and Interpretation (CAI) process relies on communication and reflexivity.

[23]See also King, D., Stangoe, C., & Cooke, L. (2012). *Scrutinising forensic services.* CPD presentation to 25 Bedford Row, at p. 18.

[24]Although the term 'match' is used, for ease of description, it should be noted that this term is abjured by many scientists and academics, who highlight the fact that DNA profiling – operating on a genuinely scientific basis – relies on statistical probabilities, rather than claims of 'match' and 'non-match', as typified by the 'pattern identification' techniques, such as fingerprinting and ballistics.

Given the above scenario, the report will necessarily be limited to statements regarding the source of the material, since no parallel interpretation of the possible causes of particular blood patterns has been carried out. Therefore, the reader will not know how much – or little – blood was present on the examined item or how it could have come to be on the item. In addition, no attempt will have been made to look for the presence of damage, or other evidence that might help the court to determine what has occurred, and which may allow the scientist to furnish propositions relating to the activity which led to the staining, as well as the source.[25]

The limitations that may result from the sole use of product 01BF derive from the fact that this product was designed to be used in simple cases, such as burglaries – or car thefts – where answers to the question of 'who', rather than 'how', are regarded as being generally sufficient. Nonetheless, this product is reported as being routinely used in more complex cases, in which, it is claimed, the interpretation of evidential material should proceed on the basis of a more thorough, and nuanced, analysis.

In addition, it should be noted that the codification, and commoditisation, of forensic-scientific products, under the West Coast Consortium Tender, extended from substantive forensic activities such as testing and analysis, to the writing of forensic reports. The tender introduced a product called an 'abbreviated' (or 'short form') statement, for use with all forensic products.[26] This product was significantly cheaper than a full evaluative statement due to the fact that the 'short form' statement contained comparatively little information. The abbreviated statement was limited to only that information which the investigating authority, and forensic scientists, considered to be important. Hence, a complete list of case items was not provided, and interpretation of the results – if present – was not thorough. Nor was the interpretation able to be conducted with any regard to the overall context of a case.[27]

As with the design of simple products, such statements were designed to be used in reasonably straightforward cases, such as burglaries or car thefts. In such cases, a DNA profile will be obtained and the abbreviated statement written, giving the basic DNA result (which will often be a full DNA profile attributable to a particular individual).[28] There is a section at the end of many of these abbreviated

[25]For a discussion of the hierarchy of propositions, see Evett et al. on the Case Assessment and Interpretation (CAI) method. Cook, R., Evett, I. W., Jackson, G., Jones, P. J., & Lambert, J. A. (1998). A model for case assessment and interpretation. *Science & Justice, 38*, 151–156.

[26]The commoditisation of forensic reports followed the introduction, by the Crown Prosecution Service, of 'staged reporting' (also known as Streamlined Forensic Reporting) for cases involving DNA. See Richmond, K. (2018). Streamlined forensic reporting: 'Swift and sure justice'? *Journal of Criminal Law, 82*(2), 156–177.

[27]Abbreviated statements should be distinguished from Streamlined Forensic Reports. The latter are frequently compiled by non-experts and contain no interpretation.

[28]King et al. provide anecdotal evidence of problems which may arise from the use of abbreviated statements:

statements stating that a full witness statement should be requested prior to the case going to court. However, it is reported that this requirement is frequently overlooked.

Thus, the codification process, in tandem with the introduction of short form reporting, may – according to the preponderance of reports – be seen as delivering efficiencies through promoting the stratification of criminal investigations – at an early stage – into 'simple' and 'complex' cases: a division which is reflected in the pricing of forensic products and which may prove potentially determinative when allocating resources. However, since the interposition of processes of 'triaging' may determine the amount of resources allocated to forensic investigation – thus affecting the depth of investigation and the nature of its conclusions – the potential must also exist for problems to arise in relation to the initial misrecognition of cases (e.g. when the concise approach is taken to a case requiring deeper analysis and thorough evaluation). Such difficulties may, it is claimed, be compounded by the lack of availability of clear criteria with which to demarcate alternative levels of seriousness and their subsequent analysis.

Conclusion

As the data have demonstrated, the creation of a rudimentary forensic science market (subsequent to the introduction, by the FSS, of direct charging to customers) is reported as having facilitated the process of informal standardisation of forensic processes. It is further reported that by making forensic investigatory processes visible to institutional agents within the CJS, forensic providers were able to deliver a degree of efficiency. In addition, it is claimed that this process enhanced the ability of the investigative authorities to dictate the course of the investigatory strategy, and to request the use of particular products, within the context of particular levels of evaluation. The standardisation, and productisation, of forensic processes is thus viewed as having facilitated 'triaging' and enabled criminal justice agencies to assign samples to different intensities, and modes, of forensic investigation, largely determined by the offence type. Given that each force had particular needs, this model led to perceived inefficiencies and an added perception that the process allowed 'inexpert' investigators within the CJS an inordinate amount of control over matters, which traditionally had fallen within the ambit of forensic science.

Scientists further reported that the convergence, and transplantation, of standardised products and practices had created tensions, which were overcome through the modification of subsisting practices, alongside site-by-site adaptation, and the use of bridging strategies. Informant's responses demonstrated the

---

> [...] we have seen examples where upon examination of the DNA profile the result is actually a mixture of DNA from which the profile of the major contributor has been deduced. In these cases there has been no comment on the presence of DNA from any other individual.

persistence of these modified local practices and the continued importance of tacit expert knowledge. Crucially, scientists also testified to the degree to which they believed that partial standardisation had served to create greater levels of variation, especially with regard to the delivery of the product. This was seen as having flowed directly from the inability of the 43 individual forces to agree to standard operating procedures and protocols (albeit that these might remain flexible enough to accommodate the particular needs of each force).

Further, informants demonstrated how the influence of codification was perceived as having shaped the subsequent process of 'triaging' which set material samples on a particular evidential trajectory and which structured the resulting analysis in terms of depth, level of expertise, and the examiner's ability to take account of contextual factors. They testified to the ways in which overarching governance structures were held to have influenced the work of expert practitioners and considered the degree to which these influences could affect the ability of forensic scientists to carry out an exhaustive – contextually rich – evaluation, which conformed to the standard requirements of the Case Assessment and Interpretation process.

Lastly, informants illustrated the ways in which processes of standardisation and productisation served to articulate the concept of customer 'value', and demonstrated how the proecccupation with efficiency created tensions between forensic scientists and institutional agents within the CJS: tensions which were shown to carry deeper implications for both the CJS and the forensic science sector.

In closing, it is claimed that – if informant perceptions are accurate – the foregoing empirical study may potentially carry significant implications for our understanding of the development of standards within emerging markets. It highlights the necessity of drafting standards as part of a comprehensive process involving all relevant stakeholders. Indeed, the empirical data raise concerns regarding the difficulties which may arise when lead agencies (or international corporations) control, and direct, the standardisation process, crafting solutions – and shaping products – which are viewed as having been tailored to providing efficiencies primarily to their members. Thus, it is probable that problems may be encountered when monopolies (or oligopolies) define standards in a way which delivers disproportionate benefits to one group. Such problems are amplified when the standardisation process is enacted against a background of market volatility, in the absence of formal, meso-level organisation.

The obstacles engendered by the incomplete, or partial, drafting of standards may potentially lead to further difficulties, related to implementation and adaptation. The data from the instant study reveal the awkward complexities of implementing forensic products, intended for utilisation within a structured investigatory process, which were viewed as having been developed in the absence of rigorous and transparent complementary protocols governing their implementation. The implications are that partial standardisation does not in, and of, itself create uniformity. The outcome will depend on additional factors which relate to the ability of those tasked with implementing the standard to do so, and which will largely determine whether a standard can ultimately be followed, absent of adaptive processes.

Further, this chapter demonstrates that the subject of standards – their production, distribution, and adoption – is of central importance, not solely to Science and Technology Studies scholars, but to those from the humanities and social sciences, particularly law. The study also demonstrates the increasing relevance of qualitative socio-legal studies of standardisation and testifies to their capacity to unearth rich descriptions, revealing the contingency of the standardisation process and of subsequent strategies of adaptation.

Chapter 5

Constructing Forensic Expertise

Chapter Summary

The focus of this section is on the restructuring of forensic expertise through marketisation and commodification. This chapter explores the perceived benefits of marketisation. In order to provide answers to the research questions, particular attention is paid to the divergence in approaches to forensic analysis brought about by the stratification of the forensic market. This chapter follows from the preceding discussion of the tendering process, which charted informant perspectives on the reported influence of historically contingent factors on the development of codification. It focusses on the perceived influence of codification, as having shaped the process of 'triaging' which sets material samples on a particular evidential trajectory and which structures the resulting analysis in terms of depth, level of expertise, and the examiner's ability to take account of contextual factors. It explores the perceived effects of overarching governance structures on the work of expert practitioners and considers the degree to which these are seen to affect the ability of forensic scientists to carry out an exhaustive – contextually rich – evaluation, which conforms to the requirements of the Case Assessment and Interpretation process. It also explores the process of market restructuring and the perception of 'de-skilling', a perception challenged by a number of professionals from allied criminal justice agencies. This chapter demonstrates the ways in which restructuring is perceived by forensic deoxyribonucleic acid (DNA) profilers as having resulted in a loss of expertise. If such perceptions are accurate, then how are the resulting tensions and paradoxes resolved? It illustrates the ways in which productisation, and the concept of customer 'value', has created tensions between forensic scientists and institutional agents within the criminal justice system. The discussion leads to a consideration of whether, and to what extent, subsisting theories of expertise offer an understanding of these processes. Again, the analysis is explicitly limited to the perceptions of informants, absent of any strong causal determinations. Further, it should be noted that the processes outlined in this chapter are not presented as being unique to the forensic science, and criminal justice, sectors. As Mirowski

Marketisation and Forensic Science Provision in England and Wales, 73–101

Published under exclusive licence by Emerald Publishing Limited
doi:10.1108/978-1-83909-123-020221005

and van Horn demonstrated, these phenomena influence 'the sphere of corporate scientific research' more generally.[1]

Pre-codification Forensic Analyses within the Public Sector

The majority of forensic scientists in Tier 1 and Tier 2 forensic science providers (FSPs) in England and Wales reported previous employment experience within the Forensic Science Service (FSS). Informants employed by Tier 1 providers tended to be less senior, having joined the FSS during the organisation's later GovCo incarnation. Nonetheless, all previous FSS employees were able to provide evidence to support their view that pre-codification forensic analyses carried out by the FSS were both comprehensive and contextual, as outlined in the previous chapter.

Notably absent from this expert's response were indications of the overarching importance of turn-around-times (TRTs) or the imposition of economic efficiencies. Rather, the investigation and comparatively rigorous forensic evaluation appear to conform to normative representations of scientific method. They are indicative of universalism, insofar as the truth claims are subjected solely to pre-established impersonal criteria. They are communist insofar as the 'customer' does not dictate the course of the investigation. And they are disinterested insofar as they are free from institutional motivations.

The responses elicited suggested that both the FSS and Forensic Science Northern Ireland (FSNI) could claim a similarly exhaustive approach to investigation, evaluation, and reporting. Both agencies made similar claims, that is, that the English and Welsh police forces, and Police Service of Northern Ireland (PSNI), were not significantly concerned with directing the course of the investigation through the selective collection of material samples. The respondents indicated an awareness of what they regarded as the possible inefficiencies of such a system, both in terms of economic and evidential value. Further, the respondents suggested that the perception of inefficiency (at least on the part of the customer) led directly towards a privileging of DNA-profiling techniques and a shift towards a more customer-directed investigatory strategy. The responses lacked the detail to make any substantive comments regarding the extent of this shift in emphasis. However, in light of the respondents' later comments on the importance of scientific method, and the perception of a continuing ability – on the part of FSNI – to carry out holistic, and contextual, analyses, it would not be unreasonable to infer that FSNI informants perceive a lesser degree of customer-led restructuring, of the type which has been reported in England and Wales.

[1]Mirowski, P., & van Horn, R. (2005). The contract research organisation and the commercialisation of scientific research. *Social Studies of Science, 35*(4), 503–548, at p. 505.

Triaging and the Privileging of DNA-profiling Techniques

The above responses suggest that the intensity of investigation and evaluation – and the concomitant granular of inference – carried out within the public sector, by both the FSS and FSNI, represents a high water mark. Further, that DNA-profiling techniques formed part of a diverse array of forensic practices. Ex-FSS employees went on to explain the ways in which DNA-profiling technologies began to be privileged, at the expense of similar bio-identification techniques and craft practices. This was facilitated by investment in DNA technologies and based on an appreciation of the ability of such techniques to deliver quick, conclusive results.

> DNA at the time was pretty expensive because we were at the beginnings of technology – big machines, big chemistry, lots of expertise, loads of training – you know, reporting was specialist because it was interpretation, so although it was very, very good wins it was pretty cost inefficient I suppose in terms of the person buying the test. So then, you invest in that area, you reduce costs, you decrease turn-around time, you increase capability, you increase sensitivity, you put a robot in a room, and suddenly that gold standard of evidence is commoditised and it allows people to spend ten pounds on the test and [to derive evidential] value from that ten pounds. (Interview with Lead Scientist: Tier 2 FSP, 2015)

Both Tier 1 and Tier 2 forensic scientists indicated that the focus on DNA-profiling techniques occurred at the expense of similar bio-identification techniques, partly as a result of budgetary constraints in relation to volume crime investigations. Investigators began to neglect peripheral investigatory practices such as fibre analysis, which began to be viewed as useful only as part of a 'fact-finding mission rather than an interpretative science'.[2] The investigative authorities began to perceive DNA-profiling techniques as the primary means through which valuable forensic results could be fed into the investigation at an early stage. Therefore, under pressure from Senior Investigating Officers – concerned with the potential loss of investigative opportunities and the availability of 'real-time' results derived from DNA-profiling techniques – forensic investigations became less systematic. A lead forensic scientist described the changing investigatory process:

> [The FSS] was moving towards being able to service that requirement. You would get items in, you would examine them quickly for blood, take the blood, put it in for DNA, get a DNA result, and link that back to the individuals for whom we had a reference sample (or put it on the database). And that's the same for semen,

[2]Interview with Lead Scientist: Tier 1 FSP, 2015.

> saliva, urine, hair: 'screen for body fluid, chuck it in for DNA, tell me who's involved'; obviously these are things that DNA doesn't say, but that was how it was interpreted. (Interview with Lead Scientist: Tier 2 FSP, 2015)

The perceived need to provide real-time results in respect of serious crimes, with comparatively rapid turn-around-times, led to the stratification of forensic-scientific investigatory processes:

> We had a standard route and a premium route and the police would pay per test. Now the premium route would be sub forty-eight hours and at the time that was a very fast route and effectively the reason that it cost more is because they were, in a sense, paying for the whole gel … you'd assign a cost to that and it would be in the thousands of pounds for a premium. (Interview with Lead Scientist: Tier 2 FSP, 2015)

The response indicates a divergence based solely on time, with investigators able to commission a rapid, or standard, evaluation. Crucially, responses indicate that the divergent approach became entrenched throughout the process of marketisation and was extended to cover, not merely the rapidity of response but the intensity and scope of the investigation. This led to the 'triaging' of cases at an early stage. Serious crimes (e.g. murder, robbery, and serious sexual offences) would automatically follow the premium, or 'bespoke' route, characterised by a lack of budgetary constraints, and charged at an hourly rate according to the time and expertise allocated to the investigation and evaluation.

> The code system doesn't apply to serious crimes such as murder. They are charged under a bespoke system according to an hourly rate.
>
> There are 'spec cases'. These are cases requiring speed, involving a quick hit routine. They tend to be volume crimes. Then there is major crime which is dealt with more strategically. But there is a creep. The police may have a jacket from a murder case and they may stick it through as a 'spec case' under the rationale that 'it's the same test'. (Interview with Lead Scientist: Tier 2 FSP, 2015)

Alternatively, less serious offences – which collectively fell under the heading 'volume crime' – would be charged on a cost-per-test basis. The volume crime route is characterised by economic efficiencies and constraints, limited opportunity for the development of investigative strategies, and direct intervention by the investigative authorities. Respondents suggested that the introduction of triaging influenced two elements of the investigatory process in particular: strategy setting and reporting.

Following the introduction of triaging, strategy meetings were no longer deemed necessary, or economically viable, in respect of volume crimes. The result is that the forensic strategy for volume crime investigations is now set by the 'customer' (i.e. the police) prior to contacting the forensic service provider:

> The strategy on many items that came in now has already been set by the police. They've set the strategy in order to say 'we want to submit that for testing' ... 'can you recover DNA from this and put it on the database?' So, the dialogue between the scientist and the strategy-setting person is lost.
>
> Context plays a part in both collection and sampling. Ideally, there's disciplinary collaboration and you develop a case strategy before beginning. (Interview with Lead Scientists: Tier 2 FSPs, 2015)

Respondents indicated particular problems due to the fact that the individual officer responsible for setting the forensic strategy is normally also the budget holder. As such, the commissioning officer may only be willing to pay for one test, with no opportunity for discussion as to the suitability of this approach. This leads to significant problems where forensic scientists require further contextual information. This is exacerbated by the codification of forensic-scientific analyses.

> If you need further information you can only contact certain named people. Often they will be named on the contract. Ideally, you contact the budget holder, who has to sign off on the work. Otherwise you don't get paid. You have to provide an estimate. The estimate has to correspond to product codes. So the codes allow the police to control budgets and compare providers. (Interview with Lead Scientist: Tier 2 FSP, 2015)

The majority of forensic scientists interviewed, in both Tier 1 and Tier 2 FSPs, indicated that the introduction of codification and triaging had led to tensions between the investigative authorities and the forensic practitioners. This was perceived as resulting in a loss of necessary contextual information. In reality, the entire responsibility for interpreting contextual information has – in respect of volume crimes – passed from the forensic practitioner to the investigative authority. This has also led to the diminishment in the role and influence of Tier 1 forensic practitioners.

> In practice, the police have budgets and scientists have turnarounds. You need thinking time ... or experience [to carry out a thorough analysis]. So, when time is short, the tendency is just to do what the police ask. You have targets to meet. You have to complete a number of allocations.

> You can't just say, 'well actually, the pattern of blood-staining is important, so I'm just going to go ahead and do that', because if you do that, you don't get paid. And if you go back to the customer and say 'd'you know what, I've even done this for free, they go 'well that's not the question I asked you to answer'. So, it completely cuts off that scientific process in some instances. (Interview with Lead Scientists: Tier 1 FSPs, 2015)

The above responses suggests a significant degree of path dependency, with a non-permeable division between the standard tests associated with volume crime and more complex testing strategies formulated in relation to serious crimes. Tier 2 providers indicated that there still exists the possibility for recursion and review but suggested that 'the process is not as open as it used to be'. Crucially, Tier 1 providers indicated that there is very little opportunity to question the forensic strategy, or to enter into any form of discussion with the 'customer', in respect of the analysis of volume crimes. Indeed, one respondent outlined an extreme iteration of attenuated volume crime reporting, whereby the absence of a budget allocation for essential interpretative work might lead directly to the failure of the forensic test.

> For a volume crime job usually it will be: 'A sample has been recovered from the crime scene. Can you load it onto the National DNA Database?' And that will come with a known cost. There'll be no thinking, no interpretation *per se*. And what's happened then is that the providers have had to develop, not only the way they report cases, but the way that they deal with results that come out the other end, because if you had a DNA result that was mixed, for example, then there's an element of interpretation there. So unless the result meets a number of criteria that are open to computer designation, computer interpretation, with a human being coming in and just verifying it, [providing a] quick win, then the result wouldn't be carried forward. So, unless it meets a certain number of criteria it would be deemed to have failed, when we're working on a commoditised test. (Interview with Lead Scientist: Tier 2 FSP, 2015)

Case Fragmentation and Quoting

A particular concern – among both Tier 1 and Tier 2 forensic scientists – was the degree of site-specific specialisation introduced through the tendering process. Respondents indicated that stratification had led directly to the segmentation of forensic analyses, which became fragmented, separated, and geographically distributed.

In assessing the problems associated with case fragmentation, it was necessary to distinguish between the organisation, and specialisation, of forensic investigations, at the meso-level, and site-specific differentiations with regard to micro-level scientific processes and protocols. The majority of respondents indicated the existence of heterogeneous communities of practice, as distinct from fragmented investigations: Many of the respondents had worked for a number of forensic providers and were able to speak to differences in culture and approach between laboratories.

> Within one protocol, different labs may develop different communities of practice.
>
> Individual labs will develop their own culture and that may affect the strength they tend to place on results. You can get a reputation for interpreting the evidence 'strongly'. That applies within FSPs to individual labs and scientists.
>
> People coming in would bring different practices, so you do get 'site by site variation'.
>
> The Met may collect samples, process some in-house, send others to an FSP, with nobody getting an overview. The work becomes less interpretative.
>
> Forensic scientists aren't getting enough *context from the police and this is getting lost* through the fragmentation of services. (Interviews with Lead Scientists: Tier 1 and 2 FSPs, 2015)

Scientists related further concerns, associated with the consolidation of the market, and the subsequent growth of an oligopoly of Tier 1 providers, resulting in functional and geographical specialisations within a single organisation. One forensic scientist provided a typical example, in order to illustrate the problems associated with fragmentation.

> A case in Nottingham centred around the discovery of a torso on a beach. The killer had dismembered the corpse, and taken parts to the beach, where he'd thrown them into the sea. The accused was the victim's boyfriend and the victim and accused lived apart. Both of them owned cats. So, in court we had DNA, blood distribution, hair, fibres, fingerprints, tool-marks, and animal hair. The prosecution experts worked in different departments of one firm but didn't know about each other's evidence. (Interview with Managing Director. Tier 2 FSP, 2015)

Forensic scientists working within the lower tier of provision highlighted the relative strengths of their holistic, and contextually rich, analyses, as compared to those carried out by Tier 1 providers.

> The defence scientists are the only ones who get to see the evidence as a whole and do the Bayesian work … The defence has the advantage of seeing what all the [Tier 1] FSPs are doing. We get good training and have to make an extra effort. (Interview with Lead Scientist: Tier 2 FSP, 2015)

This was in notable contrast to scientists working in the public sector provider, FSNI, who displayed an awareness of the advantages derived from a holistic approach to forensic analysis, particularly when these remained centralised at one site. A further negative consequence of triaging, and professional and organisational specialisation within Tier 1 FSPs, was the tendency, when writing reports, for scientists (or administrators) to quote colleagues, without having carried out an analysis in their own right. One forensic scientist expressed concerns regarding the adoption of Tier 1 DNA-profiling reports by the Metropolitan Police in-house laboratory:

> They're trying to develop a procedure where the Metropolitan Police can use the reports, or the outputs, of the DNA scientist and can incorporate that into their statement. So, with the Met lab, one scientist is simply quoting another scientist, and that is not necessarily made clear. But, by any other name, that's hearsay.
>
> Many police forces have an in-house team called the Evidence Recovery Unit. So, for the Met, the ERU send the recovered samples to LGC or Cellmark. They profile them and send the results back on a results table. The Met scientist hasn't seen the actual result or the reference sample. (Interview with Lead Scientist: Tier 2 FSP, 2015)

Quoting was deemed to be widespread, if not endemic, and was seen as directly related to the functional specialisation, and segmentation, of forensic practices, within, and between, Tier 1 providers. Particular concerns were raised regarding the loss of context.

> It's a bit of an issue. We are in a situation where [a DNA profiling match report from another practitioner] is then taken into their own statement, which is written in a particular way – about what they did, they examined a t-shirt for blood, they found blood, the DNA matches, but it doesn't provide any context as to whether there is a robust link *between* the DNA and the evidence that they saw. So, if the DNA is weak, or limited, that context is lost. (Interview with Lead Scientist: Tier 2 FSP, 2015)

Mixtures and Low-Template DNA

At this stage, it should be reiterated that the basic DNA-profiling protocol, on which the above perceptions are based, has been subject to thorough validation and accreditation procedures and has established its scientific underpinnings (see subsequent chapters). However, the same degree of trust in the accuracy of results cannot be extended to unvalidated processes, such as those involving minute traces of 'low-template' DNA, especially where these involve the interpretation of 'DNA mixtures' drawn from a number of individuals. The occurrence of DNA mixtures has risen sharply since the introduction of sensitive testing protocols (such as DNA-17 and Globafiler-24, both of which replaced SGM Plus). These are now capable of picking up trace amounts of 'low-template' DNA and have led to the routine reporting of mixed DNA profiles. Tier 2 providers maintained that they did not 'put a statistic' on very low amounts of DNA, preferring to use these for intelligence purposes. However, they indicated that this practice was not widespread.

> DNA-17 is a result of the Prum regime. It standardised tests across Europe. There is a choice of microsatellites and DNA-17 can cover all areas in Europe. In Scotland they went directly to Globafiler which tests 24 areas and has a global fit. Originally they weren't allowed to upload to the NDNAD even though the 17 necessary satellites are contained in the Globafiler 24. But that's now changed. Each new test is more sensitive, so in a commercial market a threshold is applied and anything below [the threshold] is discarded. But there's a lot of useful information there. The frequency dataset for SGM-17 was developed by the FSS. When commercial companies set up they had to develop their own datasets. That's one area that would have benefitted from standardisation. The same test can give different results depending on the company's dataset. (Interview with Lead Scientist: Tier 2 FSP, 2015)

Further, Tier 2 respondents raised concerns regarding the alleged practice of a particular Tier 1 provider, which routinely deliver results which they termed a 'non-weighted Dlugosz'. This practice bears a contradictory appellation, which would appear to contradict the ruling in *R* v. *Dlugosz*.[3]

> With mixture analysis you have to frame propositions very carefully. In certain cases you have to work through all of them. It depends on what the defence propositions are saying. Sometimes you are never given an alternative scenario, for example in 'no comment' cases. 'For two person samples you can use Bayes. Then the hypothesis becomes important. If the sample is a mixture of more than two people *Dlugosz* says we can use words instead of stats. We can provide a verbal evaluation. It's back to the CSI approach. It's much more subjective so you really need experience'.

[3] *R* v. *Dlugosz* [2013] EWCA Crim 2.

> There is also an issue with Cellmark over what's known as a 'weighted' and 'non-weighted Dlugosz'. *Dlugosz* says that you can express an opinion about very small amounts of DNA but that has to be weighted. Cellmark produce results which are not weighted. This is wrong. They call it a 'non-weighted Dlugosz' but that is a contradiction in terms The 'non-weighted Dlugosz' is an attempt to standardise across the company in order to have a common approach. (Interview with Lead Scientist: Tier 2 FSP, 2015)

The above testimony reveals concerns among Tier 2 providers with regard to the alleged practices of Tier 1 providers within the forensic science market in England and Wales. However, it should be reiterated that such concerns relate to challenges faced by DNA-profiling practitioners across all jurisdictions. Further, that such concerns may reveal long-standing problems win relation to the scientific nature of DNA profiling. The review of the national academy of science (NAS) report, and subsequent literature, *infra*, supports the assertion that it was not widely believed that DNA-profiling techniques were dynamic – rather than static – in nature. Nor that these advancing techniques – having proven their scientific underpinnings – should continue to be subject to fundamental testing and validation studies, or be required to submit to processes of accreditation, in the same manner as non-scientific 'first generation' pattern identification techniques.

Such views were dealt a severe blow by the publication of the results of the DNA (MIX05 and MIX13) studies.[4] These results – drawn from an inter-laboratory study conducted by the National Institute of Science and Technology (NIST) – had been subject to a delay, which has itself drawn criticism from practitioners and allied criminal justice agents. The study involved over 100 laboratories, which were provided with DNA samples involving mixtures. MIX05 was undertaken in 2005 and required 69 laboratories to interpret DNA data from two-person mixtures, drawn from four hypothetical sex assaults. The MIX13 study, conducted in 2013, provided 108 laboratories with data representing five 'crimes', in increasing difficulty, in scenarios involving up to four contributors and related individuals.

The results from the overall studies showed concerning degrees of variability across the results delivered by the participating laboratories. Of particular note were the results from MIX13, case 5, which purported to provide a DNA mixture from an item of clothing left behind after a bank robbery. The mixture of touch DNA was drawn from four individuals. However, due to the complex nature of the mixed sample, this initially appeared as a mixture of only two people. The labs were provided with reference samples taken from two of the four likely contributors, along with that of a fifth person. The fifth person was not in the mixture and had not been in contact with the item of clothing.

---

[4]Butler, J. M., Kline, M. C., & Coble, M. D. (2018). NIST interlaboratory studies involving DNA mixtures (MIX05 and MIX13): Variation observed and lessons learned. *Forensic Science International: Genetics, 37*, 81–94.

When the results were reviewed, it became apparent that 74 laboratories, out of 108, had wrongly included the fifth person in their mixture interpretation. A further 26 labs delivered 'inconclusive' reports, of varying levels of error. Thus, only seven laboratories correctly excluded individual number 5 from the four-person mixed sample. Even then, different reasons were given, from 'allelic drop-out' to 'PCR inhibition'.

Most were using the method of combined probability of inclusion, otherwise known as CPI, a Federal Bureau of Investigation (FBI)-approved method of separating out mixtures. However, in the instant study, further concerns were raised regarding the use of computer algorithms to de-convolute mixed DNA profiles, especially with regard to validation.

> There are two different types. Cellmark uses David Balding's computer system. LGC developed LiRa. These systems can deal with two or more people. For a while Balding's system wasn't validated but it is now. There are differences between the systems but the same system can deliver different answers depending on how the question is formed. (Interview with Lead Scientist: Tier 2 FSP, 2015)

These concerns serve to illustrate the degree of scepticism among Tier 2 providers with regard to the scientific validity of cutting-edge DNA-profiling techniques.

Commercialisation and the Restructuring of Forensic Expertise

A second aim of the empirical research was to gauge whether, and to what extent, the emergence of an emphasis on economic efficiency and codification – achieved through competitive tendering and productisation – had impacted on the framing, and exercise, of forensic-scientific expertise. Further, to outline the effect of progressive marketisation on routinised forms of forensic analyses, with an attendant restructuring of forensic personnel. One forensic scientist indicated that the managerial preoccupation with quantitative performance monitoring models and service agreements led directly to the reframing of forensic roles and practices.

A number of experienced forensic scientists began by describing the nature of training and expertise within the FSS. The emphasis was on careful interpretation, contextual evaluation, and the development of skills and forensic expertise. The structured FSS career path began as a trainee examiner.

> The examiner is entry-level. The examiner's work is directed by the reporting scientist. The reporting scientist knows the scenario and writes instructions to the examiner to carry out particular tests. The reporting scientist writes the report then presents it in court.

The FSS responded to the introduction, and rapid development, of bio-identification techniques based around DNA fingerprinting (and later profiling) by initiating a 'fast-track' scheme. This involved 18 months of intensive training as an examiner, after which the trainee became a reporting scientist. Respondents spoke of a culture of collegiality based upon mentoring and peer review.

> Peer review is so important. It's not just about finding mistakes but asking 'what more could you do? This is where laboratory culture comes from; apprenticeship, checks and counter-balances. The quicker the work, the less checking, and that affects laboratory culture.

Nonetheless, in 2002, FSS working patterns changed. The service began to segregate cases into 'homicide', 'sex', and 'hit report' (or 'volume crime', including actual bodily harm (ABH) and grievous bodily harm (GBH)), which, from that point, were serviced by three discrete teams. Respondents indicated that functional separation did not lead to de-skilling due to the potential for constant training and development.

> At the FSS the way we were trained was different. We were trained to be careful, building context into [the interpretative process]. That takes thinking time. That thinking time has been removed and when there are problems forensic sciences get blamed.

Ex-FSS employees outlined the restructuring process:

> [The FSS] went public-private partnership, then we went through to different stages. And in fact we were transforming in a very big way when we were closed, but the market had already started to change because private companies set up that were competing for the same … work … and they were building themselves up as a business, and so therefore they already knew about efficiencies and technologies, and they had backing from people with money, so if you put a government department up against a newly formed commercial provider there's no chance, because [the government department is too unwieldy]. (Interview with Lead Scientist: Tier 2 FSP, 2015)

> Out of that hundred people, the amount of expertise in that hundred people was over a thousand years of expertise. So, you can do the maths and we had people that had been with us for a couple of years and people that had been with us for forty years. However, the brain drain was enormous. Because the people who were thirty, forty years' experience just retired, took early retirement, and they got redundancy. The only reason we didn't get redundancy is because we were deemed to be aligned to the Metropolitan Police.

The restructuring of the forensic-scientific market, and the introduction of triaging, contributed to the loss of experienced forensic scientists and the stratification of forensic investigations and evaluations. The short-termism associated with peripatetic forensic contracts, competition between providers, and the spatial organisation of the market militated against the retention or recruitment of established, and experienced, personnel, the majority of whom were relatively immobile.

> [Experienced forensic scientists] are a dying breed and ... arguably we're quite expensive. You know, we've been around a little while, we've got up to a certain level of salary that we try to maintain if possible, and so it means that, when forensic providers are tendering for work, they can only have a small portion of people who are expensive and the rest of them have to be cheap, new recruits.
>
> With the tendering process there are huge shifts every few years. Some staff follow the tenders but the companies don't recruit at a senior level. So there is a large loss of staff to other parts of the industry and to teaching.
>
> Redundancies (in the FSS and LGC) mean there is a huge loss of experience across the industry, especially amongst senior staff. (Interviews with Managing Director and Lead Scientists: Tier 1 and 2 FSPs, 2015)

A number of experienced forensic scientists also expressed concerns regarding the scientific ability, values, and training, accorded to trainees subsequently recruited to the forensic sector. This concern was encapsulated by the managing director of a second Tier 2 forensic provider: 'My biggest worry is that people aren't getting the necessary breadth of training. They are too niche-focussed'. Another forensic scientist expressed concerns regarding the triaging process.

> I can give you examples of [stratification], because there are entire units now made up of people who service volume crime, and they typically will be led by someone of experience, but their reporting staff won't have the breadth of experience that you would expect in a homicide team, so they'll be trained to report DNA results up to a particular level, and anything beyond that they would say is 'uninterpretable'. (Interview with Lead Scientist: Tier 2 FSP, 2015)

In this example, the perceived loss of expertise was directly attributed to the failure of forensic analyses. More importantly, the response indicates that the potential for 'trainees' to develop skills and experience in interpretative and evaluative reporting has been sacrificed in order to service the needs of routinised, non-contextual DNA profiling. The restructuring of forensic practice in alignment with hierarchical forms of accountability entails a different role for experienced forensic scientists, who are tasked with reviewing routinised process rather than engaging in critical reflection: 'There are very set guidelines when "calling the profile" but evaluation is more mentored. When it comes to interpretation that can be influenced by senior staff'. The displacement of expertise also entailed a much-reduced role for experienced staff, with little opportunity to exercise their skills.

> Younger trainees coming into the industry are getting training but that training is basic. They don't know what they don't know. That never gets rectified as they progress. So as checkers and peer-reviewers they also lack the appropriate skills.
>
> You have less experienced staff combined with pressures to do work quicker and a pressure from the police, and it leads to a factory-line approach just to get the results out.
>
> The job I trained to do is long gone. (Interview with Lead Scientists: Tier 2 FSPs, 2015)

Further, one informant provided an example of the way in which a piece of DNA evidence, which is very strong on the source level, may be neutralised at the activity level:

> If there is no pattern, and it's only a … bloodstain, and it's perhaps in the form of a handmark, and the victim's got a bleeding nose, then suddenly you're in a situation where you've completely neutralised the evidence. (DR)

Problems relating to the lack of reliable data on DNA transfer and persistence are compounded by the increasing sensitivity of DNA-testing protocols, which now regularly pick up results from 'touch DNA', shed by (multiple) individuals, and transferred from person to person and between surfaces.[5] The following extended discussion from a field research interview highlights the difficulties posed by 'transfer and persistence':

> [When dealing with activity-level propositions] we're onto 'how', 'where' and 'when'. And this is 'transfer and persistence'. This is

[5]Jamieson, A. (2011). Case note: LCN DNA analysis and opinion on transfer: *R* v. *Reed and Reed*. *The International Journal of Evidence and Proof, 15*, 161–169; Meakin, G., & Jamieson, A. (2013). DNA transfer: Review and implications for casework. *Forensic Science International: Genetics, 7*, 434–443; Steensma, K., Ansell, R., Clarisse, L., Connolly, E., Kloosterman, A. D., McKenna, L. G., … Kokshoorn, B. (2017). An inter-laboratory comparison study on transfer, persistence and recovery of DNA from cable ties. *Forensic Science International: Genetics, 31*, 95–104.

> the bit that nobody thinks about. Because the SFR said, 'one in a billion', and the name of the individual who they got off the database. (HT)
>
> INTERVIEWER: So much concentration on what you can prove with numbers and just overlooking the simple question of …
>
> JM: … the question of transfer and persistence … Because nobody's thinking of this question and, arguably, there's no real, tenable, useful data on transfer and persistence. So, if you're provided with a reasonable avenue for DNA, from an individual, to be on something, then it goes into the hat. Because you can't 'weight' transfer and persistence. [It varies from individual to individual as well as] condition to condition, surface to surface, you know, there's just so many variables that, the fact that they're his gloves may mean that he's been wearing them every day and he's still only a minority contributor … It can pretty much wipe out DNA, that question.

It may be argued, therefore, that 'transfer and persistence' issues pose a serious threat to the ongoing utility, and legitimacy, of DNA-profiling evidence: a threat which has elicited a creative rejoinder.

The perception of de-skilling was not shared by one Queens Counsel (QC) (and former Crown Prosecution Service (CPS) strategy advisor).

> All I noticed was the conversations about it and the noise around it and, I suppose I have to declare that, although I'm not a massive fan of everything to do with market forces, I suppose being a barrister I do believe that if you're good enough you'll survive, and I don't accept, I'm afraid, and I know it's a lot of people's personal experiences, it's what they experienced therefore it's their reality, but I don't accept that that equals a brain drain. I would challenge that and the reality that I observed was that those very senior folk at the top end of the business, if you like, went off and created their own business. (Interview with QC and Former CPS Strategy Advisor, April 2015)

While the respondent challenged the assertion that restructuring had led to de-skilling, the response is founded solely on anecdotal experience restricted to the higher echelon of the forensic market. Further, the respondent acknowledges the loss of Tier 1 practitioners to Tier 2 companies, albeit managed by the same.

> I'd really rather see some less emotive data about where these people did go, rather than [listen to] the frustrations of those who wanted to just be migrated from company to company without having to demonstrate that they had the skills that were worth

> being taken forward. [The loss of staff due to competitive tendering] didn't actually happen that often. There were a few, there was like a handful of really key times when it happened to a core bunch of people. And, each time, the howl of anguish got louder. (Interview with QC and Former CPS Strategy Advisor, April 2015)

The respondent later challenged a further assertion, with regard to skills and training afforded to less experienced employees.

> I think Fordism has a lot to answer for in terms of the shortfall of personal satisfaction. However, that kind of unit approach also generates greater success in business planning, and interest from investors, so I just wonder whether that unit based approach is [a negative feature] or a natural side effect of a market place and of market forces. (Interview with QC and Former CPS Strategy Advisor, April 2015)

The respondent was candid about the fact that the de-skilling of the profession of forensic science was necessary and articulated a viewpoint that encouraged the segmentation of forensic-scientific into separate tasks that would be assigned to different individuals with different skill sets, educational backgrounds, expectations, and roles. The relative ignorance of some of these forensic technicians was deemed as unproblematic. Training would not focus on the development of expertise so much as on the ability to follow certain routines and protocols. The restructuring of training, if it did benefit the Tier 1 company, would benefit it at the level of volume crime rather at the expense of interpretative analysis.

Triaging and Forensic Science Provision in the Public Sector

As the 'preferred local supplier to the Criminal Justice System in Northern Ireland' – and the sole public sector FSP in the UK – FSNI operates from a single, centralised compound situated in the Province. Both FSNI and its main customer, PSNI, share the same premises in order to ensure the security of FSNI and its staff members. However, these two agencies are largely autonomous and enjoy a high degree of administrative, structural, and functional separation.[6]

Nonetheless, proximity between these separate agencies allows FSNI to provide an 'on-call service' to PSNI, enabling scientists to rapidly attend crime – or fatal accident – scenes in order to support the recovery of evidence for forensic-scientific investigation.

---

[6]FSNI governance structure and institutional arrangements may be contrasted with that of Scottish Police Authority (SPA) Forensics, which operates as a police support service from within the Scottish Crime Campus (a Police Scotland compound in Gartcosh, North Lanarkshire).

A priority service also allows for urgent analysis of samples, such as DNA samples taken in an alleged sexual assault. These are processed within a very short timescale: often within 24 hours. FSNI's Reporting Officers also interact with criminal justice agencies at the opposite end of the evidential trajectory, advising the Public Prosecution Service for Northern Ireland (PPS) on the meaning of scientific evidence and providing expert witnessing services to the courts in any subsequent prosecution. In addition to providing integrated forensic-scientific provision, the FSNI site is also host to the Northern Ireland DNA Database (NIDNAD).

Thus, an array of related, and disparate, parallel, contemporaneous, and successive, forensic activities are carried out at a single location. The agency notes the effect that such integrated structure and close communication can have on efficiency and quality.

FSNI currently employs approximately 200 staff, all of whom are civil servants. Of these 200, roughly 65% are scientists directly involved with casework. In total, 80% of the forensic work carried out at FSNI is categorised a 'serious crime'. Thus, the workload and depth of experience of FSNI scientists differs from that of many of their mainland counterparts, whose workload comprises mainly 'volume crime'.

The majority of the day-to-day work involves the recovery, analysis, and evaluation of evidential samples submitted in connection with a range of criminal investigations. These range from 'routine' cases involving fraud, burglary, and car crime through to murders, sexual – and other violent – offences, firearms, explosives, arson, and assault. FSNI also provides material analyses for cases involving the possession, and/or supply, of drugs and, where necessary, toxicological analyses in support of the State Pathologist's Department, in order to help determine the cause of death.

Due to the integrated and heterogeneous nature of forensic science provision, and the concentration on serious crime, the agency describes itself 'a leader in several forensic disciplines' listing particular expertise in a range of forensic practices including the imaging of latent (invisible) fingerprints, explosives, and microchemistry. The agency's portfolio of forensic specialisms also includes firearms, fires, physical methods, biology, drugs and toxicology, road traffic collisions, and the recovery of electronic data from computers and mobile phones.

The recovery and analysis of DNA from exhibits is a central activity and may encompass a multitude of interrelated activities. FSNI imposes functional separation on DNA-profiling activities, with incoming files directed towards one of two discrete workstreams – 'DNA' or 'Biology' – depending on the availability of contextual information. In circumstances where there is a known person of interest, or the sample process is investigative, or there is an actual biological stain (e.g. blood and semen), DNA recovery and analysis is carried out by the Biology team. Where there is solely a sub-source sample for loading onto the DNA database, the work is carried out by the DNA team.

> The volume is separate. In many respects the volume is separate and the volume is a simple swab coming in the door and it's going to the database, or the simple swab coming in the door where they have somebody arrested for it, and it falls into this group [indicating simple cases]. The volume – the true volume – is, as I say, the database cases coming through the door. But a proportion, because a person is known, or a person is suspected, it comes to us. (Interview with Lead Scientist: FSNI, 2015)

Thus, each team is physically and managerially separated from the other and employs different personnel, though informants are keen to highlight the benefits of proximity and communication. The custodian of the NIDNAD describes one of the purported advantages of parallel integration:

> There are pros and cons, but certainly it allows for greater agility, in that, if [the Biology team] is working on a case, and needs database searching done, there it is, it's not having to go generate forms and send them off and wait for something to come back and enter into some kind of discourse, and one of the principle advantages that we have found down the years in having the local database is, because it is inherently smaller, that actually allows greater flexibility in how you can use it. (Interview with Lead Scientist: FSNI, 2015)

Of the samples received by the Biology team, 67% are categorised as 'bio-DNA only'. The other 33% is categorised as joint and require investigatory inputs from other teams. The cases received by the Biology team can be further categorised according to the type (Table 5.1 and Fig. 5.1).

Typically, forensic DNA casework is initiated through the delivery of either a file or an evidential sample from PSNI or a similar customer:

Table 5.1. FSNI Case Types.

Case Types (FSNI Biology Unit)	Percentage of Work Received (Average 2012–2014)
Simple cases[7]	32–33%
Sexual offences[8]	17%
Complex/serious[9]	50%

[7]Assault, GBH, burglaries, robberies, and thefts.
[8](Attempted) rape.
[9]Explosions, firearms, and (attempted) murders.

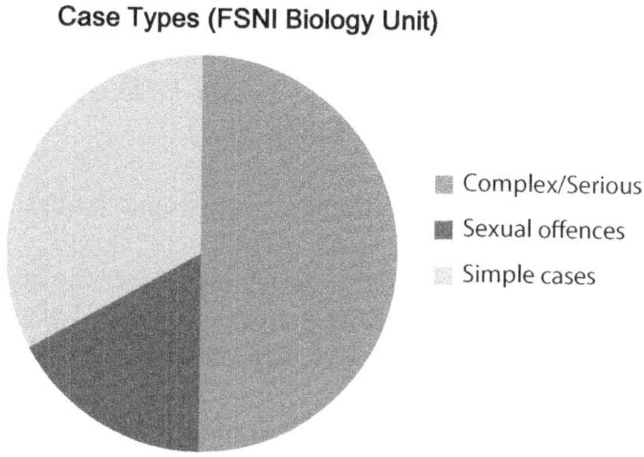

Fig. 5.1. FSNI Case Types.[10]

> We get a file, we get an item delivered. And that's the first thing we know telling us about the incident. And that then generates a case number … This is coming from the Police. So, along with that comes … a docket, which is what they have agreed to work on. (Interview with Lead Scientist: FSNI, 2015)

Customer expectations may be conditioned through the introduction of systems of codification and productisation, which render laboratory processes visible and legible to non-scientific institutional actors.

> The story coming in is brief and tells us what the police want us to do in the case. In terms of assessment we would look at this and … may adjust the strategy and adjust the products accordingly. (Interview with Lead Scientist: FSNI, 2015)

> We can recommend things. In the simplest case it's their choice what they want to send in. It is financial in some respects. They have more information than is provided to us so they're making that initial decision.

> [PSNI] state 'I want this done. It will sort out what I need to take to court'. Sometimes, we feel there's glaring issues, that what they're suggesting, in their strategy, wouldn't cover that in court. So we ask them, 'what else do you have?' We would recommend sending that in So although most of it, in the routine cases, is coming in already decided, we will assess it, and adjust it if need be.

[10]Case types (average over three-year period up to September 2015). *Source*: Lead scientist, FSNI Biology Unit.

> So they're making decisions of what they want done on that item. So [PSNI] are sending a particular item in and their decision-making process is: I want you to do ... recover DNA and analyse it. (Interview with Lead Scientist: FSNI, 2015)

Informants spoke of increasing specificity in customer requests:

> It really is case-dependent and it has changed over the last year.[11] It's become that they are making [specific requests]: I want you to take X and Y only. (Interview with Lead Scientist: FSNI, 2015)

The convergence, and transplantation, of standardised products and practices may create tensions, which are overcome through the modification of – and adaptation to – subsisting practices (alongside the use of bridging strategies). Informant's responses demonstrate the persistence of modified local practices and the continued importance of tacit expert knowledge.

> Our product coding system is based on that original ACPO/NPIA coding system ... The codes don't necessarily fit the request or the item. It doesn't easily fit the processes we do and [the product codes] have been adjusted over the years. So, each lab interprets them in a different fashion. Each lab adjusted [the codes] according to their own protocols and interpretation. (Interview with Lead Scientist: FSNI, 2015)

Subsisting theories of expertise struggle to account for these interdisciplinary translations. As will be discussed further below, Collins and Evans' taxonomy of expertises is limited by its focus on discrete bodies of esoteric scientific endeavour. However, if forensic expertise is a product of intrinsic, and extrinsic, collaborations between forensic scientists and a heterogeneous body of institutional actors within the criminal justice system, it follows that the extent, and proper categorisation, of both contributory and non-contributory experts should be gauged. Given the interpenetration of regulatory protocols, alongside standardised products and auditing practices, these may become obfuscated and difficult to discern. In order to resolve this problem, it will be necessary to concentrate on the focal points of interaction between institutional actors: in particular, the ways in which contributory forensic experts are able to influence the progress of investigations through communication with the investigating authorities. As a lead reporting scientist explains:

> Ours is a cost recovery exercise, we are not a profit-making organisation. So our products are agreed up front at the beginning of the year, how many we will do. So it's a question of how [the customer]

[11] Partly as a result of the introduction of the ICP scheme.

> uses those products, and if they use them correctly, or that what they're sending in to us actually equates to the correct product, so there is things like that have to be checked when they come in.[12] (Interview with Lead Scientist: FSNI, 2015)

However, FSNI informants stressed that, as a centralised FSP engaged in a diverse array of activities, they retain the agility to move between different forms of reporting in response to case demands and increasing complexity.

> The movement is very largely in one direction. Cases rarely become simpler. Triaging does occur but that happens outside of here in the Authorisations Unit. (Interview with Lead Scientist: FSNI, 2015)

While FSNI demonstrates a high degree of structural integration, and agility, in relation to complex and serious crimes, many forensic investigations proceed from a foundational body of rudimentary categorisations, which themselves result from processes of productisation and codification. Thus, the investigators' interactions with contributory experts are delineated solely by the interposition of forensic 'products' capable of conveying particular outputs. The enactment of forensic expertise under these conditions is, to all intents and purposes, 'black-boxed'. Therefore, errors, and categorical misattributions, are managed, and corrected, solely by the contributory experts, through a process of recursion and review.

> [...] we would redo the strategy, or we would look at the strategy ourselves to see that the items they've sent in equate with what their request is, and what our understanding of the incident is. (Interview with Lead Scientist: FSNI, 2015)

However, the exercise of contributory expertise can be curtailed by the interposition of arbitrarily defined borders and limitations. The permeability of these borders is largely dependent on the seriousness of the offence.

> Some of the restrictions might be that, if there's a lot of blood there and we're restricted to two samples then we might not find what we need to find on the item, so if it's a complex blood staining we're using our blood pattern analysis to say okay I'll take these two because if this incident has occurred it's most likely to have come from the particular person in this instance rather than the wearer.

[12]Compare England and Wales where market FSPs stated that they would carry out the customer's instructions in low-level cases even if they deemed the strategy inappropriate.

> And because of using the interpretative strategies in terms of pattern analysis we generally get this okay, but if there's two samples we're allowed we generally say okay one of them is actually Mr X's DNA profile on this garment so in terms of that we're saying, 'the blood's there – I need to choose two samples'. The choice of two samples isn't entirely random therefore the chance of getting a different profile, apart from the wearer, is quite high. (Interview with Lead Scientist: FSNI, 2015)

Thus, at the lower end of the investigatory spectrum, recursion and collaboration are circumscribed by limitations imposed on the basis of efficiency. Forensic strategies follow standard expectations, are conceived and developed unilaterally by the investigative authorities, and require forensic intervention only when they deviate grossly from standard practices or are misconceived to the extent that evidential failure may be predicted.

> So, again it's case dependent. In a quick, simple, I suppose in volume crimes it happens more …
>
> We have, in our processes – and we do have to keep reminding [PSNI] that our agreement is, that we will, if there's multiple blood there we will take two stains … And there's an agreement with [PSNI] that they will actually allow us to do that. It is getting more restricted at the moment but what I'm saying is, because of the multiple people that are bleeding, the two samples is not going to objectively tell me that there is, or is not, a contact with this particular person. (Interview with Lead Scientist: FSNI, 2015)

Given their reliance on pre-defined products and the desire to achieve particular outputs, it would be difficult to attribute the investigative authorities with interactional expertise. This relative lack of expertise may derive from the strict administrative, and functional, separation between PSNI and FSNI, which ensures that the investigative authorities are not exposed to processes of enculturation within the forensic-scientific domain (even if their aims, and activities, overlap – to some extent – with those of FSNI).

The internal process of enculturation is achieved through training and the internalisation of a diverse array of skills.

> It's a staged approach, it's the training aspect of it that you take them through the *processes* in the simpler cases first, it's easier training for them. Because this is taking them through to 'court-going' in a simple enough case.[13] It's never simple, going to court,

[13]In the following chapter, we compare the skills of inexpert administrative reporters engaged in the SFR process, who lack the ability to deliver, and communicate, comprehensive forensic analyses and evaluations.

> but in a small one-or-two-item case, so that they learn procedures of getting it in the door, of liaising with the police, checking their products, they learn the *procedures* on the simpler cases before they progress onto the more complex ones. (Interview with Lead Scientist: FSNI, 2015)

Further, the central importance of procedural conformity in forensic investigation permeates the training process:

> [...] because it's procedures, and the way for them to learn procedures, and you don't have to worry too much about the examinations and the process because you're learning the booking-in procedures, booking-out procedures, reporting procedures in the process. (Interview with Lead Scientist: FSNI, 2015)

When asked to define their role, informants replied with reference to externally imposed duties, originating from the legal field:

> We are there to assist the court: to find if there is any evidence and to explain it. My thinking is: 'If I can't eliminate it, how can I explain it?' (Interview with Lead Scientist: FSNI, 2015)

Such responses resonate with Lawless' theory of forensic-scientific endeavours, as adjunctive activities which follow structural norms of integration and are largely subsumed within the criminal justice and investigatory process.[14] However, the evidence from FSNI points to a far more substantial role.[15] Nonetheless, even if the role of FSNI forensic scientists were to be merely adjunctive, the agency operates within a rhizomatic network of criminal justice institutions, whose combined efforts lead to the co-production of contextually rich forensic-scientific truth claims.

Thus, the introduction of 'efficient' measures of proportionate, and economically efficient, modes of forensic reporting is indicative of the re-ordering of meso-structural elements within the forensic-scientific domain, in response to the macro-structural changes which shape the delivery of forensic truth claims. However, the resilience of the FSNI integrated governance structure has ensured that re-ordering has been less dynamic than that brought about by marketisation – and the introduction of Streamlined Forensic Reporting – in England and Wales.

---

[14]Lawless, C. J. (2011). Policing markets. *British Journal of Criminology, 51*, 671–689, at p. 673.

[15]All FSNI scientists are educated to postgraduate level in an appropriate scientific discipline.

The Contest and Communication Narrative – Silos and Transfer of Expertise

The data discussed above provide only partial support for the contest and communication narrative advanced by Lawless, Kelty, and members of the judiciary.[16] To recap, this popular explanation for the interdisciplinary co-production of forensic-scientific knowledge claims is predicated upon a belief that institutional agents from the legal and scientific fields are 'siloed' within their respective domains. 'Silo-ing' refers to the phenomenon whereby particular centres of organisation and activity become isolated in terms of their constituent processes and systems. These centres of organisation become self-referential in terms of their conceptualisations, leading to a lack of communication with other centres and a lack of understanding of the needs of other systems. It occurs when domains, departments, or management groups do not share information, goals, tools, priorities, and processes with other departments. Or it may occur when the networks which facilitate the sharing of goals are attenuated or unavailable. The phenomenon may therefore refer to either an intra-disciplinary or a homologous process occurring across disciplinary boundaries.

The data reveal scientific informants speaking predominantly of processes of intra-disciplinary fragmentation and stratification, and external control, which do not necessarily equate to autonomy and isolation or lend support to the assertion that enhanced communication would lead to greater interdisciplinary understanding. The process of 'silo-ing' has both descriptive and normative prescriptive dimensions. Therefore, even if it does accurately describe the co-production of forensic-scientific knowledge claims, the degree of divergence may be so deep as to thwart mutual understanding and enhanced interdisciplinarity. Further, the presence of acute power asymmetries and the instrumental uses of forensic science, as evidenced in the research data, may render any attempts impossible.

This is not true of the entire market. Tier 2 FSPs claim to maintain an overview similar to that enjoyed by the FSS, and the evidence shows that such claims are not without merit. Likewise FSNI, who do not merely enjoy greater autonomy. Although FSNI are customer focussed, they offer a more contextual and holistic service.

However, it is particularly true of the changing governance structures, and the reconstruction of forensic expertise, in respect of Tier 1 marketised providers in England and Wales. Loss of autonomy can be related to a number of complex processes of economic rationalisation, productisation, and fragmentation, all of

[16] Lawless, C. (2010). *A curious reconstruction? The shaping of 'marketized' forensic science*. CARR Discussion Paper 63; Lawless, C. (2011). Policing markets; the contested shaping of neo-liberal forensic science. *British Journal of Criminology, 51*, 671–689; Kelty, S. F., Julian, R., & Ross, A. (2013). Dismantling the Justice Silos: Avoiding the pitfalls and reaping the benefits of information-sharing between forensic science, medicine and law. *Forensic Science International, 230*(1–3), 8–15; Thomas, L. C. J. (2015). The legal framework for more robust forensic science evidence. *Philosophical Transactions of the Royal Society B, 370*, 20140258, at p. 1.

which make forensic processes visible to the customer. Within the market, these problems are exacerbated when applied to routinised analyses of so-called volume crime. The shift from a tripartite relationship, based around joint strategy-setting and co-production, and involving communication between the CPS, the FSP, and the police, to one of direct control from the 'customer' with a loss of CPS input, has displaced expertise and allowed for direct customer control.

These disparities are facilitated by the lack of a shared conceptual framework, terminological fluidity, and a lack of expert understanding of other agencies' needs. As a QC indicated,

> I think there's a lot of language used where people assume that they understand what they're saying and meaning but in fact they don't understand what each business structure within that journey actually means by it … It's simply that there are a number of walls, if you like, not just silos, but walls, that stop people from thinking laterally about what the market actually is.

The final sections of this chapter place the main conclusions of the study in theoretical perspective. In light of the problems highlighted in the foregoing discussion, these sections attempt to formulate a theory, which can provide better insights into the role of forensic-scientific expertise within the criminal justice system. The sections begin with a review the subsisting theories of interdisciplinary expertise and critiques both Edmond and Mercer's theory of 'hybrid sets' and Collins and Evans' theory of contributory expertise. This chapter concludes by proposing a new, relational theory of expertise, born from – and more consonant with – the empirical data.

Interdisciplinary Theories of Expertise

Despite the ubiquity of the term 'forensic science', it is questionable to what extent the standard body of forensic identification techniques which compose the practice of forensic-scientific expertise matches the criteria that sociological theorists – such as Collins and Evans – have generally associated with the conduct of research in the physical and biological sciences. It is also questionable whether, or to what extent, 'forensic science' can be said to meet Mertonian norms and Kuhnian demarcation criteria. Sceptisism with regard to the status of forensic-scientific practices is not new. Forensic science has been the subject of long-standing criticisms, which have tended to make unfavourable comparisons between the traditional collection of forensic practices and conceptions of 'normal science'. When judged against the standards of normal, the forensic disciplines are frequently characterised as little more than 'a loose array of police crafts graced with the aura of science'[17] and seldom viewed as proceeding in accordance with idealised conceptions of timeless, universal rationality.

[17]Lynch, M., Cole, S. A., McNally, R., & Jordan, K. (2008). *Truth machine: The contentious history of DNA fingerprinting*. Chicago, IL: University of Chicago Press, at p. 4.

What, then, is the role of the specialist forensic practitioner within the criminal justice system? Kruse states that 'the contribution [of the forensic scientist] to the biography of forensic evidence is to turn the material form of the traces sent to them into a meaningful symbolic form'.[18] However, this practice of sequential translation may be shown to have been founded upon a commitment to demonstrably ambiguous principles: primarily, the assertion that objects are unique (and the corollary, that it is possible to capture the uniquely identifiable features of any object, whether or not tied to an ineradicable bodily substrate).[19] Attempts to mobilise the concept of 'uniqueness' have attracted criticism on both the philosophical and practical levels.[20] Cole, in particular, has questioned the utility of the concept, and in light of such criticisms, it may be more accurate to define forensic-scientific practice in terms of the management of particular forms of uncertainty.[21]

Nonetheless, if the collection of techniques generally associated with forensic-scientific practice invites an invidious comparison with existing conceptions of 'pure' science, it may yet be argued that these techniques constitute an applied science. Lynch, Cole, McNally, and Jordan[22] maintain that this appellation is equally questionable, asking: 'to which branches of basic research do the fingerprint examiner, and handwriting analyst, apply?'

A more serious criticism flows from the assertion that forensic science does not constitute an autonomous field of scientific endeavour. It is answerable to initiatives, and evaluations, which emanate from external institutions, actors, and agencies (both public and private), beyond the forensic-scientific field: agencies, whom it exists to serve. Further, that the production of forensic artefacts occurs in conformation with a set of routine practices which are highly normalised and performed by agents who are 'not trusted to stand on their own two feet'. In light of these criticisms, forensic practices have frequently been viewed as a 'subnormal science'[23]: one, which is characterised by 'limited objectives, and little, or no, orientation to discovery'.[24] Crucially, the 'adjunctive repertoire

[18]Kruse, C. (2016). *The social life of forensic evidence*. Oakland, CA: University of California Press, at p. 70.

[19]Only DNA-profiling techniques can be said to have approached this criterion, albeit on probabilistic terms. See Cole, S. A., & Lynch, M. (2010). DNA profiling versus fingerprint evidence: More of the same? In R. Hindmarsh & B. Prainsack (Eds), *Genetic suspects: Global governance of forensic DNA profiling and databasing*. Oxford: OUP.

[20]Cole, S. A. (2009). Forensics without uniqueness, conclusions without individualization: The new epistemology of forensic identification. *Law, Probability and Risk, 8*(3), 233–255.

[21]Kruse, C. (2016). *The social life of forensic evidence*. Oakland, CA: University of California Press, see note 2.

[22]Lynch, M., Cole, S. A., McNally, R., & Jordan, K. (2008). *Truth machine: The contentious history of DNA fingerprinting*. Chicago, IL: University of Chicago Press.

[23]Lynch M., Cole, S. A., McNally, R., & Jordan, K. (2008). *Truth machine: The contentious history of DNA fingerprinting*. Chicago, IL: University of Chicago Press, note 1, at p. 6.

[24]Lynch M., Cole, S. A., McNally, R., & Jordan, K. (2008). *Truth machine: The contentious history of DNA fingerprinting*. Chicago, IL: University of Chicago Press, at p. 7.

of services',[25] of which these 'sciences of the particular' are composed, are not 'unified by their adherence to universal epistemological principles'.[26] Rather, analytical activities are conducted under the gaze of exogenous quality control regimes and become intrinsically limited through their adherence to routine procedures.

Forensic science may be shown to remain answerable to multiple social interests and agendas. However, this need not serve as a determinative criterion by which to judge the status of forensic practice *qua* science, since – as Science and Technology Studies (STS) scholars have demonstrated – external accountability is also a defining feature of even research science. Mirowski and van Horn highlight similar levels of regulation and normalisation in the conduct of clinical trials by contract research organisations to that experienced by forensic practitioners.[27] The justifiable intrusion of extrinsic regulatory norms (and concomitant reduction in a capacity for internal governance) also affects the work of university researchers: particularly those whose work involves human subjects.

Arguments regarding the status of forensic science would appear to be underpinned by a commitment to disciplinary purity, which may be at odds with emergent realities. It is posited that the concept of disciplinary purity may itself be paradigmatic, and thus open to review and refutation, in light of existing developments. Such a possibility is hinted at by Mercer,[28] who highlights the resilience of realist, and positivist, epistemologies – particularly within the legal system – and the concomitant tendency to attempt to show that 'there is ultimately a straightforward boundary that can be drawn around science and law to stop the distortion of scientific facts'.[29]

In counterpoint, both Edmond and Lawless highlight thecross-disciplinary co-production of forensic-scientific knowledge claims: claims whose genesis cannot be attributed solely to the application of laboratory expertise and whose application cannot be stated to have been shaped solely by the requirements of legal procedure.[30] They posit the emergence of 'scientific method discourses', which

[25]Lawless, C. (2011). Policing markets; The contested shaping of neo-liberal forensic science. *British Journal of Criminology, 51*, 671–689, at p. 682.

[26]Lawless, C. (2011). Policing markets; The contested shaping of neo-liberal forensic science. *British Journal of Criminology, 51*, 671–689.

[27]Mirowski, P., & van Horn, R. (2005). The contract research organisation and the commercialisation of scientific research. *Social Studies of Science, 35*(4), 503–548, at p. 505.

[28]Mercer, D. (2002). The intersection of sociology of scientific knowledge and law: Some themes and policy reflections. *Law, Text, Culture, 6*, 9.

[29]Edmond, G., & Mercer, D. (1998). Trashing 'junk' science. *Stanford Technology Law Review, 3*.

[30]Lawless, C. (2016). *Forensic science: A sociological introduction*. New York, NY: Routledge, at p. 3; see also Mercer, D. (2002). The intersection of sociology of scientific knowledge and law: Some themes and policy reflections. *Law, Text, Culture, 6*, at note 12; Edmond, G. (2001). The law set: The legal-scientific production of medical propriety. *Science, Technology and Human Values, 26*(2), 191–226; Lynch, M., Cole, S. A., McNally, R., & Jordan, K. (2008). *Truth machine: The contentious history of DNA fingerprinting*. Chicago, IL: University of Chicago Press, at p. 45.

result in the formation of 'hybrid sets'. According to their concept, the formation of a 'hybrid set' is a dynamic and fluid process, through which institutional actors from varying epistemological backgrounds come together to shape the form of forensic-scientific truth claims.

Applying Edmond's concept of 'hybrid sets' to Collins and Evans' theory of expertise (in the context of forensic-scientific controversy relating to DNA 'fingerprinting'), Lynch contends that the 'core-set' were temporarily joined by a 'law-set', an 'administrative set', and a 'literary set', all of whom participated in a dynamic – and amorphous – process of adjudication and legitimisation. However, Lynch's illustration may be no more than an instantiation of the banal assertion – as previously demonstrated by the STS corpus – that 'politics is never absent from the centre'.[31] Further, it should be highlighted that the creation of 'hybrid sets' was seen to have occurred in the context of a controversy relating to forensic research science, rather than as a result of its routine application.

Returning to Collins and Evans, it is reiterated that the utility of their theory of expertise diminishes significantly, when applied outwith the context of research science. The authors' normative focus forecloses discussion of scientific co-production. Further, their category of 'meta-expertises' fails to assist in the recognition of emergent forms of interdisciplinary knowledge. Attempts to apply this static theory to the interdisciplinary co-production of forensic-scientific knowledge claims – particularly instances when such activities cross epistemological boundaries – may lead only to the perception of a shifting, and abstruse, ecology of expertises.[32]

By way of example, it might be postulated that the forensic scientist is a contributory expert in the field of forensic practices (be they craft practices, such as 'ballistics', or scientific practices, such as DNA casework). However, it remains unclear whether such a specialist should be categorised as a contributory, or merely interactional, expert within the broader scientific field. It is similarly unclear whether the forensic practitioner's interactions with the criminal justice system should be classed as contributory, or interactional, or both, given the degree to which such interactions are shaped by the procedural norms, and evidential requirements, of the legal field.

It is posited that Mercer's concept of hybridisation – a chimaera born from 'the social and epistemological dynamics of law-science intersections'[33] – affords greater traction than that posited by Collins and Evans. Further, that it can be developed – and extended – to cover all expert practices, in accordance with the general theory of relational expertise outlined in the previous chapter. To restate

---

[31]See Collins, H., & Evans, R. (2007). *Rethinking expertise*. Chicago, IL: University of Chicago Press.

[32]Lynch, M., Cole, S. A., McNally, R., & Jordan, K. (2008). *Truth machine: The contentious history of DNA fingerprinting*. Chicago, IL: University of Chicago Press, at p. 44.

[33]Mercer, D. (2002). The intersection of sociology of scientific knowledge and law: Some themes and policy reflections. *Law, Text, Culture, 6*, at note 12.

the argument, expertise is located in the ability to reflexively account for heterogeneous perceptual, cognitive, and epistemological contexts. Under a generalised theory, this ability renders disciplinary boundaries permeable to expert discourses and facilitates the interdisciplinary co-production of knowledge claims through the expert's ability, not to overcome idealised conceptions of 'law' and 'science', nor to replace them with nuanced understandings of the social construction of forensic discourses, but to account for the co-existence of these conceptions within the complex matrix of social and epistemological relations which define the forensic-scientific field. Thus, the emergence of Edmond and Mercer's 'hybrid sets' may simply be viewed as a normal consequence of the contextual adaptations of forensic-scientific expertise, as outlined in the previous chapter.

Chapter 6

Swift and Sure Justice?

Chapter Summary

The previous chapter demonstrated the ways in which the extension of measures of economic rationalisation to the forensic science field, alongside the propagation of managerialist discourses across the broader criminal justice system (CJS), led to notable efficiencies within both the forensic science domain and the attendant parts of the justice system. Such efficiencies were welcomed by a proportion of institutional agents, from police officers to examining scientists. However, a significant number of respondents voiced concerns relating to the instrumental nature of these reforms and their effect upon the allied processes of forensic examination, interpretation, evaluation, and reporting. These micro- and meso-level incursions were shown to be situated within, and conditioned by, a thoroughgoing socio-economic restructuring of the forensic science field, encouraging de-skilling across the sector (most notably in relation to Tier 1 providers), while impacting negatively upon the operational and procedural aspects of expert scientific evaluation. Any discussion of these developments would be incomplete without a thoroughgoing examination of one the most contentious products of economic rationalisation in the forensic field, specifically the introduction of streamlined forensic reporting (SFR). This managerialist innovation purposefully limits the level of contextual information available to both the Crown Prosecution Service (CPS) and defence practitioners, with a view to promoting 'swift and sure justice'.[1] This chapter outlines the process that led to the introduction of this unique procedural innovation and highlights the evidential obstacles that are generated by adopting an attenuated form of forensic reporting. This chapter demonstrates the ways in which expert scientific examinations, particularly those requiring interpretation and evaluation, become limited through the deployment of a mode of forensic reporting which is purposefully designed to foreclose necessary contextual discussion. The discussion weighs the evidence and specifies the implications for managerialised forensic science provision in the English and Welsh CJS. This chapter provides evidence to demonstrate how SFR is widely

[1]Ministry of Justice. (2012). *Swift and sure justice: The government's plans for reform of the criminal justice system* (Cm 8388). London: TSO.

Marketisation and Forensic Science Provision in England and Wales, 103–128

Published under exclusive licence by Emerald Publishing Limited
doi:10.1108/978-1-83909-123-020221006

perceived by both forensic and legal professionals to detract from both the quality and content of expert scientific opinion, thus potentially limiting the court's ability to arrive at sound determinations on questions of fact. This raises concerns over the potential for SFR to contribute to miscarriages of justice. Furthermore, it is posited that the SFR scheme is legally flawed: a discussion of the compatibility of the SFR scheme with overarching – and subsisting – requirements of Article 7 Directive 2012/13/EU on the Right to Information in Criminal Proceedings casts significant doubt on the entire scheme. Thus, through this discussion, which extends beyond the domestic limitations of prior analyses, it is demonstrated that there is a significant likelihood that the SFR scheme is, in reality, unlawful.

SFR and Abbreviated (or 'Staged') Forensic Reporting

The SFR scheme was not the first attempt by the CPS to create a more efficient form of forensic reporting. Indeed, SFR was built upon a prior initiative – 'Staged Reporting'[2] – introduced by the CPS Prosecution Team in 2004. It is therefore helpful for the purposes of explication to preface a discussion of SFR with an outline of the scheme's immediate predecessor. The staged (or abbreviated) reporting initiative set out 'to minimise unnecessary work and delays by focusing on the matters relevant to the case in question'[3] and was intended to dovetail with changes to the 'CPS Prosecution Team Charging Guidance' polices, which had not previously allowed a suspect to be charged on the basis of a deoxyribonucleic acid (DNA) match report alone. However, that policy changed with effect from 1 August 2004.

> The new policy will mean that a suspect may now be charged on the basis of a DNA intelligence match, derived from the scene of the crime, and a sample of DNA kept on the National Database providing there is some further supporting evidence.[4]

The Prosecution Team DNA Guidance embedded staged reporting into the process of criminal case file preparation. As with its direct descendant, SFR, the introduction of staged reporting was justified with reference to the Criminal Procedure Rules (CrimPR) (in addition to the Criminal Justice Act 2003). Under the staged reporting scheme,

> an initial abbreviated statement is provided by the scientist simply to confirm the validity of the NDNAD match report, with a full statement only being requested where the actual issues identified

---

[2]CPS. *Legal guidance on streamlined forensic reporting*. Retrieved from https://www.cps.gov.uk/legal-guidance/streamlined-forensic-reporting-guidance-and-toolkit

[3]Nuffield Council on Bioethics. (2007). *The forensic use of bioinformation: Ethical issues* (p. 65). Cambridge: Cambridge Publishers.

[4]CPS (The Prosecution Team). (2004, July 16). *Guidance on DNA charging*.

> require full evaluation … This change provides a significant opportunity to improve the turnaround times for analysis in the laboratories and the provision of statements by the scientists, as well as greatly reducing the costs of forensic science evidence.[5]

The crucial difference between staged reporting and streamlined reporting was that, under the former scheme, the forensic report was produced by a qualified scientist, who might appear in court on the strength of the report, whereas the streamlined report (at least in its most common form, SFR1) 'is not a statement upon which the maker of the statement is necessarily qualified to give evidence'.[6] Further, while the staged report condenses 'the headlines of the [scientist's] working out'[7] and can easily be elaborated upon,[8] the SFR is often limited to a single sentence. Staged reporting is comparatively transparent as to its limitations, candid with regard to the need for contextual information, and open about the underlying methodology used and the personnel involved.[9] Thus, the relational nature of scientific evidence – directly addressed by the staged reporting process – may be hidden by the SFR process.

Following the introduction of staged reporting in 2004, the Forensic Science Service (FSS) – by that point one of several forensic science providers within a relatively undeveloped market – noted some encouraging trends. During the 2005/2006 financial year, the service received 1,887 requests for abbreviated statements based upon National DNA Database (NDNAD) match reports. These resulted in 175 requests for a full evaluative (or 'complex') statement. The cost of a full evaluative statement was, at that time, around six times that of an abbreviated statement (£600 and £100, respectively). Prior to the introduction of staged reporting, all 1,887 statements would have been fully explicated, at an estimated total cost of £1,132,200. Thus, as a consequence of using staged forensic reporting, the financial costs were reduced to roughly £293,700 (£188,700 plus £105,000). This equated to a saving of £838,500 (74%).[10]

The FSS also noted significant savings in time and resources, resulting from the introduction of staged reporting. The time taken to produce a full evaluative statement (average six hours) dropped to one hour in respect of abbreviated statements.[11] The staged reporting scheme led to demonstrable efficiencies, and it

---

[5]NDNAD. *The national DNA database annual report 2005–2006*, at p. 10.

[6]See CPS. (2015). *Streamlined forensic reporting guidance and toolkit 6*. Retrieved from https://www.cps.gov.uk/legal-guidance/streamlined-forensic-reporting-guidance-and-toolkit

[7]Interview with lead DNA reporting scientist, Oxford, July 2015.

[8]In contrast, the streamlined report is opaque with regard to its methods, and attenuated in its conclusions, providing no platform for elaboration.

[9]Staged reports contain a technical note explaining the scientific procedures used. This is absent from the streamlined report.

[10]NDNAD. *The national DNA database annual report 2005–2006*, at p. 10.

[11]NDNAD. *The national DNA database annual report 2005–2006*, at p. 10.

should be noted that it subsists: abbreviated reports are still routinely produced by some forensic science providers and are actively sought by a number of police forces in preference to full evaluative statements. However, the use of abbreviated reports is far less common than that of streamlined reports.

Background: The Ministry of Justice (MoJ) Efficiency Programme

Although not the first attempt to create an efficient mode of forensic reporting, SFR is nonetheless an innovative evidential procedure. As with its predecessor – staged reporting – SFR was introduced across England and Wales for the purpose of better case management with regard to the use of forensic evidence. Thus, the SFR scheme, as originally envisaged, was organised around modest, and achievable, goals.

It was first introduced in 2008 by the Association of Chief Police Officers (ACPO) Criminal Justice Business Group, in partnership with the Metropolitan Police Service (MPS). The scheme proceeded on the basis of a series of local pilot programmes in SFR. The initial pilot – at Woolwich Crown Court in London – was restricted to cases involving fingerprint identification, firearm and ballistic results, and DNA database matches. The forensic science provider was directed to produce a short forensic report for all cases involving these evidence types. These reports, known as Streamlined Forensic Report Stage 1 (or SFR1), were restricted to initial key findings. The reports were not intended to be presented at trial (being limited in scope, frequently based on an incomplete analysis, and possibly inconclusive). Rather, they were intended 'to elicit an agreement or to enable the defence to simply identify the real issues for trial'.[12] In the event that the case went to trial, an extended SFR Stage 2 report was presented, usually in witness statement format.

Following this year-long pilot, the evaluation found fewer discontinued cases and an increase in early guilty pleas (with attendant savings). As a result, the SFR initiative was extended. By November 2011, it included all London Courts (with the exception of the Central Criminal Court). A second review followed, focussing on cases processed through Wood Green Crown Court before and after SFR implementation. Similar effects to the Woolwich pilot were noted:

- Early guilty pleas increased from 61% to 84%.
- Guilty pleas before trial increased from 71% to 87%.
- Total guilty outcomes increased from 79% to 91%.
- Abandoned trials reduced from 9% to 2.4%.
- Additional requirement for forensic evidence reduced from 42% to 2%.
- Discontinued cases reduced from 18% to 5%.[13]

[12]CPS. *Legal guidance on streamlined forensic reporting*. Retrieved from https://www.cps.gov.uk/legal-guidance/streamlined-forensic-reporting-guidance-and-toolkit

[13]CPS. *Legal guidance on streamlined forensic reporting*. Retrieved from https://www.cps.gov.uk/legal-guidance/streamlined-forensic-reporting-guidance-and-toolkit.

However, the scheme was then brought within the MoJ's 'Criminal Justice System Efficiency Programme'. The Efficiency Programme sought 'to [modernise] the CJS by reducing or removing the movement of paper, and people, around the system'.[14] It is the implementation of the scheme through this programme – whose aims were to minimise bureaucracy and to reduce unnecessary costs and delays in the CJS – which radically altered its character. The Government White Paper, *Swift and Sure Justice*,[15] set out the objectives of the programme:

> From a so-called 'system' which operated in silos, we are moving to a criminal justice service where police, prosecution and courts work more effectively together. None of these reforms will compromise historic legal rights or important principles of justice. Rather the reverse: justice must be swift, sure and seen to be done, or it is not done at all.[16]

The targets of reforms were cases which the MoJ categorised as 'low-level, straightforward and uncontested ... where a quick response is appropriate'.[17] Such cases were to be dealt with 'promptly and efficiently'. The Ministry recognised the critical role which forensic evidence plays in bringing offenders to justice. Hence, its support for, and adoption of, the SFR scheme.

The MoJ noted the success of the pilot projects and catalogued the potential benefits which could be gained from the nationwide introduction of streamlined reporting. These included:

- A lower risk of discontinuance, likely to be due to case papers being better prepared and the defence being informed of the evidence at the earliest stage.
- An improvement in the early guilty plea rate, resulting in fewer cases coming to trial unnecessarily, helping to ease the pressure of trial dates and associated costs.
- A reduction in the number of cases requiring additional forensic evidence, saving time, and costs associated with gathering this evidence.[18]

Thus, the primary objective of streamlined reporting came to be reframed in economic terms, which focussed on the reduction of 'costs and delay associated with forensic evidence where such evidence adds no value to the administration of

---

[14]Ministry of Justice. (2012, May 14). *Defence practitioner FAQ, Version 3.92*.

[15]Ministry of Justice. (2012). *Swift and sure justice: The government's plans for reform of the criminal justice system* (Cm 8388). London: TSO.

[16]Ministry of Justice. (2012). *Swift and sure justice: The government's plans for reform of the criminal justice system* (Cm 8388). London: TSO, at p. 4.

[17]Ministry of Justice. (2012). *Swift and sure justice: The government's plans for reform of the criminal justice system* (Cm 8388). London: TSO, at p. 5.

[18]Ministry of Justice. (2012). *Swift and sure justice: The government's plans for reform of the criminal justice system* (Cm 8388). London: TSO, at pp. 33–34.

justice'.[19] The CPS then set out to actively promote the adoption of SFR across the CJS, with a target date for implementation by March 2013. As a result of these efforts, SFR was introduced throughout England and Wales on 2 April 2013.

The SFR implementation process received active support from both ACPO Criminal Justice and the CPS. The national project was led by Neil Rhodes, Chief Constable of Lincolnshire Police (and ACPO TAM Director of Strategy and Policy: SFR). The SFR governance structure is now dispersed across multiple agencies, including the Forensics Portfolio Board, Forensics Delivery Board, SFR Virtual National Board, SFR Issues and Consistency Group, and a small number of SFR Expert Networks aligned to categories of SFR evidence (DNA, footwear, drugs, and digital). The SFR programme also falls within the remit of the Forensic Science Regulator (FSR) and the UK Accreditation Service (UKAS).

Initially, the scheme was limited to cases involving forensic DNA matches. However, individual police forces were free to introduce SFR for other forensic categories, on their own cognisance, leading to the use of SFR for cases involving DNA matches, evidential drug identification tests (EDITs), simple drug tests, simple toxicology tests, firearms classification, footwear, and indecent images of children (IIoC). There are further plans to extend implementation to include forensic casework.

CrimPR

The second objective of SFR – as determined by the CPS – is to ease compliance with the requirements of CrimPR. The purpose of the CrimPR is to ensure that criminal cases are dealt with justly (as laid out in Part 1[20]). Reaching just determinations in criminal cases entails, *inter alia,* acquitting the innocent, convicting the guilty, dealing fairly with the prosecution and defence, respecting the interests of witnesses, dealing with cases efficiently, and taking in to account the complexity of the issues at hand.[21]

In order to meet the overriding objective of the CrimPR, Part 3 places a further duty on the court,[22] to actively manage criminal cases. 'Active management' is achieved through the early identification of real issues and the early identification of the needs of witnesses.[23] Part 3 also places a duty on the court to

[19]This is one of a series of *circula in probanda* deployed in support of the SFR initiative. These are discussed (*infra*).

[20]Part 1, *Criminal Procedure Rules 2015*. Ministry of Justice. A third – unstated – objective to SFR was referred to in interviews with members of HMIC: streamlined reports have been designed to act as an evidential agonist in cases where the accused exercises his (or her) right to silence. This objective receives relatively little attention in the supporting documentation but carries far-reaching implications for the conduct of criminal cases.

[21]Part 1 CrimPR 1.1(2)(a)–(g).

[22]Specifically, the Magistrate and Crown Courts, including Appeals from the Crown Court under s.3.1(2).

[23]CrimPR 3.2 (2)(a) and (b).

ensure that evidence (whether disputed or not) is presented in the shortest and clearest way.

A similar duty is placed on the individual parties under Rule 3.3, which requires that each party must actively assist the court in fulfilling its Part 3 objectives. This entails both parties entering into active communication at the earliest opportunity (and no later than the day of the first hearing) in order to establish whether the defendant intends to plead guilty or not guilty, and – in the latter instance – the parties must determine which matters are agreed and which are likely to be disputed.

Part 19 (previously Part 33) of the CrimPR places a similar duty on experts to help the court to achieve its overriding objective. This duty is not limited to expert witnesses but extends to all of those experts summoned to prepare evidence for criminal proceedings.[24] The duty is fulfilled by giving opinion which is unbiased, objective, and within the expert's area of expertise. Part 19 also places a special duty on experts to actively assist the court to fulfil its duty of case management under Rule 3.2, in particular by complying with any direction made by the court.

In the absence of direct statutory implementation, the CrimPR are imputed to provide a clear rationale for the implementation of SFR, Therefore, the SFR objectives must be read as facilitating compliance with the CrimPR. Indeed, the CPS state that the second objective of streamlined reporting (Stage 1):

> To provide a stronger basis for Stage 2 forensic reporting through compliance with Criminal Procedure Rules, rules 3.2 and 3.3, which set out the Court Case Management requirements for the early identification of real issues.[25]

The degree to which the SFR programme conforms, or departs, from the requirements of the CrimPR, in practice, will form the subject of further detailed discussion, below.

Supporting Case Law

In addition to citing the need for regulatory compliance, the introduction of streamlined reporting was justified with reference to case law. The supporting documentation listed a cluster of cases, which were cited in support of the scheme's stated objectives, and went so far as to include excerpts from leading cases. These were to be found in earlier versions of the SFR1 form (MG22b) itself. However, in later versions, these excerpts have been removed.

In particular, attention was drawn to both *Balogun* v. *DPP* [2010] EWHC 799 and *R* v. *Chorley Justices* [2006] EWHC 1795, which were cited in support of an assertion of the duty of full defence disclosure and to iterate the duty owed by both parties to identify the real issues at the earliest opportunity (as laid out in

---

[24]CrimPR, Part 19.1(2).

[25]CPS. *Legal guidance on streamlined forensic reporting*. Retrieved from https://www.cps.gov.uk/legal-guidance/streamlined-forensic-reporting-guidance-and-toolkit

the CrimPR).[26] Support was also drawn from *R* v. *Reed, Reed & Garmson* [2009] EWCA Crim LR 2698, paragraphs 128–131 of which emphasise the importance of adherence to Rule 33 CrimPR (now Rule 19). Further reference was made to *R* v. *Weller* [2010] EWCA Crim LR 724, paragraphs 16–18 of which discuss identification of salient issues; also, *R* v. *Butler, Henderson & Oyerderin* [2010] EWCA Crim LR 1269, paragraphs 209–214 on case management; the leading case of *R* v. *T* [2010] EWCA Crim LR 2439 on the duty of expert witnesses to reveal their underlying methodology; and *R* v. *Olu, Wilson & Brooks* [2010] EWCA Crim LR 2975, which deals with the SFR schedules at paragraph 45. These excerpts will form the subject of further discussion below.

SFR – Outline

As stated above, the goal of the SFR scheme is to achieve better case management through saving time and resources. However, there are other notable differences between SFR and standard forms of forensic reporting, which make the scheme unique. The most significant of these is that 'SFR1 is not a statement upon which the maker of the statement is necessarily qualified to give evidence'.[27]

Beyond that statement, it is difficult to find a consistent description of SFR(1) within the guidance notes,[28] in the supporting documentation,[29] or on the form itself.[30] SFR(1) is variously described as 'evidence'; 'a summary of conclusions'[31]; 'staged reporting'; 'not staged reporting'; 'an abbreviated form of reporting'; 'information'; 'a forensic statement'; 'not a statement'; 'a forensic report'; 'not a witness statement or an expert's report to which Criminal Procedure Rule 33 applies'; '(proportional) forensic evidence'; 'a summary of forensic evidence'; 'forensic evidence, when agreed, for the purposes of s.10 of the Criminal Justice Act 1967'; 'a vital enabling tool'; 'a key case management tool'; 'a visual prompt to the prosecution and the defence'; and 'a summary of expert evidence that is served for the purposes of securing an admission'.[32]

---

[26]See Form MG22(b) and Beckwith, J. (2014, September 23). *Digital forensics specialist group SFR*. Available on website of the Forensic Science Regulator.

[27]CPS. (2015). *Streamlined forensic reporting guidance and toolkit 6*. Retrieved from https://www.cps.gov.uk/legal-guidance/streamlined-forensic-reporting-guidance-and-toolkit

[28]CPS. (2015). *Streamlined forensic reporting guidance and toolkit 6*. Retrieved from https://www.cps.gov.uk/legal-guidance/streamlined-forensic-reporting-guidance-and-toolkit.

[29]CPS. *Legal guidance on streamlined forensic reporting*. Retrieved from https://www.cps.gov.uk/legal-guidance/streamlined-forensic-reporting-guidance-and-toolkit

[30]CPS. *Legal guidance on streamlined forensic reporting*. Retrieved from https://www.cps.gov.uk/legal-guidance/streamlined-forensic-reporting-guidance-and-toolkit

[31]CPS. *Legal guidance on streamlined forensic reporting*. Retrieved from https://www.cps.gov.uk/legal-guidance/streamlined-forensic-reporting-guidance-and-toolkit

[32]All descriptions are taken from the CPS and ACPO guidance, and toolkits, on streamlined reporting. Conflicting descriptions may be found within a single document.

Purposive definitions of the SFR are thus diverse and frequently contradictory. Nor are such definitions fixed, being provisional on both the identity of the user and the purpose for which the report is used.

> For the police investigator [SFR1] is simply used as the initial forensic report … When SFR enters a pre-trial Court Case Management hearing, it becomes a Court Case Management tool.[33]

Thus, SFR1 may be characterised as a legal chimaera designed, not solely to provide determinative answers but to flexibly serve a multitude of purposes.

Attempts to explain the nature of the forensic science provision cluster around a small number of themes. The legal and forensic-scientific professions form accessible analytic categories and have been a long-standing focus of socio-legal research, particularly in regard to their organisation, practices, and interactions. 'Neo-Weberian' perspectives have tended to focus on the composition of particular professions (through processes of inclusion and exclusion, as determined by intrinsic interests). Related studies explore the ways in which these expert communities reconstitute themselves, through the resolution of controversies and challenges.

Further intra-disciplinary studies have highlighted the ways in which members of the scientific professions resort to distinctly social practices in their efforts to distinguish science from non-science. The focus on 'boundary work' as a constitutive practice, shaping forensic science as both a discipline and profession, may serve to explain the interactions and negotiations between law and science. Scholars of expertise share an interest in processes of negotiation. They posit the creation of 'hybrid sets' of legal and scientific actors, whose temporary alignment allows for the resolution of controversies in ways which satisfy the respective interests of competing domains.[34] Thus, Mercer[35] argues that 'there is ultimately a straightforward boundary that can be drawn around science and law to stop the distortion of scientific facts'.[36] Both Edmond and Mercer highlight the necessary co-production of forensic-scientific knowledge claims: claims whose genesis cannot be attributed solely to the application of laboratory expertise and whose application cannot be stated to have been shaped solely by the requirements of legal procedure.[37] Thus, they posit the emergence of 'scientific method

[33]All descriptions are taken from the CPS and ACPO guidance, and toolkits, on streamlined reporting. Conflicting descriptions may be found within a single document.

[34]Lynch, M., Cole, S. A., McNally, R., & Jordan, K. (2008). *Truth machine: The contentious history of DNA fingerprinting*. Chicago, IL: University of Chicago Press.

[35]Mercer, D. (2002). The intersection of sociology of scientific knowledge and law: Some themes and policy reflections. *Law, Text, Culture, 6*, 9.

[36]Edmond, G., & Mercer, D. (1998). Trashing 'junk' science. *Stanford Technology Law Review, 3*.

[37]Lawless, C. (2016). *Forensic science: A sociological introduction* (p. 3). New York, NY: Routledge; see also Mercer, D. (2002). The intersection of sociology of

discourses', which result in the formation of 'hybrid sets'. According to their concept, the formation of a 'hybrid set' is a dynamic and fluid process, through which institutional actors from varying epistemological backgrounds come together to shape the form of forensic-scientific truth claims.

The 'hybrid set' theory would appear to allow for the temporary merging of science, and law, on a number of levels: cognitive, normative, and epistemological. However, other theories remain sceptical with regard to this possibility. The autopoietic perspective exhibits a similar focus on the ways in which discrete fields exchange cognitive information (through the process of structural coupling). However, autopoiesis forecloses the possibility of epistemological negotiation between discrete scientific and legal fields, both of which retain operational and normative closure.

During data collection, the overwhelming majority of scientists expressed a desire to discuss SFR. These informants tended to be critical, citing the lack of information provided on SFR1 reports as a particularly problematic feature. Deficiencies were noted in terms of both the procedural form and scientific content of the reports. The majority of expert informants were sceptical about the ability of the SFR process to meet its stated aims (delivering efficiencies by encouraging discussion and focussing on the 'real issues'):

> An SFR1 is done early in a case. Typically it will be done in a 'spec case'. [The report] is not done by a scientist. The sample goes to the evidence recovery unit [or the Forensic Science Provider]. A profile is obtained. The profile is loaded onto the NDNAD. The police DNA Unit are informed if there has been a match. They compile the SFR1. (Interview, Tier 1 Forensic Scientist, 2015)[38]

> [...] it's designed – let's be honest – to encourage a plea. (Interview, Tier 2 Forensic Scientist, Oxford, 2015)

> SFRs were meant to standardise reporting. They were supposed to save time and money by simplifying the process and to highlight

scientific knowledge and law: Some themes and policy reflections. *Law, Text, Culture, 6,* at note 12; Edmond, G. (2001). The law set: The legal-scientific production of medical propriety. *Science, Technology and Human Values, 26*(2), 191–226; Lynch, M., Cole, S. A., McNally, R., & Jordan, K. (2008). *Truth machine: The contentious history of DNA fingerprinting*. Chicago, IL: University of Chicago Press, at p. 45.

[38]All of the informants quoted in this chapter are forensic DNA experts. The cohort includes the following: operational senior scientists, lead scientists, managing director, head of operations, research and development implementation manager, principal forensic biologists, and chief reporting officer. They are all currently employed by forensic science providers in England and together represent a cross-section of the forensic science market, including both Tier 1 and Tier 2 providers. The majority of those interviewed had over 10 years' experience (frequently having spent time within the now defunct FSS). Others had received training solely within the commercial market.

> areas of disagreement. They are meant to encourage an early guilty plea. (Interview, Tier 2 Forensic Scientist, Oxford, 2015)

> There is a big push for a guilty plea – it's really like a commercial negotiation. A guilty plea saves a huge public spend. (Interview, Tier 2 Forensic Scientist, Oxford, 2015)

Lack of information with regard to 'chain of custody' was also cited as a particular source of uncertainty and confusion:

> On the SFR there is no mention of the lab who did the work or what scientist did it. (Interview, Tier 2 Forensic Scientist, Oxford, 2015)

> In one case different swabs went to two different firms. (Interview, Tier 2 Forensic Scientist, Oxford, 2015)

> In another case different swabs went to different reporters with a different URN.[39] So again there was a loss of context. The Met may have an overview but not at the raw data level. (Interview, Tier 1 Forensic Scientist, 2015)

These examples, from forensic scientists working in 'defence-oriented' (Tier 2) laboratories, reveal procedural concerns arising from tensions between the reviewing laboratory and the police, as well as with those who carried out the initial analysis. One scientist drew attention to a specific example of procedural irregularity. This involved the comparison of DNA samples with 'expired' reference profiles, in contravention of the overarching regulations.[40] The scientist viewed this as essentially an interpretative – rather than a procedural – lapse.

> Pre-2005 barcodes reflect DNA1 and DNA2[41] ... barcodes beginning 95 ... or below need a second sample to be taken. They're no longer allowed to be used in court yet they are slipping through. These are factual errors. (Interview, Tier 2 Forensic Scientist, Oxford, 2015)

Another scientist indicated that source-level attributions were being presented on the basis of sub-source analysis, providing a further example of poor evaluation based upon an inappropriately restrictive level of analysis.

---

[39]Unique reference number.
[40]See ACPO. (2005). *DNA good practice manual* (2nd ed.). London: The Stationery Office, and The Police and Criminal Evidence Act (PACE) 1984, Code of Practice D.
[41]These were the earliest forms of DNA collection kit.

> With SFRs there's no record of where the swab was taken from. They swab a stain then state that the DNA came from blood but they haven't done the KM[42] test, so we can only say that it's biological material. (Interview, Tier 2 Forensic Scientist, Oxford, 2015)

> The danger is that the division between the stain and the DNA result means that one may not be related to the other. There's no context. (Interview, Managing Director and Tier 2 Forensic Scientist, Oxford, 2015)

Informants were asked whether the deliberate separation of tasks between the forensic analysis of the sample and the subsequent compilation of the report by a police administrator represented a particular form of 'case fragmentation'. Their responses highlight concerns over the potential for the division of labour to restrict forensic evaluation and legal fact determination.

> The work is done by an administrator. The administrator hasn't seen anything but paperwork. She hasn't seen the profiles. And the scientist who created the profile hasn't seen the reference profile and compared it. (Interview, Tier 2 Forensic Scientist, Oxford, 2015)

> Many police forces have an in-house team called the Evidence Recovery Unit. So, for the Met, the ERU send the recovered samples to LGC or Cellmark. They profile them and send the results back on a results table. The Met scientist hasn't seen the actual result or the reference sample. (Interview, Tier 2 Forensic Scientist, Oxford, 2015)

> The Met may collect samples, process some in-house, send others to an FSP, with nobody getting an overview. The work becomes less interpretative. (Interview, Tier 2 Forensic Scientist, Oxford, 2015)

> With the Met lab, one scientist is simply quoting another scientist, and that is not necessarily made clear. (Interview, Tier 2 Forensic Scientist, Oxford, 2015)

The propensity for unqualified administrators to quote forensic scientists was highlighted as a particular problem. A defence scientist produced a vivid illustration of the ways in which separation of tasks, quoting, and incorporation of passages between reports may prove misleading.

> So, this individual [indicating the original examiner] has not had DNA experience ... and talks about 'the sample that *we* submitted for DNA'. She understands that a mixed DNA result was

[42]Kastle–Meyer presumptive test for blood.

> obtained, which had at least three people in it … so, she's essentially paraphrasing the wording from the original scientist. This result, this statement, doesn't give us any context on the strength and limitations of this DNA result. It just basically cuts-and-pastes from the scientist's statement. (Interview, Tier 2 Forensic Scientist, Oxford, 2015)

> So, they're now trying to develop a procedure where the Metropolitan Police can use the reports, or the outputs, of the DNA scientist and can incorporate that into their statement. But, by any other name, that's hearsay. (Interview, Tier 2 Forensic Scientist, Oxford, 2015)

Informants highlighted further problems. The increased sensitivity of analytical protocols has resulted in an increase in the reporting of mixed profiles.[43] These profiles require careful evaluation. However, scientists indicated that the interpretative process was now overly regulated, and formulaic, and that streamlining had reduced the procedure to one whereby outputs were interpreted according to a rigid, tabulated, administrative procedure. This led to inaccuracy.

> Where there is a major/minor sample, the scientist is not able to compare the two samples. The administrator has a table which s(he) consults. So the report is often factually inaccurate with regard to match probability. (Interview, Tier 2 Forensic Scientist, Oxford, 2015)

Discussions with DNA experts also unearthed more general concerns over the loss of expertise in the SFR process and the concomitant loss of contextual evaluation.

> The NDNAD was never designed to be an evidential tool. The use of SFRs mean that some [defendants] are cornered. The SFR statement is portrayed as facts and [the defendants] aren't fully informed that they aren't facts. (Interview, Tier 2 Forensic Scientist, Oxford, 2015)

> SFR1 is all factual and reads in a way that sounds very bad for the accused but it lacks context. (Interview, Managing Director and Tier 2 Forensic Scientist, Oxford, 2015)

> You are asking someone to plead on the basis of incomplete information. Even if it is complete, nowhere does it tell them about the limitations of the evidence. It's a one-size-fits-all solution. (Interview, Tier 2 Forensic Scientist, Oxford, 2015)

[43]Profiles derived from the DNA of two, or more, individuals.

Crucially, informants highlighted concerns that a complete absence of contextual, or explanatory, information made the SFR1 extremely difficult to challenge. During interviews with legal practitioners, magistrates, barristers, and solicitors, all echoed these concerns. Further, they proposed that SFR dovetails with a prosecution strategy which seeks to establish links on the sub-source and source levels while foreclosing discussion of exculpatory information on the activity level.

> Interviewer: And would you say the SFR presents things in a very factual way due to the lack of contextual information?
>
> Absolutely. Cannot agree more. And in fact, there's obviously a very strong cohort of individual scientists usually, who feel that they're misleading because a) they don't allow a scientist to talk about the context because they're very formulaic and b) they don't provide any sort of context to the findings. (Interview, Tier 2 Forensic Scientist, Oxford, 2015)

> depending on how that's put in interview, there's such a massive preconception in the general public about what DNA evidence means, whether it's fair to the defendant to just put that to him or her and how open that is left to them to contest it and realise what it does actually mean and what options they've got at that point. (Interview, Tier 1 Forensic Scientist, Warrington, 2015)

> Because there is no technical note, and so little information, it's very hard to challenge. A lawyer wouldn't know what to challenge and a defendant couldn't get the funds to challenge it. (Interview, Tier 2 Forensic Scientist, Oxford, 2015)

> [...] it must be difficult for a defence lawyer ... to themselves understand the technicalities or to be able to get the legal aid, to ... challenge it because there's just so little there. So how do you explain what they want? (Interview, Tier 1 Forensic Scientist, Warrington, 2015)

> SFR1 works well for 'volume crime' but where do we draw the line? There's a grey area. Vulnerable individuals may plead guilty on the strength of the SFR1 and these may never be picked up. Especially where they are on legal aid. (Interview, Tier 2 Forensic Scientist, Oxford, 2015)

Informants raised more general concerns regarding the loss of expertise, and resulting confusion, resulting from the introduction of SFR:

> Nobody knows their roles when it comes to SFRs. (Interview, Tier 2 Forensic Scientist, Oxford, 2015)

> The police are directing scientists to do a basic task but there's more to interpretation than numbers. The problem isn't limited to the police. The lack of awareness about SFRs among solicitors is a worry. (Interview, Tier 2 Forensic Scientist, Oxford, 2015)

> With SFRs they've taken the expert out of the process. Previously, the expert had an overview. Now, its only when the defence gets it that we have the necessary overview. (Interview, Tier 2 Forensic Scientist, Oxford, 2015)

> So, yes, as I say, I think the purpose of them and why they've come about is for very good reasons but because of the lack of understanding of all of the stake holders in it that's where it falls down. And it isn't fit for purpose. (Interview, Tier 1 Forensic Scientist, Warrington, 2015)

Informants further posited that the MoJ were relying on common perceptions regarding the probative value of DNA-profiling 'matches', rather than engaging in a more costly probabilistic and contextual scientific evaluation. These responses are listed, before the discussion turns towards their relevance to answering the research question.

> They are relying on the reputation of DNA but with none of the science underpinning it. (Interview, Tier 2 Forensic Scientist, Oxford, 2015)

> If its purpose is to identify at an early stage the issues which are going to be contested, it needs to contain, all of the issues which could possibly be contested, which isn't necessarily the statistic attached to the DNA profile. And there is that pre-conception amongst the general public that DNA is fact [probative] ... and so for a defence scientist to say, 'well I know you've got this big number on your SFR1, but I want to look at it more closely' but then the budget holder for the legal aid says 'well it's DNA': what are you going to contest? (Interview, Tier 1 Forensic Scientist, Warrington, 2015)

When summing up their views on the SFR process, informants concluded that the scheme was factually misleading and did not deliver the efficiencies that are its stated aim:

> The idea behind it, I can understand entirely and yes and I think, you know, the purpose is noble, and it's fine to try and achieve

> that, but it's entirely dependent on everybody's in the process' understanding of the purpose of that document and what it means, and what the flaws in that is, and I think where there is a lack of understanding, which the defendant is not likely to have, then that's where it falls down. (Interview, Tier 1 Forensic Scientist, Warrington, 2015)

> The SFR model is good but that model dictates there's going to be an error rate, and how do we mitigate that? At some point [in the design of the process] it has been accepted there will be a significant error rate. (Interview, Tier 2 Forensic Scientist, Oxford, 2015)

> The cost to the court is excessive as a host of reporters get called to court so the cost to the criminal justice system actually increases. (Interview, Tier 2 Forensic Scientist, Oxford, 2015)

> SFRs reduce time but the styling is very misleading. There's a dilution effect. (Interview, Tier 2 Forensic Scientist, Oxford, 2015)

> There is a long way to go before SFR is safe. (Interview, Tier 2 Forensic Scientist, Oxford, 2015)

The above responses demonstrate the ways economisation has influenced the ways in which expert forensic biologists evaluate DNA-profiling evidence in England and Wales. SFR1 reports are not sufficiently robust to meet the requirements of a genuine expert witness statement and are therefore not intended for presentation in court. The report is intended to convey only the bare minimum of evidence necessary for charging purposes. However, they are intended for production at pre-trial case management hearings and are designed to dovetail with other CPS initiatives, particularly the 'Early Guilty Plea Scheme' and the 'Stop Delaying Justice Initiative'.[44]

The 'key findings' presented on the SFR1 are brief: typically, they may be comprised of only one sentence, confirming a 'match' between a DNA sample and a reference profile. The findings are not generally accompanied by any contextual information nor by a technical note explaining the procedures from which the findings were derived. Crucially, they contain neither an evaluation nor a thorough interpretation of the purported 'evidence'.

On the basis of these findings alone, a suspect may be charged. The defence may then be invited to a pre-trial hearing. At the hearing, the key findings will be presented, and the defence may be invited to agree the content of SFR1 – presented as Form MG22 (B) – as an admission of uncontested evidence under

---

[44]The SFR scheme also operated alongside the Criminal Court Charge (abolished on 24 December 2015).

Section 10 of the Criminal Justice Act 1967. The accused may then be invited to plead guilty in order to receive the maximum sentencing discount.

In cases where the defence do not accept the content of the SFR1 report presented during the case management process, the CPS guidance places the onus on the defence to identify 'the real issues'. These issues can then be addressed in court through an SFR Stage 2 report (MG22 (C)). The SFR Toolkit states the purpose of SFR Stage 2 as being,

> [...] to provide further evidence on identified and/or disputed forensic issues emanating from the Stage 1 court case management process. Stage 2 forensic evidence provides stronger and relevant forensic evidence to address the specific case issues that have been raised.[45]

However, it should be noted that this SFR Stage 2 report is not a replacement for a full evaluative statement. It is limited solely to a discussion of those issues identified at the earlier stage of the process. Thus, in practice, the Stage 2 report is frequently replaced with a full statement:

> You could get an SFR2 as well but normally you would just go for a full witness statement. With an SFR1, you're going to court without a scientist having seen the report. (Interview, Tier 2 Forensic Scientist, Oxford, 2015)

As illustrated in the above responses, the introduction of non-expert streamlined reports has raised tensions between the forensic science community and the CJS and has attracted criticism from both fields.

The procedural innovations introduced by SFR1 dispense completely with the forensic scientist's ability to conduct an evaluation and interpretation of the DNA profile. Instead, the task of 'calling the profile' is passed to a police administrator, capable of only performing the most rudimentary interpretation (if any). This transfer of responsibilities is directly related to the process of de-skilling discussed in the previous chapter.

During a validation session, one forensic biologist took strong exception to the suggestion that the transfer of responsibilities to police administrators constituted 'de-skilling' with regard to forensic professionals, arguing that the term did not apply in circumstances where responsibilities were transferred to unskilled administrators within another field. In reply, it is argued that this assertion is wrong. The previous chapter provides ample evidence of the loss of professional cohesion within the forensic-scientific field and of de-skilling within the forensic field. Further, that these factors, alongside the introduction of standardised forensic products, have led to a decreased reliance on forensic evaluation and have

---

[45]CPS. (2015). *Streamlined forensic reporting guidance and toolkit 6* (p. 7). Retrieved from http://www.cps.gov.uk/legal/s_to_u/scientific_evidence/sfr_guidance_and_toolkit/

thus allowed for a transfer of responsibilities away from forensic biologists to institutional agents within the CJS. That is the very definition of 'de-skilling'.

Forensic scientists also expressed concerns over the ability of solicitors to engage with the evidence, due to the brevity of the streamlined report and the lack of context. During verification interviews, these same concerns were echoed by respondents from both the bar and the bench. A criminal defence barrister, and a magistrate, both expressed concern over the lack of engagement with, or challenge to, SFR1 DNA reports, by solicitors. The magistrate also expressed frustration that – from the bench – she was unable to direct solicitors scrutinise the evidence. She was therefore forced to accept the unchallenged SFR as evidence in criminal proceedings.

While these responses may be concerning, and may point to problems with the streamlined reporting system, an alternative explanation may be that solicitors are simply delivering the efficiencies that the scheme was designed to introduce. However, that assertion does not bear weight, since the frustration felt by these respondents would suggest that barristers and magistrates are alive to the issues, and limitations, that the defence solicitors are either failing to apprehend or are unable to overcome.

It may be argued, in that case, that the problem of lack of engagement does not lie solely with SFR1 but is partly due to 'forensic illiteracy' on a part of the legal profession. That may be true in some instances. However, if this were the case, then we would expect these problems to predate the introduction of SFR1. However, the data from the Wood Green Crown Court study show a significant decrease in solicitor's requests for further forensic information (from 42% down to 2%) following the introduction of streamlined reporting. It may be concluded, therefore, that while a reluctance to engage with the evidence may indeed be a contributory factor, the main drawback with SFR1 is that solicitor are rendered unable to challenge, or engage with, a report whose brevity precludes further scrutiny. In these circumstances, it is difficult to justify the use of streamlined reports in respect of DNA-profiling evidence.

One of the architects of streamlined reporting – a Queens Counsel (QC) and CPS strategy advisor – verified that there were significant problems with the system, along the lines stated above. However, the respondent stressed that these problems could not have been foreseen, and that they stemmed from the point at which the scheme came under the auspices of the MoJ Efficiency Programme, in 2012. In counterpoint, it must be noted that the data from the Wood Green Crown Court Study, and the prior Woolwich pilot study, were available at that time. Therefore, it may be asked why the significant drop in requests for further forensic information was not the subject of further scrutiny, prior to the rollout of the scheme across England and Wales. Again, it must be concluded that this justification does not stand up to analysis.

Further, the FSS data from prior studies following the introduction of abbreviated (or 'staged') reports had demonstrated the ability to deliver significant efficiencies (in time and resources and economics), while retaining the means for legal practitioners to scrutinise the forensic evidence and test the case against the accused. Given that savings could therefore already be achieved, and the aims of the CrimPR satisfied, there is little justification for the CPS and MoJ thought it necessary to introduce a novel form of reporting which actively curtails the ability to scrutinise the evidence.

Further concerns have been raised over the utility, and legitimacy, of streamlined reporting. The scheme has not been placed on a statutory basis. Therefore, attempts to clothe the SFR scheme in law, and to signal legitimacy, have relied upon the selective incorporation of quotes from leading cases, alongside endorsements from high-status members of the legal profession. These have been incorporated into the supporting documentation and the report forms themselves. The earlier versions of the SFR1 form were notable for the inclusion of the following exhortatory, and cautionary, excerpts, taken from Appeal Court cases:

> *Balogun* v. *DPP* [2010] EWHC 799: Leveson LJ: 'For my part, I do not accept that the spirit or letter of the Criminal Procedure Rules is complied with by asserting that the Crown is put to "strict proof"'
>
> *R* v. *Chorley Justices* 2006 EWHC 1795. 'If a defendant refuses to identify what the issues are, one thing is clear: he can derive no advantage from that or seek, as appears to have happened in this case, to attempt an ambush at trial. The days of ambushing and taking last minute technical points are gone'.

These were accompanied by an extract from an open letter by Goldring, LJ, endorsing the SFR process:

> SFR has high-level, national support. It is supported by the country's Senior Presiding Judge, Lord Justice Goldring: 'In short, everything suggests that SFR can deliver significant benefits to the courts, prosecution and defence. Court time is saved. Unnecessary forensic work is avoided. The defence are better able to focus on the real issues and appropriately advise their clients'.[46]

These (*obiter*) statements are cited in order to imply that a duty of candid disclosure rests with the defence. Such a duty is indeed carried by the defence, in some instances. However, the CrimPR place a countervailing duty of candour on the prosecution and require both parties to work together to identify the real issues.[47]

R v. *Reed*[48] is also cited in supporting documentation, as authority for the assertion that both parties must identify areas of agreement, and disagreement,

[46]Letter from Goldring, L. J. (2012, August). Retrieved from http://www.cps.gov.uk/legal/assets/uploads/files/Senior%20Presiding%20Judge%20regarding%20SFR%20-%20August%202012.pdf

[47]Criminal Procedure Rules Part 3.

[48]*R* v. *Reed, Reed & Garmson* [2009] EWCA Crim LR 2698.

within experts' reports. The case concerns itself with the regulation of the conduct of parties with regard to expert witnesses, under Rule 33 (now Rule 19) of the CrimPR. However, it is questionable to what degree this case may be applied to the SFR1 reports, given that these are specifically not *expert* witness statements.

A further aspect of the *Reed* judgement may have a more direct bearing on the use of streamlined forensic reports. *Reed* states unequivocally that the real issue when dealing with DNA evidence is not 'whose DNA is it?' The issue is 'how did it get there?' Given the persuasiveness of this judgement, it is difficult to see how a form of reporting – which purposefully avoids discussion of forensic DNA evidence on the 'activity level' – can be of any utility when attempting to focus on 'the real issues'.

Further, the supporting documentation states that SFR1 may be used to provoke further discussion. However, it could be argued that a partial, and incremental, approach to the disclosure of evidence in criminal investigations runs contrary to both the Practice Directions and the 'spirit and letter' of the CrimPR alluded to in *Balogun*. Given the above, it is questionable to what extent the SFR scheme can be held to conform to the CrimPR.

As stated above, Part 3 of the CrimPR places a duty on the court to ensure that opinion evidence (whether disputed or not) is presented in the shortest, and clearest, way. The SFR guidance and supporting documentation both justify the brevity of streamlined reporting with reference to this rule. However, it is debateable to what degree brevity and clarity can be conflated. During field data collection many scientists, and legal practitioners, expressed the view that the 'evidence' communicated on the SFR1 form is, in fact, disproportionately brief and hence unclear. Indeed, excessive brevity may be especially problematic when dealing with scientific evidence, which is both relational and highly dependent on context. To require experts to jettison, context may be detrimental to the needs of witnesses, contrary to the CrimPR 3.2 (2)(a) and (b). Admittedly, SFR1 procedures may sidestep this duty, since it is not a scientist, but rather the (non-expert) compiler of the report, who is frequently called as witness. Again, it is difficult to see how this inefficient approach, which may obfuscate the real issues, can be reconciled with a requirement to candidly explore these issues (in compliance with both the spirit and the letter, of the CrimPR)

It may be argued that the SFR scheme is not only procedurally – but also conceptually – flawed. Attempts to justify the process rely on a series of logical fallacies, not least the use of circular reasoning:

> [The purpose of SFR Stage 1 is to] provide a stronger basis for Stage 2 forensic reporting through compliance with Criminal Procedure Rules ....[49]

[49]CPS. *Legal guidance on streamlined forensic reporting*. Retrieved from http://www.cps.gov.uk/legal/s_to_u/scientific_evidence/sfr_guidance_and_toolkit/sfr_guidance/sfr_q_and_a/index.html

> [The purpose of the scheme is to] reduce costs and delay associated with forensic evidence where such evidence adds no value to the administration of justice.[50]

> Not guilty files and contested cases are to be built according to real issues.[51]

> [SFR1 is intended to create an] improvement in the early guilty plea rate resulting in fewer cases coming to trial unnecessarily.[52]

> [SFR] is a two stage process of which the purpose is to deliver forensic evidence proportionate to the needs of the real issues in each case.[53]

The above examples share certain common assumptions: that the 'real issues' may be easily identified; that the procedural outputs – and the inferences derived from an incomplete, and non-probative, form of forensic analysis – are sufficient to determine guilt; and that the system is self-proving. It may even be argued that a degree of pre-judgement drives the SFR process. Indeed, the following extract, taken from the SFR Toolkit, appears to address the *ultimate probandum*.

> Where the forensic evidence *proves* the charged person's involvement in an offence, SFR 1 should always be included with the Initial Details of Prosecution Case (IDPC). (Emphasis added).[54]

Further, there are strong indications that the SFR scheme encourages streaming, rather than streamlining. Scientists' concerns over the 'triaging' of cases relate to wider issues regarding the relative autonomy of the forensic, and legal, fields. Previous commentators have tended to view law and forensic science as operating in discrete silos.[55] Research has therefore tended to concentrate on the negotiations

---

[50]CPS. *Legal guidance on streamlined forensic reporting*. Retrieved from http://www.cps.gov.uk/legal/s_to_u/scientific_evidence/sfr_guidance_and_toolkit/sfr_guidance/sfr_q_and_a/index.html

[51]Beckwith, J. (2014, September 23). *Digital forensics specialist group SFR*. Available on website of the Forensic Science Regulator.

[52]Ministry of Justice. (2012). Swift and sure justice: The government's plans for reform of the criminal justice system. Cm 8388. TSO, London, p. 34.

[53]CPS. *Legal guidance on streamlined forensic reporting*. Retrieved from http://www.cps.gov.uk/legal/s_to_u/scientific_evidence/sfr_guidance_and_toolkit/

[54]CPS. (2015). *Streamlined forensic reporting guidance and toolkit 6*. Retrieved from http://www.cps.gov.uk/legal/s_to_u/scientific_evidence/sfr_guidance_and_toolkit/

[55]See Kelty, S. F., Julian, R., & Ross, A. (2013). Dismantling the Justice Silos: Avoiding the pitfalls and reaping the benefits of information-sharing between forensic science, medicine and law. *Forensic Science International, 230*(1–3), 8–15.

between the two professions, the resulting allocation of epistemic responsibility, the performance of 'boundary work', or the temporary creation of 'hybrid sets'. Lawless and Williams, for example, have addressed the relationship between law and forensic science, exploring how these fields 'combine in a mutually constitutive relationship to (in)form a mode of production of scientific commodities purchased by the police in support of criminal justice objectives'.[56]

These approaches tend to exhibit a common belief that improved communication, and a shared understanding of the respective capabilities, and needs, of both forensic science and criminal justice, may enhance the co-production of knowledge. However, the streamlined reporting scheme does not appear to conform to the 'contest and communication' narrative. Rather, SFR signals an almost complete co-option of scientific processes by the CJS, the concomitant loss of interpretative forensic expertise, and the avoidance of the allocation of epistemic responsibility. It is argued that this instrumental approach to forensic reporting is a result of the disruption, and restructuring, of the forensic profession.

> We used to have a tripartite agreement between the forensic science provider – the FSS – and the police, and the CPS, and I think we've lost that link with CPS now. There's very little input. Instead of having this triangle where we're all talking to each other I feel like we're behind the police, and the police will then talk to the CPS. (Interview, Forensic Scientist 2, 2015)

> Younger trainees coming into the industry are getting training but that training is basic. They don't know what they don't know. That never gets rectified as they progress. So as checkers and peer-reviewers they also lack the appropriate skills. (Interview, Forensic Scientist 6, 2015)

> You have less experienced staff combined with pressures to do work quicker and a pressure from the police, and it leads to a factory-line approach just to get the results out. (Interview, Forensic Scientist 3, 2015)

As before, these observations can be explained with reference to the processes of economic rationalisation. However, a more nuanced understanding of economic rationality may now be required, in order to account for innovations such as SFR. Scholars of 'neo-liberalism', and those who chronicle its effects, have hitherto been content to base their analyses on a relatively fluid understanding of the concept: one which has been used across many domains, to many ends,

[56]Lawless, C. J., & Williams, R. (2010). Helping with inquiries or helping with profits? The trials and tribulations of a technology of forensic reasoning. *Social Studies of Science, 40*, 731–755.

and is frequently accompanied by 'considerable imprecision, confusion and controversy'.[57] Garland argues that processes of economic rationalisation,

> [...] lack a strict logic or tight conceptual structure. Rather, [they form] a ragbag of techniques, models, analogies and recipes for action that are loosely bound up together by their appeal to economic rationality.[58]

Lawless and Williams exhibit just such an approach in their explorations of the forensic science market.[59] It is postulated that this approach may now be of limited utility: it is no longer sufficient to view neo-liberalism as a mere 'ragbag of techniques'. Rather, it is possible to discern distinct patterns of development, which may appear contingent in emergent phases, but which are comparatively instrumental in later, developed stages. Thus, the effects of contemporary economic rationalisation may be significantly more thoroughgoing in comparison with those previously encountered and those studies of the forensic market which do not account for these changes may now be outdated.

Economic rationalisation has disrupted techno-social 'expert' networks, to be sure. However, the purpose of disruption has been to open the forensic field to reforms focused on the organisational roles, and professional identities, of the individual forensic experts who comprise these networks. Marketisation restructures organisations in a way which renders their boundaries porous, making processes more responsive to instrumental policies, but with the strategic goal of restructuring people.[60] Thus, productisation, triaging, and marketisation are merely examples of the adaptation, and reconstruction, of processes, conditions, and which serve as the necessary precursors to the readjustment of roles, attitudes and behaviours.

Lawfulness of SFR under the European Union (EU) Directives

Notwithstanding the above, the most serious criticism of the SFR scheme is its fundamental divergence from the overarching set of EU directives designed to ensure equality of arms in criminal proceedings. Consequent to its departure from the European Union, the UK opted to retain a number of EU primary

---

[57]Brenner, N., Peck, J., & Theodore, N. (2010). After neoliberalization. *Globalizations, 7*(3), 327–345.

[58]Garland, D. (2002). *The culture of control* (p. 190). OUP: Oxford.

[59]Lawless, C. (2010). *A curious reconstruction? The shaping of 'marketized' forensic science*. CARR Discussion Paper 63; Lawless, C. J., & Williams, R. (2010). *Helping with inquiries or helping with profits? The trials and tribulations of a technology of forensic reasoning. Social Studies of Science, 40*, 731–755.

[60]See Foucault, M. (1997). *Society must be defended: Lectures at the Collège de France, 1975–1976* (pp. 243–244). New York, NY: St. Martin's Press.

and secondary legislative instruments pertaining to the CJS. The latter category consists of a set of directives conferring criminal justice rights upon suspects, the accused, children, and victims of crime. For the purposes of the present discussion, the EU directives relating to the rights of suspects and the accused[61] are of central importance, most notably Directive 2012/13/EU on the Right to Information.

The legal foundation for these directives can be traced to Article 82(2) of the Treaty on the Functioning of the European Union,[62] through which the rights conferred within the directives attain a dual character, safeguarding the criminal procedural rights of individuals while facilitating mutual recognition of judgements and judicial decisions, and facilitating cross-border police and judicial cooperation[63] (thus allowing for a comparative analysis). It is important to note that Article 82(2) provisions establish a set of minimal rules. Thus, while it becomes unlawful for Member States to introduce procedures which fall below the minimum standards enshrined under Article 82, it is envisaged that states may maintain or introduce higher levels of protection for individuals.

Article 288(3) treaty on the functioning of the European Union (TFEU) provides that directives are binding upon member states as to the result to be achieved. However, unlike EU Regulations which have direct effect upon Member States absent of any need for domestic implementation, EU directives are implemented by states through domestic legislation, the choice of form and method being a matter for the member state itself. Directives thus possess a degree of flexibility as compared with regulations. Nonetheless, an overarching obligation rests upon the Member State to confer the specific remedy upon individual citizens before the national courts. The comparatively discretionary nature of directives entails that the least burdensome obligation should be imposed.[64] Nonetheless, Member States are bound to ensure full application of the directive, to enable individuals to seek recourse in the courts where the domestic measures misapply the Directive or fall short of achieving the envisaged result.[65]

The rights conveyed under Directive 2012 are multifaced[66] and apply from the time an individual is made aware that they are suspected until a final determination.

---

[61]Directive 2010/64/EU on the right to interpretation and translation in criminal proceedings OJ L 280/1 (20 October 2010); Directive 2012/13/EU on the right to information in criminal proceedings OJ L 142/1 (22 May 2012).

[62]TFEU.

[63]Legal basis expands on Article 82.

[64]Joined cases C-6/90 and C-9/90 *Francovich and Bonifacti* v. *Italy* [1991] ECR I-5403 at [19].

[65]*See* Case C-62/00 *Marks & Spencer* v. *Commr of Customs and Excise* [2002] ECR I-6325 at [27].

[66]*See* Pivaty, A., & Soo, A. (2019). Article 7 of the Directive 2012/13/EU on the right to information in criminal proceedings: A missed opportunity to ensure equality of arms in pre-trial proceedings? *European Journal of Crime, Criminal Law and Criminal Justice*, *27*(2), 126–154; Soo, A., & Pivaty, A. (2019). Access to the case materials in pre-trial stages: Critical questions of Article 7 of Directive 2012/13/EU on the right to information in criminal proceedings. *Eucrim: The European Criminal Law Asso-*

Individuals must promptly be provided with information about procedural rights orally or in writing. Furthermore, they must be promptly provided with a letter detailing their rights in simple and accessible language. Crucially, they must be provided with information about the offence that they are suspected of committing in such detail as is necessary to safeguard fairness of the proceedings and for the proper exercise of the rights of defence. Crucially, the accused must be informed of reasons for arrest and/or detention and given free access to any essential documents. Finally, they must have free access to material evidence in due time to allow the effective exercise of defence.

Given the above, it is difficult to conclude that the SFR scheme complies with the overarching EU directives, given the attempt to curtail vital forensic contextual and technical information, and in answer to the anticipated argument that this is not withholding information, since the information does not exist until the full evaluation is carried out, it may be answered that this is a constructive default. This is demonstrably so in the case of SFR involving DNA. Since the prosecution must serve all of the evidence on which they intend to rely,[67] and courts have held that it is sufficient to find a case to answer on the basis of a strong DNA match alone, this entails that a suspect may be brought to court on the basis of a DNA source attribution conveyed on an SFR. However, in a series of cases, the Court of Appeal has begun to take cognisance of the role that DNA transfer and persistence may play in matters of evidence and of the necessity of robust activity-level attributions. Given that the court has now found that, in some circumstances, a DNA attribution may be an insufficient basis on which to found a case to answer, it may be concluded that the SFR falls further beyond the bounds of the EU directives intended to safeguard equality of arms.[68]

---

ciations' Forum, *1*, 60–65; Tsagkalidis, A. (2017). Directive 2012/13/EU on the right to information in criminal proceedings. Speech to ERA Seminar, Kraków, March 2; Arangüena Fanego, C., & Rodríguez-Medel Nieto, C. (2021). Directive 2012/13/EU, concerning the right to information in criminal proceedings. Good practices for its application. In *Procedural safeguards for suspects and accused persons in criminal proceedings* (pp. 17–37). Cham: Springer.

[67]*See, for example,* the UK Government Health and Safety Executive guidance in respect of criminal breaches of the Health and Safety at Work Act 1974.

> You should therefore serve all the evidence upon which you intend to rely, and which is available at the time of the first hearing, as part of the initial details. This would include witness statements, experts reports, copies of documentary exhibits and records of defendants interviews under PACE. (www.hse.gov.uk/enforce/enforcementguide/pretrial/procedure-advance.htm)

[68]*See,* Richmond, K. (2017, August 1). DNA profiling: Transfer and persistence: *R* v. *Tsekiri* [2017] EWCA Crim 40. *Journal of Criminal Law, 81*(4), 275–277; Richmond, K. (2019). DNA evidence alone as a case to answer: Bech, *R* v. *Court of Appeal* [2018] EWCA Crim 448. *The Journal of Criminal Law, 83*(6), 503–507; *R* v. *Jones (William Francis)* [2020] EWCA Crim 1021 (03 Aug 2020).

Conclusion

The data demonstrate that a strong link exists between the introduction of measures of economic rationalisation and the reduction of thinking time – and contextual investigation – on the part of the scientist. These limitations have been aggravated by a tendency to triage cases and by systematic attempts to avoid activity-level DNA analyses. The study exposes significant problems, related to de-skilling within the forensic-scientific field and a loss of expert evaluation with regard to the construction of DNA-profiling evidence. The study supports the view that the ultimate goal of the economic rationalisation of forensic expertise has been to disrupt, and to reform, the attitudes, and expectations, of forensic science providers and to reconstruct forensic identities in conformation with economic goals aligned to the requirements of the investigatory authorities. This disruption of techno-social expert networks has largely been achieved through the instrumental use of novel forms of forensic reporting procedures, of which SFR is the most extreme example. The study also demonstrates that such modes of reporting carry the potential to limit the quality, and content, of expert scientific opinion and may ultimately affect the court's ability to arrive at sound determinations on questions of fact, most seriously with regard to the failure of the scheme to conform to the necessary EU directives.

Chapter 7

Objectivity – 'The View from Nowhere'

Chapter Summary

The previous chapter focussed on attenuated forms of forensic reporting, introduced to the criminal justice system through the Criminal Justice System (CJS) Efficiency Programme. It discussed the introduction of streamlined forensic reporting (SFR) and the restructuring of deoxyribonucleic acid (DNA)-profiling expertise within the marketised forensic science sector. Analysis of the data demonstrated the extent to which the introduction of attenuated forms of expert discourse has been perceived as impinging upon the ability of the DNA-profiling experts to provide a contextual evaluation of the evidence, and of the potential for these attenuated forms of forensic discourse to contribute miscarriages of justice.

The third, and final, discursive chapter in this section follows a similar trajectory. However, the focus of this chapter is on the proliferating array of regulatory interventions, which now structure the processes of marketised forensic science provision in England and Wales. These interventions are indicative of the

> [...] significant (and ever-expanding) space that law has come to occupy. The result is that law is often seen as a 'thicket': a complex, fragmented, and cumulative collection of instruments, institutions, and mechanisms that requires ever greater knowledge, time and capital to navigate, thereby imposing disproportionate costs on actors, and requiring inordinate amounts of effort to move through.[1]

The marketised system of forensic knowledge production in England and Wales is a paradigmatic example of this form of legal expansion. The sector is notable for the significant degree of internal, and external, regulation, to which forensic science providers (FSPs) have become subject, to the extent that the

[1]Cloatre, E., & Pickersgill, M. (Eds). (2015). *Knowledge, technology, and the law* (p. 121). London: Routledge.

Marketisation and Forensic Science Provision in England and Wales, 129–146

Published under exclusive licence by Emerald Publishing Limited
doi:10.1108/978-1-83909-123-020221007

production of forensic-scientific truth claims, for legal consumption, is now structured around a proliferating array of disciplinary practices, including inspection, validation, quality control, batch testing, accreditation, monitoring, auditing, certification, sampling, classification, guidance, and the publication of regulatory protocols. As will be shown below, these diverse interventions converge upon the process of DNA profiling and support Laurie and Harman's assertion that the introduction of regulation imposes disproportionate costs onto individual FSPs.

The Forensic Science Regulator (FSR)

In the field of forensic science, these regulatory incursions are most closely associated with the work of the FSR.[2] The appearance of the regulator could be seen as a response to the development of diverging approaches, and variations in opinion, within a developing forensics market, and the perceived potential for those variances to affect the status, and probity, of DNA-profiling evidence. The introduction of a system of external regulation could thus be viewed as a means to retain market – and public – confidence through external validation.

The office of the UK FSR was created by the Home Office in 2008. As an independent regulatory body, the FSR was charged with the identification of quality standards, the supervision – and accreditation – of forensic laboratories (in compliance with ISO/IEC 17025 *General requirements for the competence of testing and calibration laboratories*), the determination of procedures for the validation of new technologies, development and maintenance of standards, and the management of complaints. The regulator's powers are non-statutory,[3] despite being sponsored by the Home Office, and are limited to England and Wales (although the forensic science services of Scotland, and Northern Ireland, voluntarily comply with her recommendations). The in-house laboratories of the 43 individual police forces of England and Wales operate outwith the ambit of the Office for the Forensic Regulator (OFR) regulatory regime and do not currently require accreditation.

The regulator's role has evolved, with each of the two FSRs thus far, focusing on different aspects of market regulation. During its earliest phase, the work of the FSR was largely reactive. Thus, the regulator was tasked with addressing concerns over poor laboratory procedures, which had led to notable instances of contamination[4]; the perception of an inadequate scientific basis

[2]See, generally, McCartney, C., & Amoako, E. (2018). *The UK forensic science regulator: A model for forensic science regulation? Georgia State University Law Review, 34*(4), 945–981.

[3]The Forensic Regulator Bill 2017–19, introduced to Parliament on 8 March 2018, attempts to place the Office of the FSR on a statutory footing.

[4]See, for example, *Report into the circumstances of a complaint received from the Greater Manchester Police on 7 March 2012 regarding DNA evidence provided by LGC Forensics*. FSR, 17 September 2012, Mr Andrew Rennison, MSc.

for the interpretation of low copy number DNA (LCN-DNA)[5]; and the problems associated with forensic evaluation and cognitive bias.[6] In comparison, the incumbent FSR has adopted a relatively proactive stance, propelled by the need to 'establish a baseline of quality across the forensic science market'.[7] Nonetheless, the regulator's underlying duties are not appreciably different. Primarily, the FSR is tasked with overseeing a number of regulatory protocols, as discussed below.

FSR's Regulatory Responsibilities: International Standards

The following discussion focusses on the regulator's main responsibilities. The regulator is responsible for ensuring that all accredited FSPs conform to certain international standards, in particular ISO/IEC 17020 and ISO/IEC 17025. These are United Kingdom Accreditation Service (UKAS) accreditations, which focus on the quality assurance of forensic laboratory analysis. ISO 17025 lays out the general requirements for the competence of testing and calibration laboratories and is referable to a wide range of forensic analyses, examinations, and testing activities. Accredited elements include continuity of evidence, management of case files, and storage of exhibits. In addition, accreditation determines the competence of staff, the validity and suitability of methods, the appropriateness of equipment and facilities, and ongoing quality assurance through internal quality control. A further standard, ISO/IEC 17043, introduces requirements for the competence of providers of proficiency testing schemes. It focuses on understanding and applying standard accreditation processes.

Accreditation

ISO 17025 is an essential component for FSR accreditation and is therefore a standard requirement in relation to specified functions and processes. First, any FSP processing material samples for loading onto the National DNA Database (NDNAD) must be accredited. This falls within a broader requirement, under the EU Council Framework Decision 2009/905/JHA, of 30 November 2009, which relates to the accreditation of forensic service providers carrying out laboratory activities. This decision requires FSPs to hold ISO 17025 accreditation in respect of all laboratories carrying out DNA profiling and fingerprint enhancement. It was agreed that this requirement would apply to all in-house police laboratories carrying out the specified activities, with staged implementation targets between

---

[5]Office of the Forensic Science Regulator. (2008). *Review of the science of low template DNA analysis*. London: The Home Office; Office of the Forensic Science Regulator. (2016). *Crime scene DNA: Anti-contamination guidance*. London: The Home Office.

[6]Office of the Forensic Science Regulator. (2015). *Cognitive bias effects relevant to forensic science investigations*. London: The Home Office.

[7]Office of the Forensic Science Regulator. (2016). *Regulator's codes of practice and conduct*. London: The Home Office.

2013 and 2015 (however – the UK having decided to opt out of European Union (EU) criminal justice measures – the legal obligation to comply with the framework decision is in the process of being removed).

Professional and Commercial Standards

The regulator has worked with a wide range of institutional actors, professional, and representative bodies, including the Royal College of Pathologists, the Institute for Archaeologists, the Royal Anthropological Institute, the UK and Ireland Association of Forensic Toxicologists, the Society of Chiropodists and Podiatrists, the Forensic Science Society, and the Fingerprint Society, in order to produce professional standards for those disciplines. The regulator has also worked with the British Standards Institute to develop a standard (PAS 377) for manufacturers producing consumables (DNA kits, swabs, etc.) used in the collection, preservation, and processing of forensic material.

Forensics Procurement Framework

Individual police forces, and consortia, agree contracts for provision of forensic services on a regional basis, as part of the Home Office's forensic procurement framework. Under the forensic framework, contracts require providers to hold ISO 17025 accreditation and to meet other quality requirements. This includes compliance with the regulator's Code of Practice and compliance with investigations by the regulator. Failure to meet these requirements, attracts contractually imposed penalties and may lead to the removal of the provider from the framework. The overwhelming majority of laboratories are part of the procurement framework. However, it is important to note that a great deal of forensic provision takes place out with the laboratory (this includes strategy-setting, interpretation, and evaluation). Further, the procurement framework encompasses only those services which are externally procured by law enforcement agencies (Police Forces, HM Revenue and Customs, National Crime Agency). Thus, the application of the procurement framework is partial and uneven.

Potentially serious breaches of quality, on the part of a provider, may be investigated by the regulator, whose task is to make recommendations to that provider, in order to ensure that the error is not repeated. The regulator may also investigate issues referred to her by relevant authorities. This includes ministers and the judiciary. The following section discusses the regulatory guidance issued by the FSR – guidance which serves to structure the process of DNA profiling.

Forensic Regulator's Code of Practice and Conduct and Investigation of Complaints

The FSR has published a non-statutory Code of Practice and Conduct, which applies to all agents (from FSPs to sole practitioners) tasked with providing forensic services to the CJS. The Code is non-statutory. However, 'whilst the standards are not yet mandated by law, compliance is not optional'.[8] This is due to the fact that 'all individuals reporting scientific, or technical, work to the courts (whether called by prosecution or defence) must now declare compliance with this Code of Conduct'.[9] The Code of Practice situates the requirements of ISO 17025 and gives direction on topics such as validation, contamination control, and information security. It also sets out the standards required for any organisation, or individual, working with forensic evidence, alongside detail on standards pertaining to the use of 'occasional experts', and on infrequently used methods, stipulating that – in those circumstances where agents deviate, or depart, from the requirements of the Code – they are obligated to issue the court with a 'statement of non-compliance'.[10]

The FSR stated, in response to questioning, that this body of regulatory protocols together 'serve to systematically organise a culture of competence and quality assurance'.[11] The central concept was 'quality': quality, it was asserted, goes beyond accreditation. Accreditation, in the FSR's view, is merely a baseline, onto which is added quality. Further, that 'accreditation is just an extension of scientific method'.[12] These broad statements require further scrutiny, in light of the recent development of the regulator's accreditation process and the potential for these incursions to shape the process of DNA profiling.

Quality Assurance and *Daubert* Criteria

The FSR's assertion – that quality assurance is an extension of scientific method – requires further scrutiny, as it sits uneasily within the body of Mertonian norms that form the dimensions of the scientific method. However, it is possible to argue that her assertion is correct (though the route from scientific norm to regulatory protocol is a circuitous one), and it would appear that the FSR takes the view that this, 'regulatory' form of forensic evaluation, comprises an evolved, and enhanced, form of forensic evaluation, as compared to a standard model of a forensic evaluation grounded in scientific method.

The starting point for an elaboration, and critique, of the FSR's position, is the Law Commission Report, *Expert Evidence in Criminal Proceedings in England and Wales*,[13] which, in 2011, recommended the introduction of a statutory

[8]Office of the Forensic Science Regulator. (2016). *Regulator's codes of practice and conduct*. London: The Home Office.

[9]Office of the Forensic Science Regulator. (2016). *Regulator's codes of practice and conduct*. London: The Home Office.

[10]Office of the Forensic Science Regulator. (2016). *Regulator's codes of practice and conduct*. London: The Home Office.

[11]*Interview with Forensic Science Regulator*. (2018, March). London: The Home Office.

[12]*Interview with Forensic Science Regulator*. (2018, March). London: The Home Office.

[13]Law Commission. (2011, March 21). *Expert evidence in criminal proceedings in England and Wales*. Law Commission No. 325.

'reliability' test for determining the admissibility of expert evidence. The commission recommended that admissibility be assessed by way of an enhanced *Daubert* test, of the sort encountered in the United States (see below).

While, in the various jurisdictions of the UK, the role of the expert witness is framed fairly broadly, in terms of the expert's ability to assist the court (and such experts may include scientists, individuals with specialist knowledge, and those possessing particular skills),[14] the criteria for admissibility of expert opinion evidence in many American states now differs greatly.

The US Courts used to uniformly follow the Frye standard (*Frye* v. *United States*, 293 F 1013 (D.C. Cir. 1923), which holds that expert testimony based upon scientific techniques is only admissible when these techniques have become generally accepted within the relevant scientific community. However, following the judgement in *Daubert* v. *Merrel Dow Pharmaceuticals* 509 U.S. 579 (1994), the Supreme Court amended Rule 702 (regarding the use of expert testimony) to introduce an admissibility test. Within the preponderance of US states, all expert opinion evidence must now meet the Daubert standard, measured against five criteria. *Daubert* requires that, in judging the admissibility of expert evidence, the court must look to the underlying methods used, in order to assess:

- whether a method can or has been tested;
- the known or potential rate of error;
- whether the methods have been subjected to peer review;
- whether there are standards controlling the technique's operation; and
- the general acceptance of the method within the relevant community.

Thus, the judge exercises a gatekeeping function and must now ensure that all expert testimony 'proceeds from scientific knowledge'. Indeed, the *Daubert* criteria may be viewed as a partial incorporation of Mertonian norms, as understood from a regulatory perspective. However, the introduction of the *Daubert* test caused a great many problems for forensic practitioners – particularly friction ridge examiners – whose methods were not consonant with scientific method. Therefore, in 1999, the test was extended to include methods based upon 'technical' knowledge (see *Kumho Tire Co.* v. *Carmichael*, 526 U.S. 137 (1999)).

Returning to the Law Commission's proposals, the enhanced *Daubert* admissibility test recommended in 2011 failed to make provision for the forms of technological, or 'non-scientific', evidence admitted in *Kumho*. And, after consideration, the Law Commission's recommendation was rejected by the government, on economic grounds.[15] Therefore, the common-law rules on admissibility of expert evidence subsist. However, rejection did not spell the end for the 'enhanced *Daubert* test'.

[14] *R* v. *Turner* [1975] 1 All ER 70.

[15] The government's response to the Law Commission report: *Expert evidence in criminal proceedings in England and Wales,* Law Commission No. 325, 21 November 2013.

In 2014, the Lord Chief Justice (Lord Thomas) issued a Practice Direction (effective from 7 October 2014), containing the self-same enhanced admissibility test. Thus, a test 'recognisably derived from Daubert', was 'introduced to the courts by [a] somewhat unusual mechanism'.[16]

The Criminal Practice Directions were in turn amended. Direction 19A3 now acknowledges that the Law Commission declined to introduce an enhanced Daubert test.[17] It states, however, that nothing prevents the courts from assessing admissibility using Daubert criteria. It encourages the courts to do so. However, it goes further, stating that 19A4 lists matters with which an experts report must deal in order for such an assessment to be carried out (see 19A4(h) below).

> (h) [an expert report] include such information as the court may need to decide whether the expert's opinion is sufficiently reliable to be admissible as evidence;

This may appear unproblematic. Nonetheless, the attempts to ground this procedural innovation in domestic legal precedent are arguably misconceived. The underlying guidance quotes a short passage from *Dlugosz*,[18] stating that the court must ensure 'that there is a sufficiently reliable *scientific* basis for the evidence to be admitted'. However, it may be argued that this obiter statement has been taken out of context. The discussion in *Dlugosz* centred on the evaluation of mixed DNA profiles, a singularly 'scientific' evidence type. It is far from clear that the court intended this requirement to apply more widely to all forms of forensic evidence.

Further, that inclusion from *Dlugosz* is itself founded upon the judgement in *Reed*,[19] paragraphs 111–112, which specifically refers to appropriate admissibility criteria, to be used when dealing with 'scientific evidence *of a scientific nature* ...'.[20] It may be readily inferred, therefore, that there are other forms of *non-scientific* evidence, and that these non-scientific evidence types may be judged by other criteria. This distinction has become lost along the way. Forensic practitioners are now faced with the problem of negotiating a common-law, practice-based, set of admissibility criteria, which require that all evidence – scientific, technical, or otherwise – are based upon reliable *scientific* methods (as laid out in *Daubert*).

To return to Rule 19.4, this states that a report 'must include such information as the court may need to decide whether the expert's opinion is sufficiently reliable to be admissible as evidence'. Therefore, in light of the directions above, it may

---

[16]See Ward, T. (2015, May 29). An English Daubert? Law, forensic science and epistemic deference. *The Journal of Philosophy, Science & Law: Daubert Special Issue, 15*, 26–36, at p. 26.

[17]*Criminal Practice Directions 2015* [2015] All ER (D) 134 (Sep)|CL&J at 19A3.

[18]*R* v. *Dlugosz* [2013] EWCA Crim 2.

[19]*R* v. *Reed, Reed & Garmson* [2009] EWCA Crim LR 2698.

[20]*R* v. *Reed, Reed & Garmson* [2009] EWCA Crim LR 2698. Emphasis added.

be stated that forensic reports must contain substantive evidence of the conformity of the methods used within the report with scientific method vis-à-vis the enhanced *Daubert* criteria. It may be further inferred that forensic reports must contain substantive evidence of the conformity of the evaluative report itself with scientific method with regard to the enhanced *Daubert* criteria.[21] Thus, the introduction of this unorthodox 'enhanced *Daubert*' test (following its rejection by the government) would appear to create a significant hurdle for forensic practitioners who remain unaccredited or who exercise 'non-scientific' forensic techniques. What is more, the legal requirements for admissibility imposed through the Criminal Practice Rules (and associated Directions) are met – within the forensic sector – by a regulatory stipulation on the part of the FSR.

Regulation and the 'Enhanced *Daubert*' Criteria

Alongside the requirements laid out in the Criminal Practice Rules, and associated Directions, the FSR 'suggests', in her guidance, that the courts determine the issue of whether expert evidence is 'sufficiently reliable' with reference to the presence, or otherwise, of accreditation. Further, that all methods – standard, or non-standard – be validated, and that all validations (whether in reports or as the basis of expert opinion) 'consider' 19A5 of the Criminal Practice Directions. As seen above, these Practice Directions are based on the 'enhanced *Daubert*' criteria. Therefore, due to the Regulator's stipulations, the validity, hence soundness, of expert methods is now directly referable to 'enhanced *Daubert*' criteria. And validation is inextricably linked to accreditation, insofar as accreditation is itself granted on the ability of the FSP to demonstrate the validity of their methods.

These regulatory incursions are couched in terms of 'suggestions' and 'considerations'. However, departures from these 'suggestions' may have far-reaching legal consequences. Since 2016, any forensic expert who departs from the above accreditation, and validation, requirements must now make a Declaration of Non-Compliance to the courts.[22] While the declaration has no immediate legal effect, such a declaration must – it has been suggested – be viewed negatively by the court, when judging the question of admissibility. It may be argued that this is deliberate. Indeed, it aligns with the Regulator's statement, that her task involves establishing a 'baseline of quality across the forensic sector', imposed through the 'double-check' of ISO 17025 compliance, and 'case by case scrutiny through the Criminal Procedure Rules' (interview with FSR, 2017).

---

[21]The evaluation of DNA profiling is not currently subject to a standardisation protocol. However, the FSR Annual Report (19 January 2018), paragraph 1.2, page 16, states that the development of an evaluative interpretation standard is one of the Regulator's highest priorities.

[22]Office of the Forensic Science Regulator. (2016). *Regulator's codes of practice and conduct*. London: The Home Office.

Taking the above into account, it has been demonstrated that – to the extent that accreditation requires validation in line with (enhanced) *Daubert* criteria – the FSR's statement – that accreditation is an extension of scientific method – has procedural validity. Nonetheless, it may also be argued, in counterpoint, that the Regulator's reach has only been extended by means of a somewhat abstruse series of categorisations, regulatory incursions, and administrative linkages. The next section considers the implications of these regulatory incursions, for marketised forms of DNA profiling in England and Wales. It also offers a theoretical analysis of these regulatory incursions.

Accreditation and DNA Profiling

It may be argued that the requirement to comply with *Daubert* criteria, through validation and accreditation, is merely an iteration – albeit an administrative, and procedural, one – of the grounding of forensic science in scientific method. In counterpoint, it may be posited that, this being the case, the regulatory stipulations nevertheless articulate an etiolated conception of scientific method: a conception viewed through the lens of institutional logic.

Further, when applied to the work of forensic DNA profilers, it may be argued that these requirements are aligned with – and support – the forms of high-volume, low-expertise, forensic DNA reporting that were encountered in the preceding two chapters (e.g. SFR). These forms of reporting are based upon well-established scientific methods, to be sure. However, the method of DNA profiling – at least in its routine forms – has now largely been reduced to a robotised process. It may be posited that this no longer represents an ongoing instantiation of scientific method, having been reduced to a technological process, of the sort envisaged by *Kumho,* but unaccounted for in the 'enhanced *Daubert*' schema. It is further posited that it is actually the evaluative element of DNA profiling which lies at the heart of the scientific reporting process – and it is this articulation of scientific method which is palpably missing from non-expert forms of reporting, such as SFR. Further, it is notable that the evaluative component of DNA profiling falls outwith the ambit of the accreditation process. This is a crucial omission, which will form the focus of discussion in the following section.

DNA Profiling and the Declaration of 'Non-compliance'

As stated above, the Regulator's Codes of Practice and Conduct allows for atypical analyses, 'innovative, or rarely-used methods'.[23] However, the DNA-profiling scientist who uses methods which have not been specifically validated, and brought within the regulator's Code of Conduct and Practice, must – when acting as an expert witness – make a Declaration of Non-Compliance to the court. When challenged with regard to the requirement for expert witnesses to make a

[23]Office of the Forensic Science Regulator. (2021). *Regulator's codes of practice and conduct*. London: The Home Office.

Declaration of Non-Compliance when using innovative methods (on the grounds that this prevented DNA profilers from making contextual, and holistic, analyses, from adapting or solving new challenges), the FSR robustly defended the current system, stating that:

> accreditation doesn't stifle creativity when implemented within a culture of continuous improvement.

However, this was contradicted by responses from forensic practitioners, of which the following was typical:

> ISO 17025 might show that sound structures are in place but it doesn't solve cases. That comes down to strategy.

The FSR went on to stress the central importance of 'quality': quality, it was suggested, goes beyond accreditation. The latter serving only as a baseline, onto which is added the former. In respect of DNA profilers, the regulator further stated that quality could be derived from a combination of factors: the ideal forensic actor should have 'proper documentation, and be well-trained professionals'.[24]

In counterpoint, the researcher challenged that quality is actually derived from the ability of a forensic scientist to solve problems using creativity, adaptability, and innovation, in order to utilise contextual information drawn from a palette of forensic techniques (as well as exercising core skills). It is debateable to what extent the Declaration of Non-Compliance facilitates the task of 'de-convoluting' mixed DNA samples (now frequently encountered). Or the extent to which a constrained approach can facilitate the type of high-quality, holistic analysis of the sort championed by Forensic Science Northern Ireland (FSNI).

The current framework does not adequately engage with these phenomena, and – in reality – these attributes are rendered null by the accreditation process. The regulator concedes that the current framework privileges DNA profilers working conducting high-volume analyses. Also that these forensic 'trainees' do possess neither an innovative mind-set nor the ability to design validation experiments. It may be posited that they are actively prevented from doing so by the accreditation requirements. Further, it may be posited that these forms of reporting (often carried out by police administrators, marked by quoting, and beset by case fragmentation) are now mere technological processes, in contrast to the high-level evaluations and contextually rich interpretations. Which are, in reality, more consonant with scientific method.

We might therefore discern two models of forensic DNA profiling provision: one characterised by an autonomous scientific evaluation, which retains the ability to link DNA-profiling evidence to other forms of non-expert evidence. Another, characterised by trainee following rigid standard operating procedures, aligned with the requirements of accreditation. Paradoxically, the regulatory

---

[24] *Interview with Forensic Science Regulator*. (2018, March). London: The Home Office.

model therefore allows trainees – many of whom may not have a scientific background – to facilitate technological processes grounded (or at least superficially) in scientific method, while constraining the sort of contextually driven, genuinely scientific enquiry which is grounded in Mertonian norms (and expressed in the enhanced *Daubert* criteria).

Further, to the extent that any deviation from the regulatory, to the autonomous, model, may necessitate the issuing of a Declaration of Non-Compliance, and insofar as this Declaration may be used by the court to judge the reliability of evidence, it may be posited that a form of 'regulatory objectivity' has usurped the function of the trier-of-fact and displaced a model of autonomous scientific evaluation. The phenomenon, and theory, of regulatory objectivity will be discussed further below.

Regulatory Objectivity

The attempts, on the part of the FSR, to create an unbroken chain of regulatory accreditation from crime scene to courtroom have ushered in a model of regulatory forensic provision, which has displaced the subsisting model of scientific objectivity.[25] This reconfiguration demonstrates the tendency for governments to attempt to disperse power by reshaping public services in the image of the market. Such a reconfiguration entails a different relationship between the marketised services and central government that is indirectly administrative. This ability – to 'govern at a distance' – is a characteristic feature of economic rationality, achieved by subjecting 'an ever-expanding array of spheres of activity to inspection (or self-inspection), audit, and certification'.[26] Thus, governing at a distance is associated with governing through standards.

---

[25]See Cambrosio, A., Keating, P., Schlich, T., & Weisz, G. (2006). Regulatory objectivity and the generation and management of evidence in medicine. *Social Science and Medicine, 63,* 189–199. See also M'Charek, A. (2006). Technologies of population: Forensic DNA testing practices and the making of differences and similarities. *Configurations, 8*, 121–158; M'Charek, A., Hagendijk, R., & de Vries, W. (2013). Equal before the law: On the machinery of sameness in forensic DNA practice. *Science, Technology, Human Values, 38*, 542; Stephens, N., Atkinson, P., & Glasner, P. (2011). Documenting the doable and doing the documented: Bridging strategies at the UK stem cell bank. *Social Studies of Science, 41*, 791; Jordan, K., & Lynch, M. (1998). The dissemination, standardisation and routinisation of a molecular biological technique. *Social Studies of Science, 28*, 773; Jasanoff, S. (1995). Procedural choices in regulatory science. *Technology in Society, 17*(3), 279–293; Myles, L. (2010). *Quality assured science: Managerialism in forensic biology. Science, Technology and Human Values, 35*, 283; Porter, T. M. (1992). Quantification and the accounting ideal in science. *Social Studies of Science, 22*, 833; Moreira, T., May, C., & Bond, J. (2009). Regulatory objectivity in action: Mild cognitive impairment and the collective production of uncertainty. *Social Studies of Science, 35*(9), 665–690.

[26]Gibbon, P., & Henrikson, L. F. (2012). A standard fit for neoliberalism. *Comparative Studies in Society and History*, *54*(2), 275–307, p. 275.

In the foregoing sections, it has been argued that two models of forensic investigation, and evaluation, can be discerned. The first, a holistic, and adaptive, form of investigation, which is referable to both scientific method and an underlying set of (broadly Mertonian) norms, as exemplified broadly by the analysis of DNA-profiling evidence in FSNI and by certain, more extensive, iterations within the forensics market in England and Wales. The latter comprises a comparatively more mechanistic form of investigation, procedurally determined, and limited to a set of regulatory protocols and standard operating procedures. However, while the parent organisation may possess accreditation, its methods validated, and its protocols aligned to regulatory imperatives, the DNA-profiling process is often carried out by trainees who do not possess a background in science and is characterised by a lack of evaluation and interpretation. Indeed, it should be reiterated that evaluation and interpretation – while exemplifying the scientific method – fall outwith the regulatory ambit.

Nonetheless, it might be argued that the differences in approach are merely reflective of variations in laboratory culture, rather than being indicative of deeper structural dissimilarities. Participant's responses did indicate the presence of site-by-site variations, attributable to differences in 'laboratory culture':

> Individual labs will develop their own culture and that may affect the strength they tend to place on results. You can get a reputation for interpreting the evidence 'strongly'. That applies within FSPs to individual labs and scientists.
>
> People coming in would bring different practices, so you do get site-by-site variation.
>
> There are very set guidelines when 'calling the profile' but evaluation is more mentored. When it comes to interpretation that can be influenced by senior staff. (Interviews with Tier 1 and Tier 2 forensic biologists: April–June 2015)

The above testimony from forensic biologists illustrates the propensity for laboratory culture to influence the construction of DNA-profiling evidence. However, it is argued that these variations occur in the context of micro-level interactions, and that there is no evidence that site-by-site variation structures, to any appreciable degree, the meso-level organisation of DNA profiling, nor macro-level governance structures, which retain an orientation towards the normative model discussed above.

The introduction of just such a system, to the forensic sector, has not been achieved without criticism. Indeed, recent comment, emanating from the legal sector, has characterised the Regulator's efforts as constructing a mere 'administrative paper trail'.[27] Further, as demonstrated above, the introduction of

---

[27] *House of Commons Science and Technology Committee: Forensic science.* Second Report of Session 2013–14, Volume I.

regulatory practices has also served to obscure the agency, and expertise, of DNA profilers, who must develop 'bridging strategies' in order to reconcile localised practices, and tacit knowledge, with externally imposed standards.[28]

Discussions of standardisation owe much to Foucault's theory of governmentality, with its ability to unearth the histories of the mundane techniques through which ideas materialise. The object of analysis for students of governmentality was the 'dominant strategic function' played by this assemblage of technical devices, and the ability to create an 'economy of power'[29] from 'a dec of more or less distinct practices, forms of knowledge, institutions and techniques'.[30]

Expertise is central to the reconfiguration of the 'economy of power', since the ability to govern through standardised performance measures requires the mobilisation of the professional disciplines of accounting, auditing, and quality management. These techniques allowed their proponents to evaluate existing arrangements in the public sector through comparisons with idealised private firms, using standardised forms of calculation and monitoring. Through mobile technologies, such as auditing, dispersed sites were subjected to measurement and comparison, just as organisations and subjects were reconfigured to respond to quantitative results and incentives.[31]

The re-purposing of expertise, and the encroachment of disciplinary techniques and standardised practices into the forensic sector, has had particular effects in those sectors devoted to the production of knowledge. Further, it has fundamentally altered that element most closely associated with expert judgement – objectivity. Cambrosio, Keating, Schlich, and Weisz[32] argue that the nature of objectivity has changed over time in response to governmental innovations. They argue that 'different historical periods have produced different types of objectivity that have subsequently persisted either as autonomous forms or in combination with other types of objectivity'.[33] Where once the objectivity of a statement could be inferred from the knowledge and experience of its author, 'later periods have tended to privilege mechanical or instrumental

---

[28]Stephens, N., Atkinson, P., & Glasner, P. (2011). Documenting the doable and doing the documented: Bridging strategies at the UK stem cell bank. *Social Studies of Science*, *41*, 791.

[29]Foucault, M., Senellart, M., Ewald, F., & Fontana, A. (2009). Security, territory, population: Lectures at the College de France, 1977-1978. New York, N.Y: Picador/ Palgrave Macmillan, at p. 63.

[30]Gibbon, P., & Henrikson, L. F. (2012). A standard fit for neoliberalism. *Comparative Studies in Society and History*, *54*(2), 275–307, at p. 279.

[31]Rose, N., O'Malley, P., & Valverde, M. (2006). Governmentality. *Annual Review of Law and Social Science*, *2*, 83–104.

[32]Cambrosio, A., Keating, P., Schlich, T., & Weisz, G. (2006). Regulatory objectivity and the generation and management of evidence in medicine. *Social Science and Medicine*, *63*, 189–199.

[33]Cambrosio, A., Keating, P., Schlich, T., & Weisz, G. (2006). Regulatory objectivity and the generation and management of evidence in medicine. *Social Science and Medicine*, *63*, 189–199, at p. 193.

objectivity that replaces experts' subjectivity with mechanically produced inscriptions'.[34]

Daston,[35] too, has charted the emergence of a type of objectivity – absent of any viewpoint or perspective – which 'culminates in the systematic recourse to quantitative measures'. This form of objectivity stands in opposition to earlier forms of historically contingent objectivity, which nevertheless persist.[36] Cambrosio et al. go further, arguing that regulatory objectivity is not restricted to the establishment of standard measures. In the field of biomedicine (and, by extension, forensic DNA profiling), it 'incorporates these measures and the entities measured as a basis for clinical judgment'.[37] Essentially, the *way* in which an expert judgement has been arrived at has come to replace the substance of the judgement itself. This argument may be applied to the instant case, whereby a deviation from accredited protocols – even a deviation which is beneficial and grounded in scientific method – must result in a Declaration of Non-Compliance, the presence of which may be viewed negatively by the court.

Further, this form of regulatory objectivity, based around standardised practices, has special resonance for the forensic scientist. In the radically deconstructive arena of the courtroom, the 'non-compliant' enacting of scientific expertise may be recast as nothing more than an assemblage of 'subjective, biased, messy, fuzzy, local and arbitrary practices and judgments'.[38] In these circumstances, quality assurance operates as a 'technology of trust'.[39] It

> bridges time and space, assuring lab managers … and juries that unseen work has been carried out properly. It is, thus, the defining element of an 'administrative science' designed at least in part to deal with the threat of legal deconstruction.[40]

Or, as Porter argues,

> the form of knowledge resulting from this relatively rigid quantitative protocol is decidedly public in character. Such knowledge

[34]Cambrosio, A., Keating, P., Schlich, T., & Weisz, G. (2006). Regulatory objectivity and the generation and management of evidence in medicine. *Social Science and Medicine, 63*, 189–199.
[35]Daston, L. (1992). Objectivity and the escape from perspective. *Social Studies of Science, 22*, 597–618.
[36]Daston, L. (1995). The moral economy of science. *Osiris, 10*, 2–24.
[37]Cambrosio, A., Keating, P., Schlich, T., & Weisz, G. (2006). Regulatory objectivity and the generation and management of evidence in medicine. *Social Science and Medicine, 63*, 189–199, at p. 194.
[38]Derksen, L. (2000). Towards a sociology of measurement: The meaning of measurement error in the case of DNA profiling. *Social Studies of Science, 30*, 803, at p. 806.
[39]Porter, T. M. (1995). *Trust in numbers. The pursuit of objectivity in science and public life*. Princeton, NJ: Princeton University Press.
[40]Leslie, M. (2010). Quality assured science: Managerialism in forensic biology. *Science Technology Human Values, 35*, 283, at p. 298.

> is especially useful to co-ordinate the activities of diverse actors, and to lend credibility to forms of belief and action when personal trust is in short supply. Thus, [regulatory] objectivity is a technology of distance.[41]

The data would tend to support the view that regulation serves to shape expertise and to preserve hegemonic structures. Indeed, it may be argued that a number of influential, high-status lead biologists – who occupied the upper echelons of scientific research at the Forensic Science Service (FSS) – transferred to regulatory, and policy, positions, thus preserving established hierarchies during a period of dynamic market restructuring.

> They could see it coming from 1998/99, that's why I made that point earlier about being involved in the reflective strategic groups because it then became clear that the methodology around the quality management systems, as [the FSS] progressed further towards government company status, they would need to wrap that additional layer of quality separation around themselves. So they start using that language ....

Further, it was suggested that the transition to regulatory positions enabled those scientists to structure the market to benefit those organisations which have accreditation. Insofar as this is cited as a motive, this assertion is not supported by the preponderance of data, which supports the view that the motive for regulation is enhanced quality, albeit an etiolated form of quality analysis, conforming to regulatory imperatives.

> The reality that I observed was that ... very senior folk at the top end of the business went off and created their own business. Isn't it interesting how out of that, it produced the current forensic regulator incumbent, so isn't it interesting how the organisation that was formed by those senior scientists, that the current incumbent came from, keep saying how terribly important compliance with the regulator is, that there's definitely a common language going on there.
>
> I think that's a mantra that those more senior – or seen to be more senior – and who've been in the game longer – have wrapped themselves up in, in order to preserve their gravitas and their authority. (Interview with Crown Prosecution Service (CPS) strategy advisor and Queens Counsel (QC): October 2015)

[41]Porter, T. M. (1992a). Quantification and the accounting ideal in science. *Social Studies of Science, 22*, 833, at p. 640; Porter, T. M. (1992b). Objectivity as standardization: The rhetoric of impersonality in measurement, statistics, and cost-benefit analysis. *Annals of Scholarship, 9*, 19–59.

Nonetheless, some respondents noted the tendency for accreditation to act as a scientifically meaningless, but prohibitive, economic barrier, which serves to force smaller competitors out of the market.

> ISO 17025 might show that sound structures are in place but it doesn't solve cases. That comes down to strategy.
>
> UKAS itself is a commercial monopoly … There's never usually a UKAS challenge over testing. [UKAS accreditation] fails because accreditation is ongoing and must be supported by all of the other parts of your business, including HR, marketing, etc. It's too costly [for news FSPs]. (Interview with lead forensic biologist and managing director: June 2015)

The above assertion was contradicted by QC and former CPS strategy advisor:

> [Accredited standards] are an important aspiration, they are an important target to aim towards, but they are not a binding exclusionary force that should put anybody off attempting to enter the criminal justice system market … And I think we would be a much poorer justice environment without the regulator's role and the codes of conduct and so forth. But it [should not be] the tail that is wagging the dog.
>
> 'What does the CJS ask for?' You see, in relation to expertise it's just not possible for the prosecution process to say 'we're not going to use that expert evidence because it wasn't ISO 17025'. They're not going to say 'I'm not accepting this because [the FSP is] not 17025'. They would use that as a very good cross examination tool and say 'the prosecution's laboratory has got these bells and whistles on it and your garden shed hasn't' but that still doesn't detract from what it is, is sought, is the end product of the expertise.

The above response predated the introduction for the issuing of a Declaration of Non-Compliance, on the part of unaccredited FSPs or those using non-validated methods. These subsequent developments would tend to contradict the above claims. However, the respondent did concede, on further questioning, that regulation, as currently practised, is an inefficient, and improper, way to structure forensic DNA-profiling activities.

> Yes, it's a wee bit like the idea of female genital mutilation, we've got it so you must have it, and the mantra goes round. Now, my passion about this is that people do not unpack it – certainly in the preliminary way that I've just illustrated in relation to defence practice but secondly they don't even unpack what 17020 and 17025 looks for – we were doing this work as part of the ENFSI

> working group back in 2004 and the problem with 17020 and 25 is that it doesn't deal with the requirements of the criminal justice system. It appears to, and it likes to think it does, and certainly UKAS likes to think it does because this is their lifeblood, to say this is to make sure it's CJS user friendly but it doesn't deal with any requirements in relation to disclosure, continuity, unused material, and all of those things which are actually the lynch pin for getting into the criminal justice process.

Having outlined the ways in which standardisation and regulation may condition the production of forensic-scientific knowledge claims, the next section focusses on the underlying normative factors which drive these processes.

The Normative Basis of Forensic Science

> There is no error in forensic science – 'error' only relates to the forensic scientist. (Forensic Biologist and Laboratory Manager; December 2016)

> We need to be open about the causes of error in forensic science: human error, faulty instrumentation, or systemic errors. (Regulatory Administrator; December 2016)

These typical responses, from forensic quality assurance agents, disclose an objectivist view of forensic DNA-profiling activities, which limits errors to categories generated by human action, and omission, with a particular focus on errors related to measurement and accuracy. The error thus relates to observed, and measured, phenomenon impinging on an independent reality. This approach resonates with, if it does not directly proceed from, an objectivist ontological commitment. To reiterate, the objectivist ontology views reality as a common-sense physical, or perceptual, entity. The objectivist views reality as being composed of things (e.g. a book) and social facts (e.g. a company), both of which can be observed, described, and measured, and which possess an independent existence, that lies beyond the influence, and reach, of the researcher. In other words, we see what exists, and we can capture it to produce objective knowledge. The main features of objectivism were summarised as follows:

- Reality and truth exist objectively and can be discovered and adequately measured.
- Reality is 'out there', has an identity of its own, and exists apart from our awareness.
- Reality is single, solid, and uniform: it generates the same meanings for all actors.
- Reality is 'found' by the researcher and brought to (social) awareness.
- The researcher should exercise objective detachment and value neutrality.

Therefore, the objectivist views error as being limited to issues such as contamination, cognitive bias, and faulty (or inaccurate) measurement (with regard to instruments and/or users). It is no coincidence that these three categories match the three categories of regulatory incursion taken by the FSR.[42] While remaining blind to the socially constructed nature of forensic-scientific truth claims, it nonetheless aligns with a realist epistemology; an epistemology that is based upon broadly 'Mertonian' norms. Thus, the discussion closes, as it began, with reference to the ways in which the norms of scientific endeavour continue to shape the trajectory of forensic-scientific knowledge production, in its practical, and regulatory, dimensions.

[42] Office of the Forensic Science Regulator. (2021). Regulator's codes of practice and conduct. London: The Home Office.

Chapter 8

From Biological Substrate to Digital Analyte

Chapter Summary

The instant study illuminates the contested landscape of forensic science provision in England and Wales, since the closure of the Forensic Science Service (FSS) in 2010 and the introduction of complete privatisation, the key stage in the ongoing process of marketisation. The study demonstrates the ways in which forensic scientists, working within the marketised forensic sector, have had to respond to the influence of commoditisation and cope with managerialist drives towards more and faster production. The expert informants provide evidence of the problematic influence of marketisation on the introduction of standardised practices and the commodification of forensic products and services; of the restructuring of forensic expertise and labour conditions; of the streamlining of forensic analyses, most notably deoxyribonucleic acid (DNA) profiling, and of the introduction of forms of non-expert reporting of questionable legality; and, finally, of the comprehensive regulation of these processes in ongoing attempts to ensure quality and reliability across a febrile market. The findings are given fresh impetus by recent tumultuous events within the forensic market, most notably the predicted collapse of one of the main forensic providers, and its subsequent resuscitation by the Metropolitan police,[1] followed closely by the discovery of criminal practices among forensic analysts, leading to the collapse of a significant number of trials.[2]

The foregoing data amply demonstrate the structural problems which afflict the market and the inability of the regulator to effectively assure the quality of marketised forensic analysis. A sophisticated understanding of the effects of marketisation on the evidential trajectory is therefore timely and strives to make an

[1]Hamilton, F. (2018, January 31). Police foot the bill after collapse of forensics firm. *The Times*. Retrieved from www.thetimes.co.uk/article/police-foot-the-bill-after-collapse-of-forensics-firm-key-forensic-services-limited-bg5nbxkxt

[2]Devlin, H. (2018, December 6). Convictions for drug-driving quashed in forensics lab inquiry. *The Guardian*. Retrieved from www.theguardian.com/uk-news/2018/dec/06/forty-convictions-quashed-after-investigation-at-uk-forensics-lab

Marketisation and Forensic Science Provision in England and Wales, 147–161

Published under exclusive licence by Emerald Publishing Limited
doi:10.1108/978-1-83909-123-020221008

essential contribution to understandings of the privatised forensic sector. The above testimony further suggests that marketised forensic science has followed a trajectory from scientific objectivity to regulatory objectivity, from epistemological validity to instrumental efficiency, and in reconfiguring itself around the indices of competition and efficiency has rendered itself less able to meet the challenges of a dynamic and evolving biochemical field. However, the forensic market – based upon triaging and low-skill repetitive analyses – may be configured to ably exploit the potentials of digital forensic evidence. Further research will therefore be necessary to inform debates around the future of marketised forensic science, as it begins to grapple with new methods and fresh challenges. The final chapter focusses on the central biochemical challenge facing forensic science, before considering the current shift in the forensic science field from DNA analyses to digital methods. This chapter closes with a summary.

Research Challenges: DNA Mixtures, Transfer, and Persistence

The model of forensic analysis promulgated by the FSS, while being designed to meet customer requirements, had a strong iterative element (see Part 1). In respect of DNA analysis, the propositions and expectations laid down by the evaluating scientist were necessarily subject to review, reframing, and modification in light of the results of the material analysis and the availability of new information. A framework for ongoing research, review, and expert evaluation was crucial to the field of DNA profiling, whose rapid advances, once led by the FSS, now serve to confound the static configuration of the privatised forensic market.

These issues converge in relation to the challenge of deoxyribonucleic acid (DNA) 'transfer and persistence'. The increasing sensitivity of DNA-testing protocols entails that scientists regularly encounter mixed results, from 'touch DNA' shed by (multiple) individuals and transferred from person to person and between surfaces. The following extended discussion from a field research interview highlights the difficulties posed by 'transfer and persistence':

> 'Nobody's thinking of this question and, arguably, there's no real, tenable, useful data on transfer and persistence. So, if you're provided with a reasonable avenue for DNA from an individual, to be on something, then it goes into the hat. Because you can't "weight" transfer and persistence. [Transfer] varies from individual to individual as well as condition to condition, surface to surface, you know, there's just so many variables that, the fact that they're his gloves may mean that he's been wearing them every day and he's still only a minority contributor … It can pretty much wipe out DNA, that question'. When dealing with activity-level propositions] we're onto "how", "where" and "when". And this is "transfer and persistence". This is the bit that nobody thinks about. Because the [source-level] SFR said, "one in a billion", and

> the name of the individual who they got off the database. (Interview with Tier 2 Forensic Scientist, Oxford)

It may be argued, therefore, that 'transfer and persistence' issues pose a serious challenge to the ongoing utility, and legitimacy, of DNA-profiling evidence. Particularly given the testimony from one experienced detective working within her majesty's inspectorate of constabulary (HMIC), who provided examples of the propensity for 'repeat players' to cite exculpatory DNA transfer scenarios when confronted with DNA evidence. The frequency of DNA mixtures being encountered in test results has also risen sharply since the introduction of more sensitive testing protocols (such as DNA-17 and Globafiler-24, both of which replaced SGM Plus). Tier 2 providers maintained that they did not 'put a statistic' on the very low amounts of DNA now routinely encountered, preferring only to use these for intelligence purposes. However, they indicated that this practice was not widespread.

> The frequency dataset for SGM-17 was developed by the FSS. When commercial companies set up they had to develop their own datasets. That's one area that would have benefitted from standardisation. The same test can give different results depending on the company's dataset. (Interview with Lead Scientist: Tier 2 Forensic Science Provider (FSP))

The testimony from forensic scientists indicated that further research and development is vitally necessary in order to meet such novel forensic challenges. However, de-skilling and a lack of research co-ordination, given with the pressures of operating within a competitive market sector, are constraining the ability of the market to respond. Forensic scientists operating within the forensic market stated that they are not able to conduct research in order to meet these challenges, due to economic factors which were notably absent while working within the research environment of the FSS or currently encountered in Forensic Science Northern Ireland (FSNI). Indeed, scientists and senior regulators have since suggested that while the marketised reconfiguration of the forensic sector creates a framework for efficiency and standardisation, it serves to restrict the opportunity for ongoing research, which may restrict long-term development.

DNA Mixtures, Transfer, and Persistence

The model of forensic analysis promulgated by the FSS, while being designed to meet customer requirements, had a strong iterative element. In respect of DNA analysis, the propositions and expectations laid down by the evaluating scientist were necessarily subject to review, reframing, and modification in light of the results of the material analysis and the availability of new information. The FSS stated that,

> there are many reasons why both propositions and expectations might change as a result of unexpected developments during the

> examination. There should be a continuous process of review and, where necessary, further consultation with the customer.[3]

Evett and Jackson have provided a series of case studies, which illustrate the ways in which mutually exclusive pairs of propositions may be revised and refined in order to take account of fresh contextual evidence. Further, one informant provided an example of the way in which a piece of DNA evidence, which is very strong on the source level, may be neutralised at the activity level:

> If there is no pattern, and it's only a … bloodstain, and it's perhaps in the form of a handmark, and the victim's got a bleeding nose, then suddenly you're in a situation where you've completely neutralised the evidence. (Interview with Tier 2 Forensic Scientist, Oxford, 2015)

Problems relating to the lack of reliable data on DNA transfer and persistence are compounded by the increasing sensitivity of DNA-testing protocols, which now regularly pick up results from 'touch DNA', shed by (multiple) individuals and transferred from person to person and between surfaces. The following extended discussion from a field research interview highlights the difficulties posed by 'transfer and persistence':

> [When dealing with activity-level propositions] we're onto 'how', 'where' and 'when'. And this is 'transfer and persistence'. This is the bit that nobody thinks about. Because the SFR said, 'one in a billion', and the name of the individual who they got off the database.
>
> There is so much concentration on what you can prove with numbers and just overlooking the simple question of transfer and persistence … Because nobody's thinking of this question and, arguably, there's no real, tenable, useful data on transfer and persistence. So, if you're provided with a reasonable avenue for DNA, from an individual, to be on something, then it goes into the hat. Because you can't 'weight' transfer and persistence. [Transfer] varies from individual to individual as well as condition to condition, surface to surface, you know, there's just so many variables that, the fact that they're his gloves may mean that he's been wearing them every day and he's still only a minority contributor … It can pretty much wipe out DNA, that question. (Interview with Tier 2 Forensic Scientist, Oxford, 2015)

---

[3] Cook, R., Evett, I. W., Jackson, G., Jones, P. J., & Lambert, J. A. (1998). A model for case assessment and interpretation. *Science & Justice, 38*, 151–156.

It may be argued, therefore, that 'transfer and persistence' issues pose a serious challenge to the ongoing utility, and legitimacy, of DNA-profiling evidence.[4] Further, it should be reiterated that the basic DNA-profiling protocols, on which the above perceptions are based, have been subject to thorough validation and accreditation procedures and single-source DNA analysis has thereby established its scientific underpinnings (see subsequent chapters). However, the same degree of trust in the accuracy of results cannot be extended to un-validated processes, such as those involving minute traces of 'low template' DNA, especially where these involve the interpretation of 'DNA mixtures' drawn from a number of individuals. The occurrence of DNA mixtures has risen sharply since the introduction of sensitive testing protocols (such as DNA-17 and Globafiler-24, both of which replaced SGM Plus). These are now capable of picking up trace amounts of 'low template' DNA and has led to the routine reporting of mixed DNA profiles. Tier 2 providers maintained that they did not 'put a statistic' on very low amounts of DNA, preferring to use these for intelligence purposes. However, they indicated that this practice was not widespread.

> DNA-17 is a result of the Prum regime. It standardised tests across Europe. There is a choice of microsatellites and DNA-17 can cover all areas in Europe. In Scotland they went directly to Globafiler which tests 24 areas and has a global fit. Originally they weren't allowed to upload to the NDNAD even though the 17 necessary satellites are contained in the Globafiler 24. But that's now changed. Each new test is more sensitive, so in a commercial market a threshold is applied and anything below [the threshold] is discarded. But there's a lot of useful information there. The frequency dataset for SGM-17 was developed by the FSS. When commercial companies set up they had to develop their own datasets. That's one area that would have benefitted from standardisation. The same test can give different results depending on the company's dataset. (Interview with Lead Scientist: Tier 2 FSP, 2015)

Further, Tier 2 respondents raised concerns regarding the alleged practice of a particular Tier 1 provider, which routinely deliver results which they termed a 'non-weighted *Dlugosz*'. This practice bears a contradictory appellation, which

---

[4]A challenge which has not been addressed through forensic research and has led the courts to retreat (in *R* v. *Jones (William Francis)* [2020] EWCA Crim 1021) from the high-water mark of judicial acceptance of single-source DNA evidence in cases involving DNA transfer (most notably in *R* v. *Tsekiri* [2017] EWCA Crim 40 (17 February 2017); *R* v. *Bech* [2018] EWCA Crim 448). See, generally, Richmond, K. (2017, August 1). DNA profiling: Transfer and persistence: *R* v. *Tsekiri* [2017] EWCA Crim 40. *Journal of Criminal Law, 81*(4), 275–277; Richmond, K. (2019). DNA evidence alone as a case to answer: *Bech, R* v. *Court of Appeal* [2018] EWCA Crim 448. *The Journal of Criminal Law, 83*(6), 503–507.

would appear to contradict the ruling in *R* v. *Dlugosz*. The guidance was issued in response to the use of subjective probabilistic expressions in that case. There was no dispute in the first and third appeals that DNA evidence from a mixed profile could be used simply to establish that the defendant might have been a contributor or could not have been a contributor. It was accepted that it is often useful for a jury simply to know that fact without any further elaboration.[5] However, the issues arose with regard to the framing of propositions, particularly on the activity level.

> With mixture analysis you have to frame propositions very carefully. In certain cases you have to work through all of them. It depends on what the defence propositions are saying. Sometimes you are never given an alternative scenario, for example in 'no comment' cases. For two person samples you can use Bayes. Then the hypothesis becomes important. If the sample is a mixture of more than two people *Dlugosz* says we can use words instead of stats. We can provide a verbal evaluation. It's back to the CSI approach. It's much more subjective so you really need experience.
>
> There is also an issue with Cellmark over what's known as a 'weighted' and 'non-weighted *Dlugosz*'. *Dlugosz* says that you can express an opinion about very small amounts of DNA but that has to be weighted. Cellmark produce results which are not weighted. This is wrong. They call it a 'non-weighted *Dlugosz*' but that is a contradiction in terms. The 'non-weighted *Dlugosz*' is an attempt to standardize across the company in order to have a common approach. (Interview with Lead Scientist: Tier 2 FSP, 2015)

Indeed, the UK Forensic Science Regulator's Guidance states that

> the practice of offering a qualitative evaluation in a case where, because of unresolved interpretative issues, it has not been possible to carry out a quantitative evaluation by means of validated software, should not be continued.[6]

Nonetheless, the above testimony reveals concerns among Tier 2 providers with regard to the alleged practices of Tier 1 providers within the forensic science market in England and Wales. However, it should be reiterated that such concerns relate to challenges faced by DNA-profiling practitioners across all jurisdictions. Further, that such concerns may reveal long-standing problems win relation to

---

[5] *R* v. *Dlugosz* [2013] EWCA Crim 2.

[6] Office of the Forensic Science Regulator. (2017, November 5). *FSR-G-222 guidance – DNA mixture interpretation* (Guideline 16, p. 34). London: The Home Office.

the scientific nature of DNA profiling. The review of the NAS report, and subsequent literature, infra, supports the assertion that it was not widely believed that DNA-profiling techniques were dynamic – rather than static – in nature. Nor that these advancing techniques – having proven their scientific underpinnings – should continue to be subject to fundamental testing and validation studies or be required to submit to processes of accreditation, in the same manner as non-scientific 'first generation' pattern identification techniques.

Such views were dealt a severe blow by the publication of the results of the DNA (MIX05 and MIX13) studies. These results – drawn from an inter-laboratory study conducted by the National Institute of Science and Technology (NIST) – had been subject to a delay, which has itself drawn criticism from practitioners and allied criminal justice agents. The study involved over 100 laboratories, which were provided with DNA samples involving mixtures. MIX05 was undertaken in 2005 and required 69 laboratories to interpret DNA data from two-person mixtures, drawn from four hypothetical sex assaults. The MIX13 study, conducted in 2013, provided 108 laboratories with data representing five 'crimes', in increasing difficulty, in scenarios involving up to four contributors and related individuals.

The results from the overall studies showed concerning degrees of variability across the results delivered by the participating laboratories. Of particular note were the results from MIX13, case 5, which purported to provide a DNA mixture from an item of clothing left behind after a bank robbery. The mixture of touch DNA was drawn from four individuals. However, due to the complex nature of the mixed sample, this initially appeared as a mixture of only two people. The labs were provided with reference samples taken from two of the four likely contributors, along with that of a fifth person. The fifth person was not in the mixture and had not been in contact with the item of clothing.

When the results were reviewed, it became apparent that 74 laboratories, out of 108, had wrongly included the fifth person in their mixture interpretation. A further 26 labs delivered 'inconclusive' reports, of varying levels of error. Thus, only seven laboratories correctly excluded individual number 5 from the four-person mixed sample. Even then, different reasons were given, from 'allelic drop-out' to 'PCR inhibition'.

Most were using the method of combined probability of inclusion, otherwise known as CPI, a Federal Bureau of Investigation (FBI)-approved method of separating out mixtures. However, in the instant study, further concerns were raised regarding the use of computer algorithms to de-convolute mixed DNA profiles, especially with regard to validation.

> There are two different types. Cellmark uses David Balding's computer system. LGC developed LiRa. These systems can deal with two or more people. For a while Balding's system wasn't validated but it is now. There are differences between the systems but the same system can deliver different answers depending on how the question is formed. (Interview with Lead Scientist: Tier 2 FSP, 2015)

These concerns serve to illustrate the degree of scepticism among Tier 2 providers with regard to the scientific validity of cutting-edge DNA-profiling techniques. The testimony from forensic scientists indicated that such developments were necessary in order to meet new forensic challenges, but that the level of foundational validity necessary for use in casework had not reached an optimal level. Nor were forensic scientists operating within the forensic market able to conduct research in order to meet these challenges, due to economic factors which were notably absent while working within the research environment of the FSS. Indeed, scientists and senior regulators have suggested that while the marketised reconfiguration of the forensic sector provides a framework which may restrict development, it simultaneously facilitates the shift to a new modality or 'forensic product': that new modality is digital evidence.

Participants report that the opportunity to meet the challenges of low-template DNA and DNA transfer has been circumvented by a turn to digital evidence. Thus, the sector is now seeing a further round of reconfiguration as it transitions from forensic science organised around a forensic substrate to one organised around a digital analyte. New companies have emerge to complement and displace the Tier 1 bioscientific providers, and as with their bioscientific predecessors, these private companies boast United Kingdom Accreditation Service (UKAS) certification, bid for proliferating contracts, engage in the triaging of digital material, and provide streamlined forensic reports. The ability to provide research-based solutions is also constrained by the imposition of regulatory controls, which limit the use of non-standard methods. This phenomenon is discussed in further detail below.

Summary of Conclusions

The governance of forensic science provision, its organisational structure, and the management of individual forensic science laboratories varies widely between different countries, regions, and jurisdictions. However, the provision of forensic science services (including DNA profiling), in virtually all developed countries, is through a system of public sector provision. England and Wales, alone, have transitioned to a fully marketised form of forensic science provision.

Analysis of the data elicited in the course of this research study provides support for the assertion that the disaggregation of the supply of forensic-scientific services, within England and Wales, has been welcomed by some stakeholders, due to its perceived potential to provide economic efficiencies. However, analysis of the data also revealed that it is a continuing source of tension between certain groups of Tier 2 forensic experts, criminal justice agents, and those who shape science and technology policy.

The dynamic state of the forensic market, alongside the current reliance on short-term contracts, has led to the perception of efficiency and enhanced customer satisfaction, among some criminal justice agents. However, a section of respondents reported that these same processes had led to destabilisation, and insecurity, attendant on an inability to craft long-term strategies. Given the explicitly limited nature of the instant study, it is not possible to draw any conclusions with regard to the veracity, or accuracy, of these perceptions. Nonetheless, the data do reveal concerns regarding perceived 'de-skilling' across the sector. Such concerns were widespread within Tier 2 companies but not shed by all respondents, a number of whom reported that the restructuring of forensic-scientific expertise was appropriate, especially as the result of government-led initiatives intended to deliver ever-greater efficiencies.

The empirical data, and following conclusions, cannot provide unequivocal evidence for the assertion that the institutional arrangements which structure the provision of DNA-profiling services have transformed the ways in which DNA-profiling experts set about their tasks. However, they do aggregate around particular areas of concern, setting the groundwork for further studies aimed at addressing this issue. For example, it was felt by many DNA profilers and managerial staff that the pattern of development had been volatile and had supposedly led to widespread 'de-skilling', a phenomenon which they saw as particularly affecting Tier 1 FSPs. Further, the same constituency reported reservations regarding the introduction of streamlined reporting, 'triaging', and productisation (whether it be through codification or contractual provision). These processes, they felt, had further constrained – and even dispensed with – the ability of DNA profilers to carry out high-quality contextual evaluations. Respondents from the public sector provider, FSNI, reported a comparative degree of comfort, with regard to these developments, which they viewed as particularly affecting the forensic science market. Nonetheless, some respondents within Tier 1 providers, and allied agents within the criminal justice system (CJS), welcomed these same developments.

While the above processes were viewed as having limited DNA profilers' ability to undertake high-quality contextual evaluations, a wide constituency of respondents took a positive view of the constraints imposed through the requirement for forensic DNA profilers submit to various forms of monitoring and regulation; a small number took the view that these quality assurance mechanisms actively prevent forensic experts from creatively adapting, in order to provide more holistic evaluations or in response to the fresh challenges imposed by transfer and persistence issues. Commercial imperatives have also influenced perceptions of forensic service provision within those regions in which service provision is retained within retain public ownership, with public providers reporting a willingness to embrace new management techniques, to internalise regulatory objectives, and to compete with their privatised counterparts. However, the public sector DNA-profiling provider, again, viewed themselves as being less susceptible to these influences and thus able to deliver a larger proportion of high-quality expert evaluations.

Standardisation

The data have demonstrated that the creation of a rudimentary forensic science market (subsequent to the introduction, by the FSS, of direct charging to customers) was viewed as having facilitated the 'commodification' of forensic processes. Through making forensic investigatory processes visible to institutional agents within the CJS, the latter reported that they were now able to dictate the course of the investigatory strategy, and to request the use of particular products, within the context of particular levels of evaluation. These efficiencies were viewed positively. The productisation of forensic processes was further viewed as having facilitated 'triaging', and the assignation of samples to different modes of investigation, largely determined by the offence type. However, while the customer-led model was viewed positively by members of HMIC, legal practitioners, and some Tier 1 DNA profilers, a proportion of Tier 2 providers reported tensions: given that each force sought to satisfy its particular needs, the current model was seen as breeding inefficiency and of allowing inexpert investigators within the CJS a seemingly inordinate degree of control over matters which – the scientists claimed – should rightly fall within the ambit of expert forensic scientists.

Further, it was shown that perceptions relating to the standardisation of forensic processes are highly asymmetric. Standardisation and productisation structure forensic outputs, to be sure, but these phenomena are not seen as being matched by standardisation of 'customer' demands. The study disclosed various examples in which a significant level of meso-structural variation between individual police forces was evident, each of them retaining a strong identity and demanding individually tailored requirements. This was viewed as leading to inefficiencies in terms of time and quality, which were viewed as having impacted on cost. At the time of writing, the 43 individual forces (and associated consortia) have made no steps towards agreeing standard operating procedures with regard to their forensic requirements and protocols (albeit that these remain flexible enough to accommodate the particular needs of each force).

Expertise

This study demonstrates that a significant proportion of DNA profilers perceive the existence of a strong link between the introduction of measures of economic rationalisation and the reduction of thinking time – and contextual investigation – on the part of the scientist. These limitations are seen to have been aggravated by a tendency to triage cases and by allegedly systematic attempts to avoid activity-level DNA analyses, and contextual evaluations, in respect of particular classes of offence, mainly within the 'volume crime' category.

The study exposes significant concerns among practitioners, relating to supposed 'de-skilling' within the forensic-scientific field, and a concomitant loss of expert evaluation, with regard to the construction of DNA-profiling evidence. This perception was most prevalent among Tier 1 providers. The study also revealed that many forensic DNA profilers take the view that the economic rationalisation of forensic expertise has served to disrupt, and to reform, the attitudes, and expectations, of FSPs, who view themselves as having to reconstruct forensic identities in conformation with economic goals, aligned to the requirements of the investigatory authorities.

In comparison to marketised providers, FSNI employees reported a concomitant level of flexibility, adaptability, and an enhanced ability to carry out complex and contextually detailed evaluations. This, they believed, was due to their governance structure and the retention of skilled staff members, whose training and background exhibited a grounding in 'scientific method'.

Crucially, the data have demonstrated that forensic practitioners deem it necessary to provide contextual information to support the interpretation of DNA profiles and subsequent evaluations. The data drawn from this study reveal significant tensions, and concerns, that marketisation, in general, and productisation, in particular, have negatively impacted on the ability of forensic DNA profilers to carry out these contextually aware evaluations. This is seen as having a direct effect on the administration of justice. Once more, the publicly funded provider reported that they retained the capacity to provide a significantly more robust service.

Quoting between experts within the forensic market was reported by Tier 2 practitioners as being endemic, and examples were produced in order to support this claim. It was further suggested that, as a result, many forensic DNA reports may contain hearsay and should not credibly be admitted as expert evidence. Case fragmentation was, again, a widely reported phenomenon among Tier 2 practitioners and once more attributed to marketised production, an allegedly direct result of the tendering process and of the frequent transfer of forensic activities between providers. This was seen as actively preventing scientists from conducting a holistic evaluation of the evidence. Case fragmentation is not viewed as being linked to specialisation (since all Tier 1 providers may offer similar services) – rather, it is viewed as a result of the tendering process within the forensic market. Other features were less widely reported, though nonetheless concerning. The reported use of a novel category of report – the 'non-weighted *Dlugosz*' was notable in this regard, as was the evidence of incomplete, 'pseudo-Bayesian' analyses. Again, these concerns were limited to the forensic market.

Ultimately, the study demonstrates that the perceived loss of the ability to contextually evaluate DNA profiles is viewed as having a significant negative impact on the ability of the CJS to arrive at sound determinations on questions of fact. It is also reported that this leaves the market poorly placed to adapt to new challenges, such as those posed by the sensitivity of DNA protocols, the increasing occurrence of mixed profiles, and the challenges encountered when dealing with issues of 'transfer and persistence'. Finally, it was found that the subsisting theory of expertise was unsuited to analysing the co-production of forensic-scientific knowledge. This points to the necessity to develop subsisting theories of interdisciplinary expertise, as a means to achieve a more comprehensive understanding, and evaluation, of the co-production of forensic knowledge claims.

Efficiency

This study demonstrated that one of the principle causes of the perceived disruption of forensic expert networks is reportedly the introduction of novel forms of forensic reporting procedures, of which streamlined forensic reporting (SFR) is the most extreme example. Such innovations are welcomed by a number of CJS agents, who speak of the necessity of providing efficient analyses. However, the study also demonstrates that such modes of reporting are viewed by a significant proportion of forensic science practitioners as carrying the potential to limit the quality, and content, of expert scientific opinion and may – it is claimed – ultimately affect the court's ability to arrive at sound determinations on questions of fact.

The data do not support an assertion that streamlined reporting is viewed as a benign, and apolitical, mode of scientific communication, designed purely to facilitate conformity with the Criminal Procedure Rules (in particular, the requirement for legal practitioners to manage cases efficiently and expeditiously). Conversely, it shows that, in many instances, these reports are viewed by forensic scientists as leading to the unnecessary dilation of the legal process, with an increase in attendant costs. This study is explicitly limited. Therefore, it is not possible for the instant study to demonstrate whether, and to what degree, the SFR system operates as intended. However, the claim that SFR supports 'swift and sure justice' in all instances may, if respondents' claims are grounded in fact, be treated with a degree of scepticism.

These perceived problems cannot credibly be attributed to improper implementation. The data demonstrate that forensic scientists believe that similar savings – in both time and cost – could have been made through the use of abbreviated – or staged – reports – reports completed by a forensic expert, rather than a police administrator.

In addition, the data demonstrate that many Tier 2 scientists cleave to the view that streamlined DNA reporting may pose significant dangers. The allegedly complete abjuration of forensic expertise and the brevity of the report are seen as affording no traction in terms of forensic analysis or challenge. When used at pretrial hearings, in alignment with the Early Guilty Plea scheme, it is claimed that SFR could therefore potentially lead to miscarriages of justice (especially when dealing with vulnerable suspects).

Further, due to the inability of police administrators (and low-level trainees employed by Tier 1 providers) to interpret and evaluate mixed DNA profiles, rigid demarcations have been imposed, with many mixed profiles classed as 'indeterminate'. This – it is claimed – may mask a failure on the part of the investigative authorities to fulfil their duty to properly evaluate the evidence. Again, this is a failure by omission, which carries the potential to negatively impact on the CJS and could potentially lead to miscarriages of justice.

In conclusion, it may be stated that the SFR scheme is not seen as conforming to the aims of the Criminal Procedure Rules. Further, the evidence shows that SFR – in practice – may create tensions regarding the ability of legal practitioners to adequately comply with those rules.

Regulation and Autonomy

Analysis of the data demonstrates that the Forensic Science Regulator's role has evolved, since its inception. Original concerns revolved around the issues of cognitive bias and the potential contamination of consumables. These reactive concerns have been overtaken by a perceived need to establish a 'baseline of quality' across the forensic market. The primary means of achieving this goal has been through the Accreditation process imposed by the Regulator's Code of Practice and Conduct. This processaligns with the recent amendments to the Criminal Practice Directions, both of which serve to impose a new 'enhanced *Daubert*'[7] standard on the CJS. A test through which to measure the validity, and reliability, of expert evidence. However, it may be argued that the new test fails to make a distinction between scientific forensic activities, and non-scientific forensic activities, of the sort contemplated in the *Kumho*[8] judgement. Further, that the framework relies on an inaccurate reading of the underlying case law, particularly *Dlugosz*[9] and *Reed*.[10] This issue will be explored at length in the following section.

It has been demonstrated that this regulatory framework is seen as aligning most closely with the forms of high-volume, low-expertise, forensic DNA reporting conducted by Tier 1 providers (such as SFR) while it is viewed as failing to regulate the evaluative, and interpretative, activities of expert DNA profilers which are – in reality – more consonant with the norms of scientific method (and which currently fall outwith the ambit of the accreditation process). Further, it has been demonstrated that the 'declaration of non-compliance' may serve to negatively impact upon the ability of forensic practitioners to exercise scientific creativity, and to conduct contextual evaluations, and basic research.

It was shown that the effects of the restructuring of scientific expertise (mainly afflicting Tier 1 providers) were not necessarily attributable to site-by-site micro-level variations in lab culture. Further, the study demonstrates that the introduction of standardisation, and regulation, is perceived as having served to persevere established hierarchies within the forensic profession. Finally, it was demonstrated that standard accounts of scientific objectivity have been partially displaced by a perceptions of the interposition of regulatory forms of objectivity within the forensic market.

A significant number of respondents from all disciplines claimed that the ISO 17025 standard was largely ineffectual in practical terms and allegedly did little to advance the aims of forensic DNA profiling, which could benefit from enhanced strategic capacities at the macro- and meso-levels. The data support the assertion that the regulatory framework is viewed as influencing marketised DNA profiling in England and Wales. Further, that regulation is viewed by some providers as imposing disproportionate costs on commercial forensic scientists; the former, in terms of time; the latter, in terms of both time and cost. Nonetheless, regulation was shown to aid the perpetuation of representations of normative science and rational adjudication.

Further, the attendant theoretical analysis further indicated that an awareness of the socially constructed nature of co-produced forensic knowledge claims could help to overcome the epistemological divergence exhibited by both fields. In conclusion, it is suggested that a greater appreciation of the similarities between

[7] *Daubert* v. *Merrel Dow Pharmaceuticals* 509 U.S. 579 (1994).
[8] *Kumho Tire Co.* v. *Carmichael*, 526 U.S. 137 (1999).
[9] *R* v. *Dlugosz* [2013] EWCA Crim 2.
[10] *R* v. *Reed, Reed & Garmson* [2009] EWCA Crim LR 2698.

both domains may potentially lead to a restructuring of the relationship between law and forensic science, a restructuring based upon greater autonomy and collaboration. Ultimately, it may even be suggested that forensic scientists might be afforded the same level of autonomy allowed of medical researchers, an autonomy that is viewed as the benchmark of problem-solving, progressive scientific endeavour.

Contribution of this Study to the Literature

This study illuminates the landscape of forensic science provision in England and Wales, since the closure of the FSS in 2010 and the introduction of complete privatisation, as an integral part of the process of marketisation. The study examines the ways in which DNA profilers working within the marketised forensic sector perceive the key elements of marketisation. These informants provide a hitherto unstudied account of the introduction of standardised practices and commodification of forensic products and services, of the restructuring of forensic expertise and labour conditions, of the streamlining of forensic DNA profiling and the introduction of non-expert reporting, and of the regulation of these processes in an attempt to ensure quality and reliability across a febrile market.

As yet, no researcher has tackled these topics as they come to fruition within a mature forensic market. Nor has any researcher considered how these changes impact on the perceptions of those tasked with upholding the central plank of forensic-scientific endeavour. Recent developments add urgency to this study. The collapse of one of the main forensic providers, and its subsequent resuscitation by the Metropolitan police, followed closely by the discovery of criminal practices among forensic analysts leading to the collapse of a number of trials. These demonstrate the structural problems which afflict the market and the inability of the regulator to effectively assure the quality of marketised forensic analysis. A sophisticated understanding of the perceptions of DNA profiling is therefore timely and essential to understanding of what has happened post-2010. As such, this study makes a distinct contribute to the field and will help to inform debates around the future of marketised provision forensic science in the UK. It will also add to the scholarly understanding of what has happened in the UK since 2010. No other scholarly work has hitherto addressed this.

From Biological Substrate Towards Digital Analyte

Contemporary evidence appears to show that the forensic science field, having failed to fully account for emergent problems relating to DNA-profiling analysis, is facilitating a shift to a new modality or 'forensic product': that new modality is digital evidence. Participants and regulatory agents report that that the obstacles described above may be circumvented through a turn to digital evidence. Thus, the sector is now seeing a further round of reconfiguration as it transitions from forensic science organised around a biological substrate to forensic science organised around a digital analyte. New companies have emerged which complement, compete with, and displace the Tier 1 bioscientific providers on whose model they are founded. As with their bioscientific predecessors, these private companies boast UKAS certification, bid for proliferating contracts, engage in the triaging of digital material, and provide streamlined forensic reports.

Thus, the above testimony suggests that marketised forensic science has followed an economically determined trajectory from scientific objectivity to regulatory objectivity, from epistemological validity to instrumental efficiency, and in reconfiguring itself around the indices of competition and efficiency has rendered itself less able to meet the challenges of a dynamic and evolving biomedical field but may be well placed to reconfigure around, and exploit, the potentials of digital forensic evidence. Further research will therefore be necessary to inform debates around the future of marketised provision forensic science, as it begins to grapple with new methods and fresh challenges.[11]

Karen McGregor Richmond

[11]Morgan, R. M., & Levin, E. A. (2019). A crisis for the future of forensic science: Lessons from the UK of the importance of epistemology for funding research and development. *Forensic Science International: Synergy*, *1*, 243–252; Horsman, G., & Sunde, N. (2022). Unboxing the digital forensic investigation process. *Science & Justice, 62*(2), 171–180.

References

Bijker, W. E., Bal, R., & Hendriks, R. (2009). *The paradox of scientific authority: The role of scientific advice in democracies*. Cambridge, MA: MIT Press.

Cambrosio, A., Keating, P., Schlich, T., & Weisz, G. (2006). Regulatory objectivity and the generation and management of evidence in medicine. *Social Science and Medicine, 63*, 189–199.

Cook, R., Evett, I. W., Jackson, G, Jones, P. J., & Lambert, J. A. (1998). A model for case assessment and interpretation. *Science & Justice, 38*, 151–156.

Flyvberg, B. (2006). Five misunderstandings about case study research. *Qualitative Enquiry, 12*(2), 219–245.

Gibbon, P., & Henrikson, L. F. (2012). A standard fit for neoliberalism comparative studies. *Society and History, 54*(2), 275–307.

Jackson, G., Aitken, C., & Roberts, P. (2015). *Practitioner guide 4 – Case assessment and interpretation of expert evidence*. London: Royal Statistical Society's Working Group on Statistics and the Law.

Jasanoff, S. (1995). Procedural choices in regulatory. *Science Technology in Society, 17*(3), 279–293.

Jordan, K., & Lynch, M. (1998). The dissemination, standardisation and routinisation of a molecular biological technique. *Social Studies of Science, 28*, 773–800.

King, D., Stangoe, C., & Cooke, L. (2012). *Scrutinising forensic services*. CPD Presentation to 25 Bedford Row.

Lawless, C. (2010). *A curious reconstruction? The shaping of 'marketized' forensic science*. London School of Economics Centre for Analysis of Risk and Regulation (CARR) Discussion Paper 63.

Lawless, C. (2011). Policing markets: The contested shaping of neo-liberal forensic science. *British Journal of Criminology, 51*, 671–689.

Lawless, C. J., & Williams, R. (2010). Helping with inquiries or helping with profits? The trials and tribulations of a technology of forensic reasoning. *Social Studies of Science, 40*, 731–755.

McAndrew, W. P. (2012a). Are forensic science services club goods? An analysis of the optimal forensic science service delivery model. *Forensic Science Policy & Management: An International Journal, 3*(4), 151–158.

McAndrew, W. P. (2012b). Is privatization inevitable for forensic science laboratories? *Forensic Science Policy & Management: An International Journal, 3*(1), 42–52.

M'Charek, A. (2006). Technologies of population: Forensic DNA Testing practices and the making of differences and similarities. *Configurations, 8*, 121–158.

Moreira, T., May, C., & Bond, J. (2009). Regulatory objectivity in action: Mild cognitive impairment and the collective production of uncertainty. *Social Studies of Science, 35*(9), 665–690.

Morgan, R. M., & Levin, E. A. (2019). A crisis for the future of forensic science: Lessons from the UK of the importance of epistemology for funding research and development. *Forensic Science International: Synergy, 1*, 243–252.

Myles, L. (2010). Quality assured science: Managerialism in forensic biology science. *Technology and Human Values, 35*, 283.

Porter, T. M. (1992). Quantification and the accounting ideal in science. *Social Studies of Science, 22*, 833.

Richmond, K. (2017, August 1). DNA profiling: Transfer and persistence: *R v Tsekiri [2017] EWCA Crim 40*. *Journal of Criminal Law*, *81*(4), 275–277.
Richmond, K. (2018). Streamlined forensic reporting: 'Swift and sure justice'? *Journal of Criminal Law*, *82*(2), 156–177.
Richmond, K. M. (2019). Customer-driven standardization in the forensic science market in England and Wales. In K. Jakobs (Ed.), *Corporate standardization management and innovation* (pp. 218–232). Hershey, PA: IGI Global.
Stephens, N., Atkinson, P., & Glasner, P. (2011). Documenting the doable and doing the documented: Bridging strategies at the UK stem cell bank. *Social Studies of Science*, *41*, 791.
Yin, R. K. (2003). *Applications of case study research* (2nd ed.). Thousand Oaks, CA: Sage.

Government Reports and Regulatory Guidance

Association of Chief Police Officers. (2005). *DNA good practice manual* (2nd ed.). London: The Stationery Office.
Crown Prosecution Service (CPS). (2015). *Streamlined forensic reporting guidance and toolkit 6*. London: CPS.
Committee on Identifying the Needs of the Forensic Sciences Community, National Research Council. (2009). *Strengthening forensic science in the United States: A path forward*. Washington, DC: National Academy of Sciences.
Forensic Science Regulator. (2017, November 5). *FSR-G-222 guidance – DNA mixture interpretation*. London: The Home Office.
Forensic Science Regulator. (2019, March 15). *Annual report November 2017–November 2018*. London: The Home Office.
House of Commons Science and Technology Committee. *Forensic science on trial* (seventh report of session 2004–05 HC 96-I).
House of Commons Science and Technology Committee. *The forensic science service* (2011 HC 855).
House of Commons Science and Technology Committee. *Forensic science* (second report of session 2013–14 HC 610).
House of Lords Science and Technology Committee. (2019, May 1). *Forensic science and the criminal justice system: A blueprint for change*. 3rd report of session 2017–19 (HL Paper 333).
President's Council of Advisors on Science & Technology. (2016). *Forensic science in criminal courts: Ensuring scientific validity of feature-comparison methods*. Washington, DC: Executive Office of the President.

Legislation and Cases

The Police and Criminal Evidence Act (PACE) 1984, Code of Practice D.
The Forensic Science Regulator Act 2021.
R v. *Dlugosz* [2013] EWCA Crim 2.
R v. *Tsekiri* [2017] EWCA Crim 40.
R v. *Bech* [2018] EWCA Crim 448.
R v. *Jones (William Francis)* [2020] EWCA Crim 1021.

Index

Note: Page numbers followed by "*n*" indicate notes.

Printed and bound by CPI Group (UK) Ltd, Croydon, CR0 4YY

16/09/2026

14963021-0003